Journeying Forward

Dreaming First Nations' Independence

Patricia A. Monture-Angus

Fernwood Publishing

Editing: Brenda Conroy
Cover photo: Denis Okanee Angus
Design and production: Beverley Rach
Printed and bound in Canada by: Hignell Printing Limited

A publication of:
Fernwood Publishing
Box 9409, Station A
Halifax, Nova Scotia
B3K 5S3

Fernwood Publishing Company Limited gratefully acknowledges the financial
support of the Ministry of Canadian Heritage and the Canada Council for the
Arts for our publishing program.

Le Conseil des Arts   The Canada Council
du Canada   for the Arts

Canadian Cataloguing in Publication Data

Monture-Angus, Patricia.

    Journeying forward

    Includes bibliographical references.
    ISBN 1-895686-97-0

1. Native peoples -- Canada -- Politics and government.* 2. Native
peoples -- Legal status, laws, etc. -- Canada. * I. Title.

E92.M66 1999   323.1'197071   C98-950004-7

Contents

For Eleanore Kathleen Townshend
and
Earl Harold Monture

Denis Okanee Angus

for every time you have said:
"do what you have to do."

and with special thanks to
Marion Cornwall

for sharing with me that my parents
are proud — my walk has
changed with that knowledge.

Preface

In My Circle

The little girl going forward down a path on the cover of this book is my daughter Kate. She is wearing a coat that my grandmother made, without a pattern, for my cousin Sharon, from the worn-out woolen bathrobe of my grandfather. My Aunt Dorothy (Sharon's mother) passed it along to me. This picture speaks to me about family, about relationship, about history and about sharing. It speaks about the creativity that the people have used to survive. These are some of the themes that are pressing in this book. The photograph is also the old combined with the new, with the hope. My girl holds my hope for the future.

The name for this book eluded me until I went looking for the photograph to use on the cover. Kate's father, Denis, is a photographer. The first thing I did after learning this manuscript was to be published (after I squealed and jumped around) was to raid my partner's stash of photographs. I found the cover easily and knew it as soon as I saw it. The day after I picked the photograph, the title of the book came to me as I drove through an April first Saskatchewan blizzard.

This book is born out of antagonism and frustration. It is born out of the pain I carry every day because of what I see happening in our communities and to the lives of our children. It is this pain that took me to looking at self-government as a solution. This book contains the thoughts of more than a decade.

There is a different group of people than usual that must be thanked for this book. I acknowledge the support, both in inspiration and in challenges, they have given me. As a teacher, my thoughts have been influenced by the many students I have taught over the last decade. They have always encouraged and inspired me. Their dreams kept me going on days when my own gifts seemed too heavy to carry.

Many colleagues and friends have also supported and challenged me. Understanding an idea such as self-determination is not a task that can be completed in the isolation of academia. It is a task which must be nurtured by community. I am grateful to William Anderson (Uncle Billie), Constance Backhouse, Russel Barsh, Gerald Bisschop, John Borrows (Anishnabe),

Sheldon Cardinal (Cree), Patricia Doyle-Bedwell (Mi'kmaq), Willie Ermine (Cree), Sakej Henderson (Chickasaw), Michael Jackson, Bev Jacobs (Kanien'kehaka), Darlene Johnston (Anishnabe), Kiera Ladner (Cree), Debra Laliberte (Cree), Tracy Lavallee (Cree), Irene Linklater (Anishnabe), Leroy Little Bear (Blackfoot), Noel Lyon, Janice Many Grey Horses (Blackfoot), Ron Marken, Denise McConney, Kent McNeil, Canadace Metalic (Mi'kmaq), David Monture (Kanien'kehaka), Michael Monture (Kanien'kehaka), Andrea Bear Nicholas (Maliseet), Shirley O'Connor (Anishnabe), Bonnie Pelletier (Anishnabe), Donna Phillips (Oneida), Tracey Robinson (Cree), Rupert Ross, Les Samuelson, Leona Sparrow (Salish), Ronald "Bud" Sparrow (Salish), Eleanore Sunchild (Cree), Darrell Tait (Cree), Tobasonakwut (Peter Kinew) (Anishnabe), Nin Tomas (Maori), Andrea Tunks (Maori), Mary Ellen Turpel-Lafond (Cree), Gloria Valencia-Weber and John Whyte. The danger of a long list of acknowledgments is to leave someone behind. However, it is important for me to note that Aboriginal ideas do not generate themselves in isolation. There is no way to footnote the many conversations I have had with people who have helped me along the way. Those who have walked with me will see themselves in these pages. These few words are my small acknowledgment of your presence and assistance. Of course, I alone carry the responsibility for the ideas and challenges in this book.

I have also learned in ceremony and from traditional teachings. Many of the Elders who encouraged, taught and supported me have passed to the other side. I shall follow tradition and not name them here. I still remember your teachings. I also understand that I do not always do justice to them.

Over the last few years, I have spent many evenings at the kitchen tables of Tracy Lavallee and Denise McConney. Our chatter is usually unfocused and jumps through topics of relationships, law, identity, anguish, Indian politics and politicians, worry, children, school, all at random. No matter where our chattering goes, and we are sometimes joined by other friends and family, it always sustains, supports and frequently challenges me. Without Tracy's and Denise's friendship and concern, my road would have been lonely. This book would have been more difficult to complete.

This book would not have been possible without my family. My children have been asked to make many sacrifices. They have always accepted my work and my dream chasing with kindness and generosity (and to a degree that continually amazes me). Nadia, Brandon, Genine, Blake, Kate and baby Jack (who missed the first book), I thank you. I honour you. Leonard Sapp and Joey Lewis are also important parts of this family. And to Denis who always keeps the home going in my many absences, much thanks. I am grateful for the comfort and courage that comes to me because you are the man in my circle.

In My Circle

Without my circle of extended family this book would not have been possible. It is this relationship that sustains me most fully. More than this book depends on the sustenance I receive from Denise McConney (and daughter Wynonah), Tracy Lavallee (and son Dene Cree), David Monture, Michael Monture, Patricia Tait Sasakamoose (and daughter Tara), Leona Sparrow and the ancestors we all call upon for guidance.

And of course there is the Fernwood family. Errol, you never lost your faith in me through all my delays in finalizing this manuscript. Your support and encouragement extends well beyond the publisher/author relationship. You truly know the meaning of friendship. Brenda, your editorial skills have truly made this book a better one. Your editing is kind and patient and I have learned a lot from your comments and corrections. Bev's layout and design skills have also contributed greatly to this book. Your artistic touch is greatly valued.

I would also like to thank those of you who have waited so patiently for this book. I am honoured by your interest in my work.

Thunderchild First Nation and Grand River Territory
June 1999

Introduction

Where I Am Standing

In recent years I have had to make my own choices about how I believe we can locate self-determination in our communities. My interest in self-determination began as a legal and academic pursuit. Perhaps if my early years had not been dominated by the exhausting need just to survive, my experience of self-determination might have been a lived one much earlier than now. More recently, I have realized that self-determination is both a personal issue and a collective yearning.

As I have come to understand it, self-determination begins with looking at yourself and your family and deciding if and when you are living responsibly. Self-determination is principally, that is first and foremost, about our relationships. Communities cannot be self-governing unless members of those communities are well and living in a responsible way. It is difficult for individuals to be self-determining until they are living as part of their community. This truth has been the hardest for me to accept and has resulted in great changes in my personal circumstances.

I intend no disrespect to urban Aboriginal people; one can successfully live "Indian" in the city, and I have been part of this statistical category for the majority of my life. However, we must recognize the limited choices available to people who reside on the reserve. I could not have pursued a legal education while I lived on the reserve. In fact, I assume that, as long as I continue to be a university teacher, being at least a part-time urban resident will be a fact of my existence. It does not matter if I aspire to that reality or not. That is the reality. The lack of opportunity for people living on the reserve is not an argument to abolish the reserve system. It is one consequence of colonialism I will keep because having space that is "Indian country" is essential to my well-being. I also recognize this is my choice. Other Indian people face the same dilemma and choose the city. I do not believe that being part of your community necessarily is as simple as locating yourself and your family on reserve. I do recognize that living at home (or at your partner's home) is the easiest way to establish the relationships that self-determination requires.

I also recognize that the realities of adoption, section 12(1)(b), incarceration, residential schools, and domestic and sexual abuse (by which every Aboriginal family is touched) make it very difficult for many individuals to return or remain home. These facts must be incorporated into any analysis which discusses linking the rights of Indians to reserve residency. We must all recognize that the reserve is a colonial construct and not an Indian one. This issue of reserve residency as a requirement of Indian rights is a different issue (albeit an important one) from the responsibility I am speaking of. The responsibility I am speaking about is the responsibility we carry for maintaining our families and our communities.

In the summer of 1994, I left my position at a Canadian law school in Ottawa, Ontario, although not because of any particular, individual experiences at that law school. I left because of some of my experiences and my children's experiences living in the nation's capital. I left because it became too difficult at that point in my life to live in a city and maintain a true connection to "Indian" reality. I am not saying it is impossible; it was just too difficult for me. I left and went to the closest university to my husband's home. Close is a three-hour drive and at least two or three days a week, eight months a year, away from my home and my family. And I consider myself fortunate. Just a little further north and there would be no road access to my adopted community and no hope that my family could reside in the community full-time while allowing me to pursue my career objectives. This decision is a constant struggle for us.

Before I left the law school in Ottawa to join the Native Studies Department at the University of Saskatchewan, I survived for five years as a law teacher.[1] Leaving law schools behind was not an accident but a conscious choice. This followed my realization that law contains no answers but is in fact a very large and very real part of the problem Aboriginal people continue to face.[2] Law is one of the instruments through which colonialism continues to flow. This is a problem that is both vast and elusive. Leaving legal education in my wake was a personal act of resistance calculated (and prayed upon) as an act of survival, but more importantly as an act of renewal. Perhaps leaving law teaching was more about personal strength (or the lack thereof) than I understood at the time.

The move from law to Native Studies[3] has not completely resolved the tension and contradictions I experience at the university. Even in a department such as Native Studies, I remain an "outsider." I know that is full of irony. If anywhere in the university there is a place and space for Indian people and the knowledge systems we were raised in, it is Native Studies. Native Studies allows me to commit all of my teaching energy, as well as my research and writing, to Indian people and issues. I can now live more fully in my Indian intellect. At the law school, most of my energy was committed to mainstream constitutional and property law regimes. Aboriginal education in law was relegated to the margins (or one "special topics" course a year). The move to Native Studies accomplished

9

the centring of my teaching and thinking on Aboriginal people. In this way I overcame one aspect of disconnection. However, I do not (yet) understand all that this means for me in the future.

This personal confessional may bewilder some, but I understand best when knowledge is personal. This is the lesson of "double understanding." We must think and feel to truly gain knowledge. I came to understand that law is not the solution to oppression during the time (more than a decade) when I survived legal education. This book documents the detail of that understanding. Because I believe that knowledge is personal, my life choices must reflect the knowledge I have gained, even when that specific knowledge was not what I was seeking. When I understood that law was *the* problem, I also realized that by continuing to teach law, I was cooperating too fully in my own oppression. This evolution in my own thinking and career aspirations has particular consequences in my understanding of the visionways to self-determination for my people and other Indigenous nations. I suppose it is possible for me to imagine returning to law teaching. All I know now is that standing outside of legal institutions for these past five years has provided me with a necessary opportunity to understand the multiple ways in which Canadian law is oppressive, to me individually and to First Nations collectively.

My everyday experience of law as a profession is theoretical. I think about law. I study carefully and often painfully the outcome of individual incidents in Canadian law and how they are applied to Aboriginal people. I do not spend day upon day entering Canadian court rooms. This is important to understand as it describes the place where this book comes from. There will always be a need for front-line legal warriors as long as the land needs protecting, the children are being apprehended, and Aboriginal people are being arrested. Long ago I discovered that I could not ever comfortably experience the practice of law on a full-time basis. My skills and gifts are better put to use in other places.

I became involved in law because I believed in it. I believed that justice could be achieved through law. That sounds terribly naive to me now. Although I still believe in justice and peace, I no longer have the faith necessary to maintain a close relationship with Canadian laws, lawmakers or judicial resolution of disputes as we know them all today. This book is very much an examination of the reasons for which I was unable to maintain my individual faith in Canadian law. Law was and is my ultimate lesson in colonial oppression. I am not seeking escape but rather a way to put my understanding of colonialism and law to better use. Just as I would not accept being a victim of abuse during adolescence, I cannot accept that my relationship with law (and my experience in law schools) will always be about my daily survival. I seek renewal.

As I struggled with the pain in my life and in the lives of those I am close to, I became more and more determined to understand the process of colonialism and colonization. If colonialism brought our nations to this point, then undoing the damage of colonialism must be the answer. I now understand this thinking to be much too linear (image that!) to be helpful. It is not just the colonial relations that must be undone but all of the consequences (addictions, loss of language, loss of parenting skills, loss of self-respect, abuse and violence, and so on). Colonialism is no longer a linear, vertical relationship—colonizer does to colonized—it is a horizontal and entangled relationship (like a spider web). Now, sometimes the colonized turn the colonial skills and images they learned against others who are less powerful in their communities, thus mimicking their oppressors.

Colonialism undoubtedly is a significant cause of the struggle and strife in First Nation communities. However, ending colonial relations against First Nations (such as the *Indian Act*) will clearly be insufficient to remedy the full impact of those relations. When I considered the consequences of colonialism, including suicide, conflict with the criminal justice system, child welfare apprehensions and intrusions, violence against women and children, sexual abuse, and so on, I began to notice that all the consequences had one thing in common—that is, the creation of varying and multiple degrees of disconnection.[4] The obvious solution to the relations of disconnection, and these are relations (alcoholism would be an example), is to create or reclaim relations of connection. I wonder if this answer is too individualistic or perhaps even too simplistic.

At first, I did not see a clear relationship between what I had come to understand as a framework for self-determination and what has to be done within our relationships to deal with disconnection. This bothered me and set me thinking again. It was here that I returned to the writings of Paulo Freire. I now understand that both self-government and perhaps self-determination have become too elitist and too political in the worst sense of the word to assist me in thinking myself out of oppression. My goal, my dream for my children is that they may have freedom and independence. I have replaced in my vocabulary the concepts of self-government and self-determination with the standard Freire suggested, independence.[5] This gives rise to the title of this book.

This book was first visioned[6] as a discussion on self-government or self-determination. It was first completed as a discussion paper for the Royal Commission on Aboriginal People.[7] It has evolved considerably since then. I was not comfortable sharing all my thoughts and ideas on the pathways forward with the Royal Commission because I experienced the Commission as a non-Aboriginal space.

My concern with the troublesome elements of self-determination and self-government is not simple. Mere days before I packed up my family and moved cross-country to the Thunderchild First Nation, I spent two very frustrating and illuminating days at a self-government think-tank sponsored by the Royal Commission on Aboriginal Peoples. This think-tank was struck to discuss pressing and unresolved issues regarding Aboriginal self-government. I tried to listen patiently to often dry academic prattle about the meaning of self-government. More than half of the people present had never experienced daily life in any Aboriginal community. Most were non-Aboriginal scholars. Only one individual present was a current resident of a First Nation community. It was a discussion carried on against all odds. It was painful to listen, knowing what the realities were in my home community and in my partner's home.

I do not fault the Commission or individual Commissioners (but I do note they had the power and choice to do things very differently). I now understand that even a Royal Commission is a construct of colonial power. At the beginning of their term they spent day after day travelling to communities to listen to the people. Some of this information made it to the final report. However, to be true to First Nations processes would require an opportunity for communities (as communities) to come to a consensus on what the solutions are. Rather, the Royal Commission on Aboriginal Peoples only ended up mimicking the earlier efforts of research scientists. The Commission took information from the people, then returned it to Ottawa to craft solutions in isolation behind closed doors. *The* solution is *not* about constructing a single (national) model. Because it cannot involve even a majority of the people it will be applied to, such an initiative is more about reinventing colonialism 1990s style than it is about real change. Change is going to come from the people in the communities. Change will come when we rebuild our relationships on traditional principles, such as the Anishnabe ones of caring, sharing, truth and strength. This is the real meaning of the concept of community-based.

For the Commission to have been something different, less emphasis should have been placed by the Commissioners on what the Canadian government would accept. This severely limited the opportunities and vision of the Commission at the same time as it created a pressure toward status quo solutions and processes. The over-reliance on academics and other professionals to the exclusion of Indians at the community level is a conventional solution to conundrums faced by Canadian governments. The individual goodwill of Commissioners, their Aboriginal knowledge, or their desire to learn about Aboriginal Peoples are not sufficient to topple years of accepted colonial practice or colonial relationships. I began to understand that my experience at the Commission was just another lesson in colonial oppression. How can a Commission established by government order, with its mandate drafted by a former Supreme Court of Canada justice (no matter how sympathetic to Aboriginal Peoples), merely in consultation with Aboriginal Peoples, be seen as a solution. Their mandate was broad, but it remained one-sided. As reflected in the Commissioners' desire to come to a solution that Canadian governments would accept, the Commissioners did not disturb existing power relationships between the Crown and the Indians. It is precisely this relationship that needs disturbing. This is in fact the mirror image of the lesson I learned about Canadian law. (Thankfully these days I am catching on faster.)

That year, 1994, was an illuminating one for me. It seems to have been my year to confront colonialism head-on (and the fact that many of these lessons arrived during the Year of Indigenous Peoples is an irony which is not lost on me). I rested that summer and drenched myself in as many things "Indian" as I possibly could. I taught sixty-three wonderful and courageous Aboriginal students who were chasing their dreams about law school. I chased pow-wows from north to south and east to west. I took my family to old historic sites, each having a particular significance to my adopted community, around what is now known as Saskatchewan. By walking the territory we chose to put our family down upon, I learned lessons from the long-distant past. I spent time reflecting on my years of law (colonial survival). I tried to distance myself from every thing and everyone who was not healthy for me. I reflected that summer on many experiences of mine over the years that there had been no time to consider when my energy was consumed by the legal institution that surrounded me. That summer of wandering and thinking often led me to ponder the kinds of changes that would make a difference to Aboriginal people. In other words, I spent a great deal of time thinking about self-government (even though this was not really conscious at that time).

What is left to share now are some stories about personal experiences which fundamentally shaped my thinking about self-determination and the journey to independence. My thinking did not just revolve around my personal situation and my personal dissatisfaction with my professional life. At all times, it is necessary for me to remember and acknowledge the privileges (such as income, employment and post-secondary education) I possess.

During that summer, I also took hard looks at the structures which we must rely upon to "lead" us to self-government. I am referring specifically to the national, provincial and territorial organizations which represent Aboriginal people. At least that is the claim. Taking the best known as an example, I looked at the Assembly of First Nations. This organization is an assembly of elected *Indian Act* chiefs. I seem to be doing much apologizing, so again, I intend no disrespect to the many men and women who have suffered long and hard to ensure that our collected Indian voices have national volume. Unfortunately, it is not essential that there is anything really "Indian" about an *Indian Act* chief[8] or the office that they occupy. These people draw their limited authority from a piece of federal government legislation. If they act on their inherent Indigenous authority, those actions are either disallowed by the Department of Indian Affairs or worse yet are penalized (such as by the withholding of discretionary band funding). This, of course, is the recurring theme of colonial intrusion.

I concluded that the Assembly of First Nations, owing largely to its origins in a piece of colonial legislation (that is, the *Indian Act*), is not the answer. At least one national chief, Ovide Mercredi, has also pointed out this contradiction. Of even more concern is the fact that the Assembly of First Nations, in common with other provincial, territorial and tribal council bodies, is not democratic. First, elected chiefs answer to the Minister of Indian Affairs under the provisions of the *Indian Act*.[9] This inverts the relationship between the people and the leaders.

The second example is more disturbing. First Nation communities elect the chiefs. The chiefs then gather and elect the tribal council, and the provincial, territorial and national leaders. How can we continue to listen to bold assertions that they represent the people? These Indian organizations were not formed by the people, but by the chiefs. Our provincial and national leaders are not raised by the people (and particularly not by the women as would be the custom of my people). This has the consequence of removing our tribal, provincial and national leadership from the ground, as their first line of accountability is to other chiefs. It sets the principle, presuming a provincial or national chief wishes to be re-elected, that the other chiefs, *not* the people, come first. This is the most unacceptable of all the structural consequences of governing from within a structure not our own. Elitism amongst the leadership must be recognized as a recurring theme. This elitism is fostered because of the structure of the government system we have been forced to participate in. It is also a theme I see as being a significant part of perpetuating colonial relations in the 1990s.

In a recent work by Kanien'kehaka scholar, Gerald (Taiaiake) Alfred, this analysis of the position and role of our current leaders is taken further:

> The hard truth is that many of those who hold positions of authority in Native communities have come to depend on the colonial framework for their power, employment, and status. How many of them would still hold their positions if the criteria for leadership reflected Indigenous values instead of an ability to serve the interests of mainstream society? Very few contemporary Native politicians can honestly claim to possess the qualities and skills needed to lead in a non-coercive, participatory, transparent, consensus-based system. The hunger for power, money, and status prevents many people from seeing what is best for the community in the long run. But even when the people who seek that power do so with the best intentions, for the good of the people, *the fact remains that holding non-consensual power over others is contrary to tradition.* (Alfred 1999:27–28. Emphasis added)

Although I concur fully with the analysis quoted, I have some difficulty embracing all of Alfred's conclusions. Alfred believes, and this is the focus of his book, that the solution lies in the leadership. He believes that the way forward is to raise a different kind of, a more traditional, leadership. Although, I agree that this may be part of the solution, I do not believe it is a full solution. Although Alfred has done a better job in his second book in presenting the issues and roles of Kanien'kehaka women, the inclusion is still not complete in his work. I believe the fact that his work is written from the male "perspective" (the only place he can speak from as the only place I can speak from is as a woman) diminishes the role he sees for the community. The leaders, after all, are nothing without the people (and especially the women) standing with them.

As an aside, I think it is very important that scholars who are First Peoples comment on each other's work. Most of us work in institutions where there are few if any First Nations academics we can consider our colleagues. I am, however, encouraged that we have come to a time where there are enough First Nations scholars that this discourse can now be offered in written form.

I do not believe that the Assembly of First Nations (formerly the National Indian Brotherhood) is without purpose (or worse, has only harmed the people). The truth is that most of these leaders have done the best they could within a structure that is limiting, colonial and denies the true source of a leader's authority. The structure holds tremendous potential to turn the person who is leader, inside out. These organizations do serve, in my opinion, an essential purpose for First Nations citizens. They are the "tail-gunners" in the Indian "army." (Although this war imagery is generally not what I encourage, as I am both a woman and come from a tradition where peace is a paramount value, it does seem appropriate here.) These chiefs' organizations keep track of the few successes and powers we have to ensure that we do not lose any more ground. They are the pillars that allow people like me to have the space in which to dream. This realization about the role of our political organizations of chiefs led me to another conclusion.

I began to understand that real change must come from the community. This is the only way to really change things for Aboriginal people. Real change will come when the women stand up. When the women stand up, the men and children will also soon be standing. The experience of the community of Alkali Lake in British Columbia may be one of the best popular examples of this process. One woman sobered up and it rippled through the entire community.

Over the summer, I also reflected on the experiences I had had of the Charlottetown Round of constitutional renovation. Much of this process was disturbing to me. I found it disturbing to watch the "divide and conquer" politics used against our leadership since the time of contact unfold in full public view, as if we were the authors of those disputes. The best example of this colonial phenomenon is the gender divisions which exist among and within our national organizations.[10] For much of this process, I sat thankfully outside the arena. From time to time, I was forced to field calls from curious journalists. Like many others in the country, my experience of the latest round of constitutional oblivion was to turn on the TV and watch the "Journal" or the "National."

During the preamble to the Charlottetown Round, which might be "ancient" history[11] by now, I learned lessons from the process which are still important for me to remember and share. I was asked by the Assembly of First Nations to do some contract work for them. I organized (on very short notice) four constituent assemblies on women, youth, urban residents and Elders. This project was just one component of the First Nations Circle on the Constitution. Two of these assemblies, the one for youth and the one for Elders, brought to me some important teachings.

During the youth assembly, several of the committee I worked with came to me on the first day of the conference and asked if they could re-organize the conference. Rather than merely repeating the morning workshops, they wanted to bring them together. The five workshops would be combined to make three and this would be the afternoon schedule. The self-government and the law (constitution) workshops would be combined, as would education and culture. Left to stand by itself was the justice workshop. I was elated. Whether the youth realized it or not (and I do not know if they did because we never discussed it), they were following an age-old tradition of consensus building used by Aboriginal people. Small groups of peoples (families) reach a consensus and then several groups (clans in the case of the Kanien'kehaka) are brought together to continue the process. This was a lesson of encouragement.

Sitting beside the elation, I also was greatly disturbed that justice fit nowhere in this new conference structure. I was disturbed enough that I made certain I had some time in the afternoon to listen in on the justice workshop. This workshop was very poorly attended. There were maybe a dozen young people in the room when I walked in, shortly after the workshop started. Most of the people present were young men who'd had first-hand experience of conflict with Canadian law. In and of itself this did not surprise me. What surprised me was that the workshop had developed into an airing session on personal injustice and experience. Although I see this as necessary to the healing process, it was clearly not what a justice workshop at a self-government conference was intended to accomplish. The Elder left unhappy with the individualized nature of the discussion. I knew he was disappointed that the youth could not get past their personal pain to see the patterns of colonialism and oppression in their experiences. Nor did anyone discuss how these issues would impact on self-governing justice relations.

Where I Am Standing

I walked away from the room knowing the place where justice (broadly defined) sat. It sat in the centre of the circle surrounded by education and culture, and self-government and law. I began to see, in the way the relationship was inverted, that justice, written Indian style, was the key. I developed an unhealthy fear that we would be successful in amending the constitution. I knew that the constitution might be an answer, but it was an answer to the wrong question. The question ought to be: How do we achieve justice for Aboriginal Peoples domiciled in Canada? To concentrate too long and hard on constitutional amendment focuses too much attention on Canada and leaves Aboriginal people only further oppressed and marginalized. How can a process that capitalizes on our oppression be seen as a viable solution? This teaching was furthered by my experience at the Elders' gathering in Morley, Alberta.

At the Elders' Assembly, I was equally set back in my place. I was assigned the duty of facilitating a workshop on the question of Indian status (or membership). I assumed this was going to be a women's workshop and used that to counter-balance my fear of being the facilitator for a group of Elders. At my age, it was cultural suicide to believe I could facilitate such a group. When I walked into the room where the workshop was scheduled there were no women. All of my panic returned as the workshop progressed. I learned that the Elders present (about ten) were all Cree men. These men were very concerned about any agreement to new constitutional provisions. They each told that they saw a familiar pattern of legislative oppression (and these are my words). They spoke in Cree about how the treaty cards had been taken away from them and replaced with status cards earlier this century. They told of how that moved the source of their rights away from the treaties their ancestors had signed and prayed over to the *Indian Act*. What they foresaw was the evolution from the *Indian Act* to a new form of oppression that would be inflicted under the *Charter* and the constitution. Perhaps, they chose to live with the evil they knew but I do not think this was the case at all. They wanted to move toward a truly new time in the relationship between settler nations and First Nations. They wanted to move toward the treaties and the just implementation of those agreements. All of the arrangements that are required for peaceful co-existence between first and founding nations are found in those treaties, if not in words, in spirit. It is the will to implement the treaty relationship that is missing from Canada's various constitutional negotiation packages.

One further comment on my intentions for this book is essential. I write for Indian people. To the best of my ability, I try to write about law in a way that creates the greatest amount of access for the average Aboriginal person. This is the audience that I first and foremost imagine reading my work. I see their faces as I write. This is not to say that I do not think about the non-Indian people who might also pick up this book. I hope that some of these readers will come to know this Indian person (and my ideas) a little better. I also know that some of these non-Indian readers will take offence at my words, feelings and ideas. I could choose to allow this to soften some of the things I say, or worse, to completely silence me. If I allowed this to happen, I could not say I write for my people, first and foremost. I would ask those readers to understand that my intent is not to hurt anyone.[12] There are hard words in this book for the Indian audience as well. In my opinion, the offence must be read through and understood against the very real power relationships that exist in this country as a result of colonial oppression

The lessons I have learned over the years have led me to two broad objectives for this work. The first is to begin the task of articulating a theory of Aboriginal and treaty rights in Canadian law. As Charles Wilkinson[13] noted with reference to "Indian law" in the United States, no such theory presently grounds the resolution of Aboriginal claims in Canadian courts. This is an unacceptable vacuum. The first step in addressing this failing is to undertake a careful examination of cases to determine how far the courts have gone in articulating a comprehensive theory. The second objective is related to the first. Before any consideration of a theory of Aboriginal and treaty rights is possible, it is essential to consider the knowledge base and understanding that I, as an Aboriginal person, possess of "right relationships."

Notes

1. It is interesting to note that three women were the first "Indian" professors to be appointed at Canadian law schools, on July 1, 1989. It is interesting that it took so long. All three of us (Darlene Johnston, Mary Ellen Turpel-Lafond and myself) are currently "retired" from law schools.
2. I am far from convinced that I have found an intellectual home in Native Studies but that is a topic for another piece of writing. See Monture-Angus 1999c, and on a similar topic, Monture-Angus 1999a.
3. Given the fact that I believe both Métis and Inuit experience the department differently from how I, as an "Indian" person experience it, I here intend my comments to be specific and not inclusive.
4. It was the writing of Rupert Ross (1996: especially pages 131 to 135) that really emphasized the importance of understanding the "disconnected" state of many Aboriginal lives and communities.
5. I adopted independence as a goal because Aboriginal self-government is a politically loaded and narrowly defined term. I do recognize that in other political contexts, such as the aspirations of some Quebecois, independence is a loaded term.
6. Throughout this text I will take certain liberties with the English language. I have a need to create verbs from nouns as Indigenous languages are verb, not noun, based.

7. This earlier paper is titled: "The Familiar Face of Colonial Oppression: An Examination of Canadian Law and Judicial Decision Making" (Monture-Angus 1995).

8. In describing the situation at the Thunderchild Reserve after the Rebellion of 1885, Jack Funk states:

> What these charges demonstrated more than anything was that the whiteman did not understand the Indian system of band allegiance or how a chief gained his position. They thought that band leadership was a hereditary position. They did not understand that a chief only had the authority which the band members chose to give him. The whiteman thought that a chief had absolute power over his followers, like a feudal king. Hence, they considered Thunderchild to be "hostile" because he had been unable to control all of his young men all of the time. (Funk 1989:1–2)

9. This description provides some insight into the gap that exists between what we know today as the *Indian Act* chief and the traditional role and responsibilities. Examples include: section 28(2) which gives the Minister the power to issue permits for the occupation of band lands; section 32(1) provides that "a transaction of any kind whereby a band or a member thereof purports to sell, barter, exchange, give or otherwise dispose of cattle or other animals, grain or hay, whether wild or cultivated, or root crops or plants or their products from a reserve in Manitoba, Saskatchewan or Alberta, to a person other than a member of that band, is void unless the superintendent approves the transaction in writing"; section 42(1) gives the Minister the exclusive authority over "deceased Indians"; section 65 gives authority to the Minister to make certain payment from capital moneys; section 79 gives to the Governor in Council the power to set aside an election; and most importantly, section 83(4) gives the Minister the power to approve or set aside band by-laws.

10. In my own experience, gender relationships in our political organizations do not mirror how I have seen these organizations described in the press. Perhaps I am just fortunate. Perhaps there is a problem with the absoluteness of the characterization.

11. My friend and colleague, Denise McConney, who teaches Indian History courses at the University of Saskatchewan, tells me that "it is not history if it happened in my lifetime."

12. I want to thank an old high school friend, Gerald Bisschop, who by coincidence (if you in fact believe in coincidence), I recently crossed paths with again. I shared with him a copy of my last book, *Thunder in My Soul*, which he read. One of the comments he made to me was about how angry I had become since we had last seen each other as young adults. This comment troubled me and has stayed with me. I continue to reflect upon it. I want to walk away from this anger (or thunder as I prefer to think of it) but it is trapped by and imbedded in incidents of continued pain and oppression for Indian people, both individually and collectively. Sometimes, what is called my anger is white guilt transformed so that I, the member of the oppressed class, feels shame and am silenced. It takes a considerable amount of energy

to overwhelm this silencing and thus, the response often comes out sounding harsh. I am trying to tame my anger and know it would be a much easier task to accomplish if more people picked up their guilt and forced the government to deal with the issues that still have negative effects on Indian lives. And Gerald, thanks for the nudge (knowing that probably was not a comfortable thing for you to tell me).

13. For a full discussion please see Wilkinson 1987.

Chapter One

To Break With The Past
Searching For The Meaning
Of Self-Determination

This book is both a journey and reflections on what I have learned about Canadian law and the degree to which I now see the laws of Canada as an obstacle for the governance aspirations of Aboriginal people and Aboriginal nations. It is a book also very much about dreaming a future for Aboriginal people. I mean to be controversial in writing this book. In fact, I have struggled through two years of terror[1] at my university to come to the place where I can regain my controversial voice and to again exercise it with confidence. This book is intended to invoke critical thought on self-government rather than agreement and acquiescence. I understand from many of my Aboriginal teachers that change for our communities will only come out of flux or chaos. If this book creates an intellectual maelstrom for either Indian or white readers then I have accomplished my goal. In my opinion, we have become much too ambiguous in our visioning and in dream chasing our Aboriginal futures in what is now known as Canada.

As Aboriginal Peoples (that is, Indian (First Nations), Inuit and Métis) are not homogenous, there is no single Aboriginal "perspective" on anything, let alone governance. This is a significant challenge to the work of creating discourse and shared understandings on which our future visions can be built. To complicate matters further, homogeneity does not even exist within the First Nations, Métis or Inuit. Likewise, Canadians are not a monolithic entity. Therefore, the work of creating "self-government" is both layered and detailed. In this book I am interested in articulating one Aboriginal view of what the pathway (or pathways) away from oppression might look like. It is understanding the nature of our oppressive relationships with governments that I see as the first and central task of this broader goal. The book begins by examining the past and what Aboriginal people have tried to accomplish on our journey toward reclaiming our individual and collective identities.

This book is one perspective, mine, on what some would call self-government. It is, therefore, an understanding that is strongly influenced by the fact that I am Mohawk. It is also influenced by the fact that I have now spent five years of my life in Cree territory. This book is not the Aboriginal perspective as no such thing exists. The simple understanding of perspective is that it cannot be singular because of the diversity of Aboriginal peoples. However, it is more essential to understand that the idea of perspective diminishes and disappears the fact that each Aboriginal nation always had systems of knowledge and understanding, law and government. These distinct systems of knowledge do form into a common pattern with shared concepts and beliefs. Perspective connotes something that is lesser and perhaps emotional. It is opinion based. It is an inappropriate label to apply to Aboriginal ways of understanding which are in fact knowledge systems.

When Aboriginal Peoples discuss the meaning of self-government and/or self-determination, we are forced to do it in a language that is not our own. We must express our ideas in English or in French, both of which epitomize our colonial experiences. It is almost solely Aboriginal energy that fosters the accommodations that are required to carry on both the political and legal dialogues in either of the Canadian colonial languages. This is a particular experience of colonial oppression. At the same time, the languages that were brought to our territories have benefitted Aboriginal people, in an odd kind of way, as we are able to more fully share our ideas beyond Indigenous boundaries.

Reclaiming our self-governing relationships sometimes means remembering, and in other places means putting back into practice, traditional systems of governance (or responsibility). It requires the commitment of Canadians to allow Aboriginal Peoples to lead the way to the future. Canada does not have the answer for us, and it is essential that Canada recognize this because to do otherwise is not only to continue colonial relations but also to entrench colonialism even further in the relationship between Aboriginal nations and Canada. Canadians must carefully examine their past and present relationships with Aboriginal Peoples in an effort to take themselves to the place where they understand what is required to move beyond the colonial relations on which this country is based. Canadians must come to understand what the true history of this country is and how they (as well as their ancestors) are complicit in both the overt and more subtle forms of colonialism and oppression Aboriginal people have survived as individuals and as nations. Canadians cannot fix or help Aboriginal people until they have both stopped (and undone) their multiple forms, thoughts and practices of colonialism.[2]

However, this is not what this book is about. The commitment to examine Canadian responsibility is the task of Canadians and their governments. It is not my Mohawk place nor my responsibility to discuss or detail it, but rather merely to acknowledge that I know such a responsibility exists. To do more would be a fundamental violation of my responsibility as a Mohawk woman to respect Canada's authority to govern itself. A reversal of intellectual conquest and colonialism is not the answer. At the same time, I stand on my right (and responsibility) to reject Canadian forms of government which for more than a hundred years have been imposed without consent on my people.

Neither is this book a litigators' guide to Canadian case law, Aboriginal rights or treaty rights. I am most conscious that I do not possess a fine technical legal mind; nor have I ever aspired to this goal. It is not a natural way of thinking for me. I do not think in fragments and lines. I do not choose to devote the energy to developing my mind in this direction as it flows contrary to the Aboriginal teachings I follow. Rather, this book is about the impact of Canadian law on Aboriginal nations.

This is also not a book which examines existing or historical government policies on Aboriginal people. We have had enough of this form of external study. It is not about the current negotiations for self-government that are occurring in some Aboriginal communities. It is not a critical discussion of the Royal Commission on Aboriginal Peoples and its recommendations.

This is a book that is located in Aboriginal thought and heart. It is about the consequences of political and legal oppression on Aboriginal people, our communities and our nations. It is a book about the visionways for the future. It is about the path that I see before Aboriginal peoples. It is a book written with soul and from soul.

There is often a hesitancy and a reluctance in response to the suggestion that a renewed historical understanding is required for a new relationship between Aboriginal Peoples and Canada to truly take shape. However, it is unlikely that a new relationship can be forged without acknowledging and then remedying historical wrongs. Aboriginal experience of this country's history is not linear; the past is not simply the past. Aboriginal people still suffer the inter-generational consequences of these historical wrongs, in part because Canada has never significantly tried to remedy in full the consequences of colonial imposition.

Residential school experience easily demonstrates this point. Children were removed from their parents for ten months of the year and placed in institutions. In such artificial environments, they did not learn how to be caring parents (or responsible self-governing adults). Their children in turn learned dysfunctional parenting patterns. In the residential schools, many children were criminally assaulted, and this is the way the activities in those schools must be understood.[3] Dr. Maggie Hodgson describes the reality of the residential school experience as follows:

What would you do if you were a child being removed from your parents' arms? Would you scream, "Mom, help! Mom, help!"? What would you do if you saw your parents standing there help-lessly? Would you feel, "They should have stopped them from taking me"? What would you feel if you arrived in that big building where there were people speaking a funny language and when you spoke the language you knew, you were hit and told to speak in that strange language? What if your culture taught that your hair was part of your spirit, and the strange people cut off all your hair and scrubbed your head with something that burned your scalp to get rid of "lice"? What if you were bathed in a public washroom? What would you do with the shame? What would you do if you saw your brother or sister and you ran to them and were hit for speaking to them?

How much fear and loneliness would you feel? Probably the same amount as those children did. In residential school, grieving over loss of contact with parents often had to happen under your blankets or in your pillow—it would be repressed in order not to give the people who took you away the benefit of seeing your pain. It's natural for children to cry when they are hurt, scared or need attention. If in your home of origin you experienced paren-tal response to your crying, you would expect to receive a re-sponse now. What if the only response you got for crying was being hit? Maybe the occasional nun or priest would pay atten-tion to you. But whom could you trust? Whom could you trust? (1992:105)

This terror of residential schools is not a terror of the past alone; it constantly recreates itself and continues to transform Aboriginal commu-nities. The loss of parenting skills in one generation, for example, impacts on generation after generation until the loss is fully addressed. However, it is not just the loss of skills that is the legacy of residential schools. The loss of the human ability to trust is a paramount concern. The real conse-quence of this imposition is the creation of peoples who do not remember how to live in peace and with peace.

It is not enough, although it may be essential, to "apologize" to the victims of the physical, spiritual, linguistic and sexual abuse that occurred in residential schools. The harm done to First Nations cannot be measured by counting and perhaps compensating these victims. This is to individu-alize a harm that has also had significant impact on entire communities.[4] This impact is greater than the sum of the individual wrongs. The harm of residential schools extends to all First Nations, both as individuals and as communities. As I understand my family history, my grandparents left the Six Nations community and moved to the city because they wanted to protect their children from the "mush-hole," the school that served our community. As a result, their grandchildren are well educated but, in my family, we suffered dislocation from our home community, the clan, ceremony and the language. These are harms that I see as directly and centrally caused by residential schools even though my parents, aunts, uncles and cousins did not attend them.

In my opinion, there has been enough written that focuses on the specific harms, often cataloguing the crimes, inflicted on First Nations children. This very narrow focus operates to conceal the outcomes and impacts those schools have had on our families and communities. My point is not to minimize the harms done to individuals but to make clearly the point that these crimes are just a small portion of the actual impact. One of the things that needs to be considered is the simple fact that we did survive the genocidal educational attempts of Canadian authorities. Beyond this simple fact, First Nations need to begin discussing the ways in which we survived.

One example clarifies my position. Sitting in a circle with some prisoners at Saskatchewan Penitentiary (a medium security federal institution in Prince Albert), I heard one man speak of his experiences in residential school. However, the quality of his comments differed from what I had heard previously. He spoke of surviving by looking the other way at night when things happened in the bed beside him. Our children (many of whom are now the adult leaders in our communities) survived by looking the other way. This behaviour may have helped them survive the incidents of abuse in residential schools, but it now has a larger negative consequence for our communities. Many reports document the catastrophic levels of violence and abuse against women and children that occur in First Nations communities. It is not just violent behaviour that was picked up in residential schools, so was the ability to look the other way. This is not solely the individualized responsibility of male leadership in the community; it is actually a consequence of colonialism. The catch is that a behaviour adopted to help you survive as a child may not be a beneficial behaviour today. However, behaviours that have helped us survive (even when they are dysfunctional) are difficult to identify as part of the problem and more difficult to let go.

The experiences, such as residential schools, left as legacy to Aboriginal people abject terror. On the days when I am able to remain conscious of the world and space around me (often white space), I am conscious of my own individualized terror, as well as the terror of those around me. In her book, Killing Rage, bell hooks notes:

> Even though I live and move in spaces where I am surrounded by whiteness, there is no comfort that makes the terrorism disappear. All black people in the United States, irrespective of their class,

status or politics, live with the possibility that they will be terror-
ized by whiteness. (hooks 1995:46)

Although I do not presume that Blackness and "Indian-ness" occupy the
same location, portions of the way I experience whiteness as a Mohawk
woman, I suspect, mirror the location of Blackness as bell hooks describes
it.

Today the results of these historic experiences, such as residential
schools, have spread and multiplied within society to other social correctional systems, such as child welfare, young offender and criminal justice.
To try to address the present-day manifestations of the historical oppression as singular, distinct and individualized, without a clear understanding of colonial causation and the subsequent multiplication of forms of
social disorder, is to offer only a superficial opportunity for change and
wellness to occur in Aboriginal communities. Such remedies, as they are
incomplete, do not offer any real change. The need for historical honesty
is not a need to blame others for the present-day realities, but a plea for
the opportunity to deal with all of the layers and multiplications of
oppression that permeate Aboriginal lives and Aboriginal communities
today. When non-Aboriginal guilt becomes the focus of any process
meant to address historical wrongs, Aboriginal pain is appropriated and
then transformed. This transformation is a recreation of colonial relationships.

On behalf of Canada, the Minister of Indian Affairs, Jane Stewart,
stated in 1997:

> Sadly, our history with respect to the treatment of Aboriginal
> people is not something in which we can take pride. Attitudes of
> racial and cultural superiority led to a suppression of Aboriginal
> culture and values. As a country, we are burdened by past actions
> that resulted in weakening the identity of Aboriginal peoples,
> suppressing their languages and cultures, and outlawing spiritual
> practices. We must recognize the impact of these actions on the
> once self-sustaining nations that were disaggregated, disrupted or
> even destroyed by the dispossession of traditional territory, by
> the relocation of Aboriginal people, and by some provisions of
> the *Indian Act*. We must acknowledge that the result of these
> actions was the erosion of the political, economic and social
> systems of Aboriginal people and nations. (Minister of Indian and
> Northern Development 1997:4)

This kind of apologizing accomplishes more in the direction of massaging
white guilt than in alleviating Indian pain. In fact, in the aftermath of the
so-called apology, I was witness to an unleashing of memories and pain in

Indian communities—communities where existing social services and health resources were largely inadequate to deal with the memories that were turned to the surface by the Minister's apology. (Acknowledging that "whiteness" is a constant terror in my life, how do I accept the white psychologist, resource teacher, principal or director of health as someone who brings help and hope rather than as a representative of the oppression and terror I survived?)

Although the apology may be a step in the right direction, the accompanying action is insufficient. The "Statement of Reconciliation" was the first official response to the six volume report on the Royal Commission on Aboriginal Peoples (RCAP 1996c). Second, $350 million was pledged to a healing fund. RCAP noted that "unless economic conditions and welfare programs on reserves change radically and soon, the bill for social assistance will reach $1 billion by 1999 and $1.5 billion by 2002" (1996B:46).

The oppression, colonizing and labelling as inferior has left a large imprint on Aboriginal lives. The call for the "right" of self-governing powers by Aboriginal people is equally a call for the opportunity to remedy the consequences of colonialism and the corresponding oppression we carry as individuals and collectively. This in fact makes discussions and negotiations for self-government very difficult, because part of what Aboriginal people seek, the right to heal, is not considered by all a self-governing function. Often, I believe, this aspect of the Aboriginal understanding of self-determination is not visible to those who negotiate on behalf of the Canadian state.

The call for remedies cannot be seen as culturally (or Aboriginally) specific, for there is a familiar maxim that lawyers hold dear: Every right has a remedy. The call for remedies to follow along with our Aboriginal (or treaty) rights is not an *inherent* Aboriginal right as found in Canada's constitution, as we had no need for remedies (or traditions) which addressed colonial impacts prior to contact. It extends beyond the call for "government" relationships as Canadians would understand it. This is one of the significant problems with existing political and legal processes which have as their aim increasing the recognition of self-government powers held by Aboriginal nations. Much of what Aboriginal people load into the definition of self-government is not understood by Canadians as having anything to do with governance. Therefore, much of the cultural political understanding that Aboriginal people possess regarding the meaning of self-determination remains invisible to cultural outsiders.

There are a number of other faulty assumptions, stereotypes and invisibilities that undermine existing relationships between Canada and Aboriginal nations. One example demonstrates this. Diversity of views is seen as a cornerstone of Canadian democracy. The suggestion that Canada should embrace only one political perspective and therefore abolish the party system would be instantly decried. Yet I have been asked repeatedly why all the "Indians" do not support the national chief (whomever he might have been at the time). The parallel question, "Why don't all Canadians support the prime minister?" is obviously ridiculous to most people. This alarming requirement foisted on Aboriginal politics requires Aboriginal people to meet a standard of absolute unanimity prior to having our visions of government received as legitimate. Canada, on the other hand, does not claim to aspire to such accountability or organization. The same point can be made each time chiefs' organizations are criticized for the lack of women who participate. The faces in Canadian legislatures do not look much different from the ones in Aboriginal political arenas. These are examples of intolerable double standards.

Understanding that the standards placed by whites on the acceptance of Aboriginal agendas are unreasonable also exposes a further problem. The idea that Aboriginal people only have one perspective not only reinforces white ideas of Aboriginal inferiority but limits the opportunity of Aboriginal people to develop full and complete lives based on our dreams and visions, systems of knowledge, values and beliefs. Whites can accept that Aboriginal people have politics (albeit perhaps not fully) but do not recognize that we equally have theologies, epistemologies, knowledge systems, pedagogy and history. These are all collapsed into mere "perspective," thus, making actual the white fallacy of Aboriginal inferiority.

The respect (albeit only partial) that Aboriginal politics and Aboriginal politicians have gained is perhaps part of the problem. Growing up to be chief (politician) was the only professional career option available and visible to many Indian people for far too long. Having a singular (and single) career option has assisted in creating the narrow vision which encapsulates much thinking about employment options. In a similar fashion, to recognize political ambition as the only way to gain credibility and respect from whites narrowed and constrained the visibility and viability of other realms of Indigenous being (for example, spiritual, intellectual). The dreaming and "crying" for self-government as a right has not yet entered more than the political discourse. This is a problem of great magnitude.

Many people use the phrases self-government, self-determination and sovereignty interchangeably. However, the three phrases do not hold exactly the same meanings from any of the Aboriginal points of reference. A single Aboriginal tradition or notion of self-government only appears to exist when it is juxtaposed against the dominant non-Aboriginal system. Presenting the two worldviews as diametrically opposed takes us further away from the solutions as the competing understandings create distance rather than relationships. Unfortunately, it is difficult to discuss these issues concisely in the English language without falling into the trap of polarization in defining Aboriginal ways of being, defining and governing. Seeing loss of language as a condition of my colonial reality, I make no apology for the few appearances of constructing dichotomies. Once this country proceeds beyond creating colonial relationships, perhaps some other forms of dialogue will be possible.

Many traditional people, in my experience, hold a disdain for the phrase, self-government. (I use the word, traditional, to refer to those Aboriginal Peoples who strive to understand the ways of life as they were originally given to us. To be traditional does not mean to live in the past. This is another well kept myth. The values and ways of Aboriginal cultures are as viable today as they were centuries ago.) The definitions of and relationships between the terms, self-government and nationhood, are superbly articulated by Vine Deloria Jr. and Clifford Lytle:

> When we distinguish between nationhood and self-government, we speak of two different positions in the world. Nationhood implies a process of decision making that is free and uninhibited within the community, a community in fact that is almost completely insulated from external factors as it considers its possible options. *Self-government*, on the other hand, implies a recognition by the superior political power that some measure of local decision making is necessary but that this process must be monitored very carefully so that its products are compatible with the goals and policies of the larger political power. *Self-government* implies that the people were previously incapable of making any decisions for themselves and are now ready to assume some, but not all, of the responsibilities of a municipality. Under self-government, however, the larger moral issues that affect a *people's* relationship with other people are presumed to be included within the responsibilities of the larger nation. (1984:13-14)

For me, self-government as a goal feels too much like admitting defeat— not only accepting Aboriginal misery but agreeing that a full solution is the Aboriginal ability to self-administer that poverty and oppression. This must been seen as unacceptable because it is the ability to subordinate that creates the opportunity to colonize. Further, self-government that only allows Aboriginal people to assume some but not all powers of Aboriginal governance actually operates to further imbed destructive colonial relationships in our communities, all the time under the guise of offering real change and hope. Accepting such a limited form of governance continues into the future the false belief of Aboriginal inferiority, and through such solutions the confinement of Aboriginal nations continues.

The term sovereignty (and nationhood) is the political preference of many First Nations and other Aboriginal people. However, at least one scholar points out that the concept can never fully embrace Aboriginal beliefs as it rests on the idea "that there can be a permanent transference of power or authority from the individual to an abstraction of the collective called 'government'" (Alfred 1999:25). Self-determination more easily conceptually includes the wealth of concepts and relationships that a narrow definition of politics or government excludes. Self-determination is really about fostering what Anishnabe people call the "good life" in our communities. This includes all four aspects of life—mental, emotional, physical and spiritual.

Many Aboriginal people believe that the right to self-determination has never been and cannot be extinguished, that is to say that the right to self-determination is *inherent*. Others suggest that their right to self-determination is protected by the numbered treaties that were signed. The differing views of traditional and treaty people (as they call themselves) are the essential difference between the phrases self-determination and self-government as they usually appear in isolated and individualized political debates. In the Canadian context, the meaning of self-government has become attached to the agenda of the federal government to provide municipal-style governments on "Indian reserves." From a traditional understanding, this is unsatisfactory as it does not mirror our Aboriginal understanding of our relationship with this territory.

It is often easier to articulate what self-determination is not than what it is. This is not an excuse for my own inabilities, but rather a condition of more than five hundred years of colonial practice on the continent and the resulting suppression of Aboriginal ideas, governments, territories and being. Any effort to move toward self-determination which focuses on the reserve as the sole basis for any form of jurisdiction[5] will be unsatisfactory to urban and Métis groups. It should also be unsatisfactory to Indians. After all the reserve is *not* a good Indian idea. Any plan or model that accepts without question the reserve as a basis for government powers entrenches colonialism. This realization acknowledges that reserves are non-Aboriginal creations and are, in fact, colonial institutions.[6] What seems to be common to all Aboriginal Peoples, despite our vast differences, is a desire to continue to exercise our authority in political, social and legal ways, at least amongst our own people, following our own understandings of our (political) authority.

A decade or so ago, I believed that law was a (perhaps *the*) solution to the Aboriginal struggle for political freedom. Since then I have learned that there are many examples of law's complicity in the oppression of Aboriginal Peoples. Canadian laws established residential schools, outlawed ceremonies, denied women their birthright, and outlawed our forms of government. There can be no full solution to the "problems" of "Indians" if the role that law has played in our oppression and colonization is immune from scrutiny and remedy. Until this reconstruction of Canadian history is a reality in the courtroom, judicial decisions based on this history are not objective. Judicial decision making as an objective practice is a mere myth of the western cultural variety.

The history problem is not a simple one. In the Supreme Court's judgment in the *Delgamuukw* case, which considered the nature and scope of Aboriginal title for the first time, much was made of the fact that "oral history" was to be given as much legal weight as written history. However, the words surrounding this evidentiary breakthrough illuminate that a small legal rule has been nominally changed to include Aboriginal people, nations and ways. The recognition that the problem is one of larger magnitude is not discussed by the court. The rules of evidence have been "adapted" to "accommodate" Aboriginal peoples. It is not that there is anything wrong with the rules and, therefore, a small re-jigging of the rules will suffice. This sees the Indian, and not the methods of history or law, as the problem. In a similar fashion Neal Salisbury notes:

> For while the convention of distinguishing Indians and whites as two different species of humanity is largely outmoded, a vestige of it survives in the assumption that Indians have not participated in "history," except in their encounters with the whites who actually "made" that history. (1987:46)

The problem with history is the same as the problem with law. History is also grounded in the belief in the "natural" superiority of Europeans (and their descendants), and this must be fully and finally disposed of. Meaningful negotiations can only occur between the first and founding nations, when those we negotiate with believe in the principal of respect and inclusion (perhaps some would think about this as equality). Unfortunately, this will not be enough to purge our relations of the notion of one race's natural superiority, because that belief is currently embedded in the structure and practice of Canadian institutions of government and law.

Related to the faulty idea of one people's natural superiority is another obstacle on the path to self-determination—the Canadian preoccupation with defining equality. Definitions of equality often fail to recognize that not all people or peoples are the same (although I grant that Canadian courts are getting better at seeing the nuances required to realize meaningful equality). Respecting difference cannot be guaranteed by formal equality, but rather, from an Aboriginal location, must be understood as creating relationships of balance and harmony (or peace). In her essay, "Patriarchy and Paternalism: The Legacy of the Canadian State for First Nations Women," Mary Ellen Turpel-Lafond writes:

> Equality is simply not the central organizing political principle in our communities. It is frequently seen by our Elders as a suspiciously selfish notion, as individualistic and alienating from oth-

ers in the community. It is incongruous to apply this notion to our communities. (1993:180)

Canadian definitions of legal equality which rely on the rule of law[7] often guarantee only rights of sameness. This thinking, when extended to the political realm, casts Aboriginal difference as a form of special rights. The argument is then constructed that no one deserves special treatment and rights. This reasoning must be understood for what it is—the colonial mentality.

The definitions, all the definitions, that have developed within Canadian legal and political systems must be considered suspect as they were all developed on presumptions of Euro-Canadian superiority and/or the rules of a foreign legal order. All the presumptions and the concepts built on the presumptions must be renegotiated to reflect the participation of all parties in this new "legal" dialogue. The difficulty with coming to the understanding that definitions are a significant part of the problem in resolving Aboriginal claims in law is the fact that there is no mechanism in the Canadian system that has the power to address this shortcoming (other than litigating each and every definitional difficulty, a task which would assume much time and millions of dollars). Because law is backward looking, judges look to previous decisions to shape the answers to current legal questions; thus the problem with definitions is easily perpetuated, and incomplete definitions are (re)affirmed.

As colonialism is not a static relationship between oppressor and oppressed, it is not just the beliefs of the Euro-Canadian that must be carefully examined. The spirit of colonialism now also sadly vests in some Aboriginal people and Aboriginal organizations. As Paulo Freire noted some two decades ago:

> In this situation the oppressed do not see the "new man" as the person to be born from the resolution of this contradiction, as oppression gives way to liberation. For them, the new man or woman themselves become oppressors. Their vision of the new man or woman is individualistic, because of their identification with the oppressor, they have no consciousness of themselves as persons or as members of an oppressed class. It is not to become free that they want agrarian reform, but in order to acquire land and thus become landowners—or, more precisely, bosses over other workers. It is a rare peasant who, once "promoted" to overseer, does not become more of a tyrant towards his former comrades than the owner himself. *This is because the context of the peasant's situation, that is, oppression, remains unchanged.* In this example, the overseer, in order to make sure of his job, must be as tough as the owner—and more so. This is illustrated in

our previous assertion that during the initial stage of their struggle the oppressed find in the oppressor their model of "man-
hood." (1996:28, emphasis added)

Freire thus provides an explanation of the occurrence in Aboriginal communities of solutions that mimic the manner in which white people govern
themselves. Especially in the areas of child welfare and justice, this trend
is notable. Despite the many attempts to create programs which "accommodate" Aboriginal people in the Canadian criminal justice system, the
overall rates of Aboriginal over-representation have not decreased and in
fact, have continued to rise (RCAP 1996a:28–29).

The essential and often overlooked step in creating a renewed relationship between Aboriginal Peoples and Canadians is an examination of
the meaning of the concepts we are building our relationship with. (And
this failure means that Aboriginal difference is not being respected.) This
necessarily involves an analysis of the ways in which individuals and
institutions attain the legitimacy and authority to have their definitions
accepted. If we are not certain that we are constructing a conversation
based on a common understanding of both the legal and political terms,
we cannot be certain we are turning the page in the history of the absolute
legal and political oppression of Aboriginal Peoples. If we cannot even
have a conversation, then how can we hope to build a relationship, legal or
otherwise? The dominant system's monopoly on the definitions of both
legal and political terminology holds the book open to a page where the
oppression of Aboriginal Peoples is still writ large.

The problem with the monopoly on terminology extends as well to
process. Courts rely on precedent, or decisions made in previous cases, to
resolve legal issues, including the claims brought by Aboriginal people,
communities or nations. Catherine Bell and Michael Asch note:

> Despite the existence of mechanisms to distinguish and reinter-
> pret these decisions, Canadian courts challenged to recognize
> new rights remain openly deferential to the past. The result has
> been judicial denial of the contemporary existence of an inherent
> right to government and legislative power. This approach is par-
> ticularly appealing to a lower court or a judge with an emotional
> and intellectual commitment to the status quo as it allows one to
> empathize with the discriminatory treatment of Aboriginal people
> and at the same time declare helpless bondage to fundamental
> principles firmly established in the common law. (1997:45)

These recognitions lead to an important conclusion. The process of
reconciliation must first recognize and then ameliorate the power imbal-
ances between Canada as a nation and First Nations. This is another way

of noting that ideas of Euro-Canadian superiority are no longer accept-able. A system built on such a belief cannot continue to be seen as democratic. It is not. Some of the equities, such as access to financial resources, are quite obvious. Others, such as recognizing that language (English or French) reinforces the unequal power base, are more subtle.

The structure of negotiations between Aboriginal governments and the Canadian government is fraught with obstacles. One of the major obstacles, as well as a major irony, in the search for a renewed relation-ship, is the Canadian government's insistence on negotiating self-govern-ment arrangements only with the political representatives that are statutorily recognized (until recently, this was only chiefs with an Indian Act man-date). The problem arises when one recognizes that the Indian Act system of government was one forced on Indian nations. In *Logan* v. *Styres* (1959), the Hereditary Chiefs of the Six Nations community challenged the authority of the Indian Act chiefs. The court held that:

> I am of the opinion that the Six Nations Indians are entitled to the protection of the laws of the land duly made by competent *au-thority and at the same time subject to such laws.* (at page 424, emphasis added)

This is a problem that originates in Canada's constitution. Sections 91 and 92 divide legislative authority between the federal and provincial govern-ments. Under section 91(24) the federal parliament has authority over "Indians and Lands Reserved for Indians." Indian people (and our lands) are objects of Canada's legislative authority, nestled in between "Copy-rights" and "Naturalization and Aliens." As long as s. 91(24) remains a part of Canada's constitution, Indian people will never be free of our subordinated position. This again exposes the myth of "equality" within Canadian society for what it is.

Some Indian people would be very surprised that I advocate the repeal of s. 91(24). They believe that this section entrenches the "nation to nation" relationship between Indian peoples and Canadians. This is a strained and overly generous understanding of Canadian constitutional law. Furthermore, section 91(24) is unnecessary to sustain the legal valid-ity of the "nation to nation" relationship, as Aboriginal peoples can rely on both the *Royal Proclamation of 1763* and on treaty. In some areas of the country the *Royal Proclamation* must be seen as treaty and not as a unilateral Crown act (Borrows 1997:161).

It is not just Indian nations that have had their right to traditional forms of government interfered with. Both the Métis and the Inuit have been historically excluded from the regime of *Indian Act* control. How-ever, this does not diminish the reality of colonial imposition on those peoples. Since the signing of the *Manitoba Act* in 1870, until 1982, the leaders of the Métis were considered legal non-entities. Worse yet, after the so-called Riel Rebellion (a better word is resistance) many Métis leaders were declared criminals.

Acknowledging the contradictions and being brave and resourceful in the face of the challenges that all governments in this territory will confront is a continuous process of renewed commitment. Aboriginal nations must shake loose all the shackles of oppression. Canadians must learn to live free of false assumptions of superiority. There are no immediate or simple answers. The commitment required involves understanding that change will come in small steps, much like a young child learning to walk. Final solutions cannot be fully articulated as the walk has just begun. How new this walk is becomes obvious when it is remembered that we have been living with the constitutional protections of Aboriginal and treaty rights for less than two decades. Even the history of colonialism and imposition appears short when understood against more than ten thousand years that Aboriginal Peoples understand as their history.

It is from this history (or these histories)—and I have heard over and over again from the Elders that you must know where you come from to know where you are going—that the Aboriginal sense of relationship with land and territory arises. My sense of self-determination (or sovereignty) arises from understanding these relationships. Yet, when I say sovereignty it has much the same effect as when I use the word racism (Monture 1990:38). The reaction is defensive posturing and denial—especially on the part of people in the federal government who are supposed to have a sacred "trust" responsibility with my people.

The denial of Aboriginal self-determination arises because people are afraid that Aboriginal sovereignty will mess up their territory (the lines they have arbitrarily drawn around and in Canada). Canada and Canadians do not want us to pull the country apart acre by acre. The debate, when it is expressed in this way, becomes grounded in western notions of individualized property rights (and I would reiterate that what Aboriginal Peoples are more interested in is land rights). Sovereignty must be about territory and the control of that territory because Canadians say that is what it means. I say sovereignty is about my right to be a Mohawk (and, equally a woman). This requires some explaining.

First, sovereignty is another example of the disparate meanings that are attached towards by Canada and Aboriginal Peoples. Whenever I engage in legal discourse there is a translation process going on in my head. Even though my first language is English (and it remains the language of my fluency), I do not understand the words in the same way many Euro-Canadians do. So, I am translating twice every time I try to speak law to you. This is a lot of work for anyone to do merely to engage in a conversation (and for those whose first language is Aboriginal the issue of translation becomes even larger). There is often a negative reaction to my English words, such as sovereignty, a reaction I am not going to assume full responsibility for. Sovereignty, when defined as my right to be responsible, is really a question of identity (both individual and collective) more than it is a question of an individualized property right. Identity, as I have come to understand it, requires a relationship with territory (and not a relationship based on control of that territory).

Second, rejecting a western territorially based definition of sovereignty is not to say that Aboriginal Peoples do not aspire to having a land base that will make our nations economically stable and self-sufficient. It's hard to be sovereign when you cannot even feed your own children from your own resources. Because our notion of land is not merely about individual ownership of property, Aboriginal people have a notion of community "ownership" of land which very much combines the spiritual with any notion of individualized ownership. Constructing dichotomies of individual versus collective ownership diminishes the relationship that Aboriginal people understood existed between the two. At the same time it must be remembered that ownership is just one choice in the spectrum of possibilities of relationships with land.

Sovereignty (or self-determination) then is not about "ownership" of territory in the way that Canadian politicians and lawyers would define those words. We have a Mohawk word that better describes what we mean by sovereignty and that word is "tewatatha:wi." It best translates to "we carry ourselves" (Kane and Maracle 1989:10). This Aboriginal definition of sovereignty is a definition which is about responsibilities and not just about rights. I have heard many other Aboriginal people from many other Aboriginal nations say that this is also true, or similar, in their languages and beliefs.

What sovereignty is to me is a responsibility. It is the responsibility to carry ourselves; collectively as nations, as clans, as families as well as individually, as individual Mohawk citizens, in a good way. In order to be a self-determining nation, you must have self-disciplined individuals. You must have individuals who understand who they are and how to carry themselves. Unfortunately this is precisely what policies such as residential schools have interfered with amongst Aboriginal peoples. What must be understood then is that the Aboriginal request to have our sovereignty respected is really a request to be responsible. I do not know of anywhere else in history where a group of people have had to fight so hard just to be responsible. It seems so absolutely ridiculous.

For my people, this very much means understanding the "Great Law of Peace."[8] It means understanding the various treaties we have signed with other nations, be they Aboriginal Peoples or settler nations. One of the most important of our treaties in this day and age is the "gus-wen-qah." It is also referred to in English as the "Two-Row Wampum." It is the treaty which governs the relationship between the Six Nations Confederacy (respectfully called the Haudenosaunee) and the settler nations. The gus-wen-qah became an important symbol to the Penner Commission on Self-Government in 1983 and appears on the cover of this report. More recently, it was relied on by National Chief Phil Fontaine in response to the "Statement of Reconciliation":

> It took some courage on the part of the Minister and government to take this historic step, to break with the past, and to apologize for the historic wrongs and injustices committed against our peoples. It is therefore a great honour for me, on behalf of the First Nations, to accept the apology of the Government and people of Canada. Let this moment mark the end of paternalism in our relations, and the beginning of the empowerment of First Peoples; the end of assimilationist policies, and the beginning of mutual respect and cooperation. *This, after all, was the intention of our forefathers who agreed in the historic wampum treaty to paddle their canoes in separate but parallel paths.* (Office of the Treaty Commissioner 1998:2, emphasis added)

The gus-wen-qah is vastly complex but is visually quite simple. It is two rows of purple shell imbedded in a sea of white. One of the two purple paths signifies the European sailing ship that came here. In that ship are all the European things—their laws, languages, institutions and forms of government. The other path is the Mohawk canoe and in it are all the Mohawk things—our laws, institutions and forms of government. For the entire length of that wampum, these two paths are separated by three white beads. Never do the two paths become one. They remain an equal distance apart. And those three white beads represent "friendship, good minds, and everlasting peace."[9] It is by these three things that Aboriginal Peoples and the settler nations agreed to govern all of their future relationships.[10] It is very easy to see how this treaty has been disrespected by all of us, Indian and settler alike.

There is a reason why we recorded our laws, our agreements and our treaties in shell; and it was not because we were inferior peoples. I do not believe that writing everything down is necessarily a very advanced idea or a sign of great humanity. This is not how I experience it. When you write things down they are easily forgotten, as you assume the paper will do your job of remembering. When you write things down they are easily destroyed, for example by fire. But, if a wampum belt is thrown into the fire, the shells will still be there when the ashes are cool. If you have learned well, you will be able to put that wampum belt back together again. This is the standard of knowing the law that all Mohawks will be responsible to. The only way that you can destroy a wampum belt is willfully. It cannot happen by accident. Those shells will last a very long time and the law of the people will be taught from those belts.

Returning to the gus-wen-qah and the paths that belong to each of our nations, the descendants of the settler nations have their laws and beliefs, their institutions. These things will be kept on the Canadian path. Canadian people have their own way of doing things and they have the right to be that way. It is parallel to the right to be a Mohawk woman, which is in fact the only right that I have (Monture-Angus 1995:87). It is the right to be in that canoe on the other purple path with all the Mohawk laws, ways, language and traditions. Those paths do not become one. Nowhere have my people ever agreed to live governed by Canadian laws or Canadian ways of thinking and being. Nor have my people tried to change the way Canadians govern themselves. That is our respect for Canadian rights. This is the place where my people wish to remain, living in respect of the Two-Row Wampum Treaty.[11]

One of the best and simplest definitions of the right being asserted by Aboriginal Peoples is expressed by Oren Lyons, a traditionalist, of the Haudenosaunee Confederacy. In a speech from the 1979 Montreal Conference on Indian Government, Lyons stated:

> Sovereignty—it's a political word. It's not a legal word. Sovereignty is the act. Sovereignty is the do. You act. You don't ask. There is no limitation on sovereignty. You are not semi-sovereign. You are not a little sovereign. You either are or your aren't. It's simple. (cited in Hill 1992:175)

Just as the notion of self-government carries with it a derogatory meaning for many Aboriginal people, the phrase sovereignty carries with it a particular cultural and legal meaning which causes non-Aboriginal people to be fearful. Solutions lie beyond the defensive posturing found in the mere semantics of the majority of discussions on self-government or self-determination.

Notes

1. I am grateful to bell hooks and her work *Killing Rage* (1995). She has given me courage, language and inspiration.
2. Several scholars have written on this topic. Please see the work of Russell Barsh, Dara Culhane and Denise McConney.
3. For a fuller discussion please see Chrisjohn, Young and Maraun 1997.
4. Thomson Highway's novel, *Kiss of the Fur Queen* (1998), although fictional, provides a good account of the family impact of the removal of children and their placement in these schools.
5. It is not essential to define self-determination within the confines of territorial limits. There are a number of exceptions to the territorial integrity of a

nation state which are already recognized in domestic law. Among others, the exceptions include income tax provisions, criminal law and admiralty law. A fuller discussion is found in Geoff R. Hall 1992:302.

6. I had never thought of reserves as "institutions" until one of my students mentioned this to me. Thank you Michael Blackmon for your insight and wisdom.

7. The rule of law is a rule about formal equality. It suggests that it is wrong for both kings and beggars to steal bread and sleep under bridges.

8. An excellent resource (although I do have some concerns about the way gender relations are represented) is Chief Jacob Thomas 1994. For a discussion of the current situation in Haudenosaunee communities please see Robert B. Porter 1998.

9. This interpretation is the one presented by Jacob E. Thomas in his publication "The Friendship Treaty Belt and the Two Row Wampum Treaty" which was compiled for his library on November 13, 1978. A copy is on file with the author.

    I have also heard the treaty explained to mean that the three beads represent friendship, truth or respect or honesty, and kindness. As the treaty was signed on separate occasions with the Dutch, the French, the English and the Americans it is understandable why several interpretations exist. It is also understandable because of the difficulty in translating complex Mohawk words into simple English ones.

    It is essential to note that I have not earned the right in the Mohawk way to give the sacred teaching about this wampum. This is a brief discussion and not the detailed information necessary for true understanding and knowledge.

10. This explanation was provided to the Special Committee on Indian Self-Government in 1983:

    > When your ancestors came to our shores, after living with them for a few years, observing them, our ancestors came to the conclusion that we could not live together in the same way inside the circle.... So our leaders at that time, along with your leaders, sat down for many years to try to work out a solution. This is what they came up with. We call it Gus-Wen-Qah, or the two row wampum belt. It is on a bed of white wampum, which symbolizes the purity of the agreement. There are two rows of purple, and these two rows have the spirit of our ancestors; those two rows never come together in that belt, and it is easy to see what that means. It means that we have two different paths, two different people. The agreement was made that your road will have your vessel, your people, your politics, your government, your way of life, your religion your beliefs—they are all in there. The same goes for ours.... They said there will be three beads of wampum separating the two, and they will symbolize peace, friendship, and respect. (As cited in Johnston 1993:349–367 at 351)

11. This treaty is also recorded in the European style in the Treaty of Fort Albany.

Chapter Two

Theoretical Foundations And The Challenge Of Aboriginal Rights

Despite living the last decade of my life outside of my territory, being Kanien'kehaka remains at the center of my identity. Choosing to study Canadian law did not diminish my need to live as Kanien'kehaka. Any information or knowledge that I have gained from my involvement in Canadian universities and Canadian legal institutions over the last two decades is always brought to this core of my Kanien'kehaka identity where I compare and contrast new information to the values and teachings of my culture. This is my duty as I understand it. As a young woman, the Elders taught me that white things were not of necessity wrong but to take care and ensure that I was picking up only the "good stuff."

In order to understand the way I have processed the recognition and affirmation of existing Aboriginal (and treaty) rights in Canada's constitution, the basics of Haudenosaunee political thought must be briefly established. As I understand it, in this knowledge tradition it is difficult to separate intellectual, spiritual, political and legal realms. This is unlike the manner in which Canadian structures of state, church, law and academia are premised on separation as a fundamental and necessary value in a civilized society. John Mohawk notes of Iroquoian political thought:

> For this plan to work the Peacemaker was required to convince a very skeptical audience that all human beings really did possess the potential for rational thought, that when encouraged to use rational thought they would inevitably seek peace, and the belief in the principles would lead to the organized enactment of the vision.
>
> The test of this thinking is found in the converse of the argument. If you do not believe in the rational nature of the

human being, you cannot believe that you can negotiate with him. If you do not believe that rational people ultimately desire peace, you cannot negotiate confidently with him toward goals you and he share. If you cannot negotiate with him, you are powerless to create peace. If you cannot organize around those beliefs, the principles cannot move from the minds of men into the actions of society. (1989:221)

The central object of social arrangements for my people is significantly about living in the way of peace. This peace is defined much more broadly than living without violence.

Living in peace is about living a good life where respect for our relationships with people and all creation is primary. The "Great Law of Peace," which at least partially parallels the role of law in Canadian social organization, is a principle which translates to "the way to live most nicely together."[1] Kanien'kehaka scholar Gerald Alfred expands on the leadership principles entrenched in the Kaienerekowa (Great Law) and notes:

> In the Rotinoshshonni tradition, the women of each family raise a man to leadership and hold him accountable to these principles. If he does not uphold and defend the Kaienerekowa, or if the women determine that his character or behaviour does not conform to the leadership principles, he is removed from the position. As in other traditional cultures, the moral definition of leadership focuses on a person's adherence to the values of *patience, courage, fairness, and generosity.* (1999:90, emphasis added)

If these are the qualities—patience, courage, fairness and generosity—of individuals who are (political) leaders, then these qualities are also the ones on which Kanien'kehaka politics are built.

The beliefs of the Haudenosaunee clearly influenced the Europeans who came to the shores of what we knew as Turtle Island. John Mohawk notes in the same essay quoted above:

> When the *White Roots of Peace*[2] was first published it became immediately apparent that the author had accomplished a pioneer work of sorts. Wallace exhibited astonishing insight when he alleged that prehistoric Iroquois had constructed a political philosophy based on rational thought. Not many writers on anthropology or oral history have found rational thought a prevalent theme among their subjects. Many professionals in this field operate on an expectation that rational thought is found only in the west.

Such cultural blindness is unfortunate because it automatically denies most of the academic and literary world access to the best thinking of many of the world's cultures. This unspoken doctrine helps to promote the tradition in the West that non-Western people are non-rational people. Wallace's work was an honest and commendable effort to go beyond that. He saw good rational thinking in a place where such thinking was not expected to exist and he promoted his discovery, almost breathlessly, to a disbelieving world. (1989:218)

The Haudenosaunee influence on what have come to be known as western ideas about democracy has been made invisible by the operation of rules of academic discourse and the bias of those involved in that discourse.[3] Because I do not intellectually disenfranchise Aboriginal thought and intellectual traditions,[4] the continuity of Haudenosaunee influence remains an important thread in this work, which crosses conventional interdisciplinary boundaries.

Obviously then, when the categories of discourse (law, politics or academia) are inappropriately applied without consideration to the different structural bases of the worldviews of Aboriginal people, diminishing of the political sophistication of Aboriginal thought and intellectual traditions (the rational mind) occurs. When the world is looked at in a holistic way, everyone's opinion carries with it a similar weight. The way voice is legitimated in Aboriginal society is vastly different from that of the societies that settled here. A number of consequences flow from this observation. For example, an Aboriginal academic does not have credibility in their home community based on their academic qualifications but rather on what they have earned in the Aboriginal way in their community. In fact, sometimes their academic credentials operate as a liability in relationships with other Aboriginal people. The artificial dichotomies between community member and activist, academic, politician or technician must be questioned. Any absolute dichotomy must be suspicious as no dichotomies exist in the natural world. The creation of dichotomy as a condition of existence is a colonial manifestation.

Historically, Aboriginal Peoples have been controlled by a variety of means, including our exclusion from the systems which have determined the meaning of concepts such as justice, sovereignty and rights. Howard Becker explains:

> control based on the manipulation of definitions and labels works more smoothly and costs less.... The attack on hierarchy begins with an attack on definitions, labels, and conventional conceptions of who's who and what's what. (1973:178)

Although the study of deviance is not analogous to the topic of this book, Becker's conclusion persuades me of the significance of his comment to the study of rights and governance. The pathway to a new relationship is paved with the long-term commitment to share the definitional power that creates the legitimacy whereby words and phrases gain their accepted meaning. It requires the free giving up of control over Aboriginal lives, with careful attention to the way language (that is English) presupposes a framework of meaning that is at least hierarchical and gendered. I also experience it as colonial. No definition can be taken for granted as inclusive. The re-examination of the way language sanctions particular worldviews and understandings is central to this process of change. This is particularly true if the framework of study is Canadian law, as law is the study of words.

As someone trained in the law, I turn to the written text of the Canadian constitution as one possible framework to consider when determining if my aspirations as an Aboriginal person and the way I understand my people's political position can be situated within that existing legal framework.[5] This may or may not be the appropriate starting point. Perhaps, it would be more logical to start with developing a true understanding of both history and the provisions of the treaties. At this time, I will leave the work of history to the historians, both tribal and/or those academically trained. I must note though that it is essential to understand one's own history or there is no future.

In 1982, when Canada repatriated its constitution, a provision which protects the rights of Aboriginal Peoples was included in that package.[6] This provision did not receive the unanimous support of Aboriginal people nor our governments, and in particular many Haudenosaunee people were opposed to it. However, given the fact that the provision does exist in Canadian law, it seems logical to use it as a starting place for discussion. The reality is that Canada's existing constitutional provisions will have a dramatic impact on the ability of and degree to which Aboriginal people and Canadians will be able to craft a new relationship based on mutual respect and co-existence. Further, it is naive to think that the entrenchment of Aboriginal and treaty rights in Canada's constitution will not have an effect on Aboriginal nations, communities and individuals. In some cases it may enhance dreaming. Or it may limit our vision making and cause fear.

There are two principles that must govern the intellectual examination of the meaning of section 35 from an Aboriginal place. This work must be completed with a respect of all peoples and in a way that brings colonialism, past and present, to account. If colonial relations cannot be challenged and changed, then there is no hope for any kind of renewed relationship. The degree to which I will eventually embrace section 35(1) depends on the degree to which it creates space for Aboriginal intellectual and political traditions. Does it foster peace? Does it create the space for the recovery of Aboriginal nations from colonial impositions and manifestations?

An examination of the historical relations between Aboriginal Peoples and Canadians (especially their government representatives), clearly indicates that the philosophical grounding of the relationship is based on a misplaced notion of Euro-Canadian superiority. More fundamentally distressing, allowing Euro-Canadian superiority to remain ingrained in the fabric of Canadian society, including Canadian legal relations, ignores the trust-like responsibility of the Canadian government to Aboriginal Peoples. A "trust" relationship does not necessarily have to be built on a notion of one party's superiority or the other's vulnerability. This is another colonial myth.

During the 1950s the courts, in fact, began to articulate the notion that Canada has a special responsibility to Indians:

> The language of the (*Indian Act*) embodies the accepted view that these aborigines are, in effect, wards of the state, whose care and welfare are a political trust of the highest obligation. (*St. Ann's Island Shooting and Fishing Club* v *R.*, 1952:232)

Minimally, we would now recognize the idea of wardship as overly paternalistic (or grounded in the notion of supposed European superiority). The idea of wardship has developed into what is now legally recognized as a fiduciary responsibility (see the discussion in *Guerin* v *R.* 1984:501) and more recently as a trust responsibility by the Supreme Court of Canada in *R.* v. *Sparrow* (1990:180–181).

In the *Sparrow* decision, Justices Dickson and LaForest opined:

> the Government has the responsibility to act in a fiduciary capacity with respect to aboriginal peoples. The relationship between the Government and aboriginals is trust-like, rather than adversarial, and contemporary recognition and affirmation of aboriginal rights must be defined in light of this historic relationship. (1990:180)

And later in the decision the Justices declared:

> we find that the words "recognition and affirmation" incorporate the fiduciary relationship referred to earlier and so import some restraint on the exercise of sovereign power. (1990:181)

No matter how offensive the idea of "wardship" or the evolved and modern notion of "dependency" is to me, the fact of the matter is that there is a relationship of dependency between First Nations and the

Crown. This *is* the reality that is the result of colonialism. As the ability to move away from these dependent and colonially inspired relations will not happen overnight, the fiduciary duty remains an interesting legal concept that might prove beneficial to First Nations' efforts to move toward truly independent and self-sustaining relationships with Canada.

In addition, the court in *Sparrow* noted:

> We cannot recount with much pride the treatment accorded to the native people of this country. (1990:177 affirming the decision of MacDonald J. in *Pasco* v. *Canadian National Railway Co.* 1986:37)

The assumption of superiority must be fully stripped away from all the current legal and constitutional interpretations with respect to Aboriginal Peoples and this requires more than dismissing history as unfortunate and lacking in pride. This is particularly true for section 35 as this section "recognizes and affirms" "existing Aboriginal and treaty rights." The constitutional provision requires that a standard of equality[7] be incorporated in all legal analyses.

The concept of "equality" in law has a long history in both Canadian law and in political theory.

> As used in 'liberal democracy,' the word 'liberal' connotes 'equal,' the fundamental equality of all human beings. A corollary of this ideology is the idea that each individual is free to achieve her or his own free and independent development in a free market. Liberal treatment also implicitly meant 'non-violent,' once again in reference (and in deliberate contrast) to the United States and its violent Indian policy. Chancellor Boyd, also in his *St. Catherines Milling* opinion, referred to a legal policy that promoted the immigration of Europeans in such a way so that 'their contact in the interior might not become collision.' Non-violence was implicit in the ideology of liberalism: *people treated equally, according to the law, did not need to resort to violence.* A just society was also a non-violent society. Canadians were committed to a frontier without the kind of warfare that they saw just below their border. This commitment had underlying reasons of economy as well as morality, for as some nineteenth-century observers noted, the cost of Indian wars to the United States in the decade of the 1870s exceeded the entire Canadian budget. But it was also a moral policy. (Harring 1998:12, emphasis added)

The problem with this kind of thinking, that less violence is better (and frankly I do not know how to understand the colonial process, past or present, as anything but violent) is how it acts to conceal the truth about certain events of this country's history. Carol Aylward has noted that "[w]hile the doctrine of 'colour-blindness' has promoted the myth that racism is no longer a factor in American society, the same doctrine has promoted a prevailing myth in Canada that racism was never a factor in Canadian society" (1999:76). In the United States, that "the west was won" (from the Indians) is the popular myth. In Canada, the myth is that the removal of the Indian nations from their territories was somehow peaceful (that is non-violent). Asserting a non-violent (or less violent) pattern of conquest seems to equate to suggesting a more advanced and civilized society. But, the truth of the matter is Canada has not always treated people with respect and dignity. For me, this exposes the degree to which Canada's foundations are *not* built on a principle of equality.

I understand too painfully well that asserting that Canadian notions of equality, particularly historically and legally, are more fiction than fact is a dangerous proposition. What passes for equality talk in Canadian jurisprudence is generally a conversation about power (and why one group has the power to keep it). Sherene Raczack notes:

> Rights in law are fundamentally about seeing and not seeing, about the cold game of equality staring. Talking about women's lives in the language of rights is a cold game indeed, a game played with words and philosophical concepts which bear little relationship to real life. In spite of these doubts, the game is always enticing, perhaps because it seems to hold out the promise that something about the daily realities of oppression will eventually emerge from under the ice. Equality staring, however, as Patricia Williams poetically describes, feels like a non-win situation. The daily realities of oppressed groups can only be acknowledged at the cost of the dominant group's belief in its own natural entitlement. If oppression exists, then there must also be oppressors, and oppressors do not have a moral basis for their rights claims. If, however, we are all equally human, with some of us simply not as advanced or developed as others, then no one need take responsibility for inequality. Moreover, advanced, more civilized people can reconfirm their own superiority through helping those who are less advanced. (1998:23)

From my own experiences, many times over, I know her words reflect the reality that I have lived. It is not this form of equality that I aspire to but rather the simple fact that all four human races have a fundament right to respect and self-respect. It is through this cultural standard that I approach any kind of legal analysis (including an analysis of equality).

Section 35(1) of the constitution provides that the "existing aboriginal[8] and treaty rights" of Aboriginal Peoples are "recognized and affirmed." From the outset it is important to recognize that section 35 is not part of the *Charter of Rights and Freedoms,* nor is it a guarantee given to Aboriginal Peoples from the Government of Canada. It must be emphasized that the consent of Aboriginal nations to our position in the Canadian federation, including the application of Canadian law, is still an outstanding issue. In my mind, section 35(1) merely advances the possibility that such a conversation can now take place. Unfortunately, this is not what I see or understand to be happening in Canadian politics and Canadian courts.

A guarantee, such as the guarantees Canada provides in the *Charter,* is something qualitatively and quantitatively different than a recognition or an affirmation as found in section 35(1) of the constitution. When a recognition or an affirmation is made, the thing being recognized or affirmed already exists. In this specific case of legal-political relations, this relationship was *just* being seen by the drafters of the Canadian constitution for the first time. The rights, however, pre-exist the Canadian recognition of them. If section 35 were a grant of rights, this would ensure the ability of Canadian law to continue to embed the Euro-Canadian superiority myth. A grant is a gift of rights to the people from the Crown. As noted, section 35(1), recognizes and affirms certain rights of the Aboriginal Peoples. The words, recognize and affirm, are not intended to be the equivalent of granting rights. "Recognize" means to acknowledge something that already exists. "Affirm" means to embrace the rights which are now being recognized. To not accept that the words "recognized and affirmed," at a minimum, move us beyond thinking that western or European is superior renders the constitutional words meaningless. As a legal standard, the recognition and affirmation sets a serious goal. It requires complete rejection of the belief in Euro-Canadian superiority, the belief that denies Canadians a pride in their history.

Aboriginal Peoples have always understood that our rights are inherent. All that Canada can do is to begin to take responsibility for their historical and ongoing failure to respect the authority and legitimacy of Aboriginal governments. Now that this simple task of recognition has been completed by the entrenchment of section 35(1), the more pressing and onerous question of how to implement and respect this responsibility is without full answer in either political or legal realms. I would also point out the parallel to the situation of treaties. It is not that the agreements are "bad." It is that their implementation has been ignored.

The Canadian government has not gone (and could not go) further (such as a *Charter* style grant) than the recognition and affirmation of Aboriginal (and treaty) rights. It is because section 35(1) respects the Aboriginal view that our rights are inherent and pre-date the concept of Canada that a new relationship can be established based on (and preconditioned by) the 1982 constitutional entrenchment. This is the reason for which I suggest that section 35(1) holds promise. The way has been cleared to do Canada differently, to do Canada in a way that also includes Aboriginal people. This is the ultimate irony of section 35(1). Section 35(1), in my opinion, changes the political relationships between Aboriginal people and the state. However, section 35(1) has seen much more activity as a judicial mechanism than it has as a revolutionary political device.

In my mind the failure to secure Aboriginal consent to this constitutional provision is not fatal to the goal of establishing a renewed relationship. If all section 35(1) accomplishes is to recognize the independent relationship of Aboriginal rights to the Canadian governments, then logically no Aboriginal nation needs to consent. Consent only becomes a primary issue after the passing of section 35(1) because Canada first had to acknowledge the truth about its relationship with Aboriginal Peoples. Section 35(1) does not change, touch or interfere with in any way the Aboriginal view of the world, our values, beliefs, laws and systems of government. It is a long overdue promise by Canada, a "solemn commitment" to Aboriginal Peoples, as the court in *Sparrow* noted (1990:180).

The issue of outstanding consent to participate in Canada remains one of the principal keys to opening the door to a new and revitalized (truly a "nation to nation") relationship with Aboriginal Peoples. The entrenchment of section 35(1) creates the necessary pre-condition which now allows us to proceed to the more important question of how we will choose to relate to each other. In my view, section 35(1) is a mere invitation.

Unfortunately, as I noted before, I would not characterize the almost two decades of judicial activities since the entrenchment of section 35(1) as revolutionary. Clearly the problem with creating revolution through judicial activity is the fact that the judiciary is intended to be a stabilizing force, not a revolutionary one. Because it is adversarial by nature, litigation has not yet allowed Aboriginal Peoples and Canada to step outside "us versus them" relationships. There have been a number of attempts by the Supreme Court of Canada to specify the meaning of section 35(1). In my opinion, and this book will detail, these attempts have not yet provided a clear definition of the idea or theory of Aboriginal rights. More importantly, the judicial decisions have not lived up to the potential that exists in the words contained in section 35(1). My concern is that the fundamental principles (in the case of the Kanien'kehaka, peace, friendship and respect, as articulated by the Two-Row Wampum) required to create a "nation to nation" relationship must remain in our focus.

In *Sparrow*, the Supreme Court of Canada stated: "When the purposes of the affirmation of aboriginal rights are considered, it is clear that a generous, liberal interpretation of the words in the constitutional provision is demanded" (1990:179). In addition the law requires that the interpretation of documents (such as treaties) regarding Aboriginal Peoples must be construed liberally and any "doubtful expression be resolved in favour of the Indians" (*Nowegijick* 1983:94 and affirmed in *Sparrow* 1990:179). First, this strengthens the assertion that constitutionalizing Aboriginal rights moves us beyond assumptions of superiority. Second, it emphasizes that it is impossible to identify and deal with ambiguity without understanding the historical context in which the documents were drafted. If judicial interpretation of the section 35(1) commitment is to live up to its potential, the interpretation must also rely on Aboriginal understandings of our relationship with this land and with the state. Recognized and affirmed are relationship words more so than they are the standard jargon that lawyers associate with rights discourse.

The Aboriginal understanding of this historical context must become as important as the western understanding. I am not convinced that the Supreme Court's decision in *Delgamuukw,* where "oral history" is pronounced equal to written history in weight, is a sufficient commitment to accomplish this task. Embedded in this pronouncement is the idea that western written history is the same as oral history. It is not. Oral history must not be diminished against the standard accorded to written history in Canadian law. Oral history cannot be interpreted in the same way. Treating these forms of history as the same will likely lead to further imposition on the Aboriginal forms of history.

As a Kanien'kehaka woman and a member of two First Nations communities, I use my lived experience to help me accomplish this task of recognizing mono-culturalism in Canadian law. Obviously then, this recognition points to another problem with the reliance on Canadian law as the mechanism to resolve Aboriginal claims. Canadian law is not objective but rather grounded in Euro-Canadian cultural assumptions that are neither more nor less valid than the cultural assumptions of First Peoples which support our systems of law. I am not a "cultural" authority but rather a lawyer using my skills of legal reasoning to determine the degree to which the system I have been trained in is capable of understanding and respecting diverse cultures.

The discussion that follows is not built solely on the methods I learned during my years of legal study. Legal method was insufficient to meet my needs as an Aboriginal person, and my understanding of the proper way to look at the world. It requires that the scholar analyze the words of the judicial decision and not the cultural and social value systems embedded in the judicial pronouncements and their legal reasoning. I am concerned with both the ability of the courts to apply specific cultural and social values to Aboriginal Peoples as well as with the imposition of foreign government structures and laws on Aboriginal nations. Therefore, this realization must be accompanied by an attempt to adopt the legal method as I learned it as a student at the same time as I balance this skill against my understandings as a Kanien'kehaka woman. This skill is not necessarily unique to Aboriginal legal analysis. Dara Culhane writes:

> What I consider *not* readily accessible to common sense, and not a reflection of good sense, and therefore in need of explanation and criticism, are the Crown's positions and the evidence and theories relied upon to support them. This book is therefore a project in the anthropology of European colonialism: a study of power and of the powerful. I turn my anthropologist's spyglass on the law, an institution that quintessentially embodies and reproduces Western power. (1998:21)

This problem of the dominant cultural monopoly is pervasive throughout Canadian law and is a repeated theme in this discussion. One poignant example is offered here as demonstration of this concern. In the Gitksan and Wet'suwet'en trial. (*Delgamuukw*) Chief Justice Allan McEachern, in his closing, made somewhat personal comments (and these kinds of comments are unusual for judges to make):

> The parties have concentrated for too long on legal and constitutional questions such as ownership, sovereignty, and "rights," which are fascinating legal concepts. Important as these questions are, answers to legal questions will not solve the underlying social and economic problems which have disadvantaged Indian peoples from the earliest times.
> ... This cacophonous dialogue about legal rights and social wrongs has created a positional attitude with many exaggerated allegations and arguments, and a serious lack of reality. Surely it must be obvious that there have been failings on both sides....
> It is my conclusion, reached upon a consideration of the evidence which is not conveniently available to many, that the difficulties facing the Indian populations of the territory, and probably throughout Canada, will not be solved in the context of legal rights. Legal proceedings have been useful in raising awareness levels about a serious national problem. New initiatives, which may extend for years or generations, and directed at reducing and eliminating the social and economic disadvantages of Indians are now required. It must always be remembered, however, that it is for elected officials, not judges, to establish priorities for the amelioration of disadvantaged members of society. (*Delgamuukw* v. *The Queen* 1991:276)

The first difficulty I have with McEachern's analysis is the manner in which he characterizes the "national problem" which Aboriginal people have become. It is a problem of "social and economic disadvantage." He, in addition, benevolently agrees "that there have been failings on both sides" accepting for the "state" a certain degree of responsibility. Nonetheless, this is a fundamental mischaracterization of the issue which was litigated in *Delgamuukw*. The Gitksan and Wet'suwet'en people were litigating (at least at the trial level) the issue of title to land and the question of jurisdiction (or which government has authority over the territory—Gitksan and Wet'suwet'en, provincial or federal).

Simply put, this is the offence in McEachern's judgment. He uses the robes of his judicial authority to manifest power, in my opinion colonial power, to trivialize the nature of the problem and the case before him. This judgment impairs the rights of Aboriginal people by turning them into "social and economic problems," when they were brought by the people as, and should be understood as, fundamental constitutional issues. These issues rightly deserve to be heard within the sphere of the "supreme law of the land." I am not suggesting that there are not pressing social and economic difficulties which Aboriginal nations must address, but rather simply that these were *not* the issues that the Gitksan and Wet'suwet'en chose to place before the courts. Not only does McEachern attempt to toss away from the judiciary any responsibility for the valid legal issues placed before the court by mischaracterizing those issues as social and economic problems, he then correctly points to the fact that programs for the amelioration of disadvantage of "members of [Canadian] society" (which I do not believe is an accurate description of how the Gitksan and Wet'suwet'en peoples see themselves) are the responsibility of "elected officials." This is tantamount to a whine suggesting that the judiciary should not have been bothered with these issues in the first place!

There are other examples in McEachern's short comments here quoted that demonstrate his unquestioned absorption of the colonial mentality. McEachern locates the economic and social disadvantage of Indian people in "earliest times." This must be a reference to the early period of European contact, as it is with contact that the conditions of disadvantage arose. It is historically incorrect, if not simply ridiculous, to refer to this as "earliest times." The people and the land were here long before European "discovery." Understanding time only through what Europeans knew about the world is one of the many ways that presumed European superiority is still being manifest.

There is a further significant issue that concerns me. I believe that Justice McEachern's quoted comments are intended to shield him from criticism of a decision that he must have known would be actively criticized. Otherwise, I am at a loss to explain the presence of those comments. He attempts to accomplish this goal in several ways. McEachern privileges his access to the evidence by stating: "it is not conveniently available to many." This may be true of the average Canadian but it is certainly not true of the access and expertise of the people themselves. McEachern, however, chooses to acknowledge his superior expertise as the source of differing opinions in an attempt to legitimize his decision and suggest that criticisms are the result of lack of information and knowledge. This strategy is reinforced by his comments in the second quoted paragraph. The logical implication of comments such as "positional attitudes" and "exaggerated allegations and arguments" is that they are also attempts to diminish the validity of critics' comments. According to McEachern, those critics operate from a position of "a serious lack of reality." If this is the degree to which Aboriginal people can rely on the judiciary to justly assess Aboriginal claims, then a serious problem of judicial credibility will continue to exist. It does not matter to me if McEachern intended these implications and consequences. Intention has little to do with racist and colonial attitude and talk.

It is precisely this form of thought that precipitates the dominant ideological monopoly, which results in the oppression of Aboriginal Peoples.[9] Justice McEachern attempts to distance law from the colonialism and oppression that First Nations have faced in Canada. Unfortunately, declaring this so does not make it true. Despite the fact that McEachern and I agree that law alone cannot fix it, law was and remains a central tool in delivering oppression and colonialism to First Nations. The judiciary, of whom McEachern is but one example, despite its convenient claim to objectivity and neutrality, must come to understand that the Canadian system of law is complicit in the oppression of Aboriginal Peoples. Further, and perhaps more important, judicial neutrality must be seen for what it is, a legal principle of great convenience. It is a principle that assists in the writing of colonial judgments such as McEachern's which are based on political judgments and moral reasoning.

Courts consider cases to be individual and isolated phenomena, and are rarely able to assess them within their historical and contemporary contexts. Yet this task is necessary to the just resolution of Aboriginal claims.

Aboriginal people turn to the courts for a number of reasons, including the recognition of their relationship with oppression and/or colonialism and the law. After all, law has always been the tool by which oppression/colonialism have been delivered to Aboriginal people in this country (Monture-Angus 1995:174). The day where Canadian law is experienced by Aboriginal people as freedom and justice has yet to arrive. It is not because Aboriginal people have faith in the Courts that legal action is commenced. It is generally because the people have no other perceived way of protecting their rights.

In addition, the artificial separation of political and legal spheres in the delineation of responsibility for ensuring the protection of "existing aboriginal and treaty rights" serves only to ensure that the government and courts are able to continue to side-step, in a complementary fashion, their concurrent responsibilities. For many Aboriginal people, the separation between courts and governments is unclear, arbitrary and of little sense. And in the result, both these branches of Canadian sovereignty can be seen and often are seen as equally oppressive.

This pattern of complimentary side-stepping of responsibility is overly familiar to Aboriginal people. During the 1970s when Aboriginal people desired to see reforms in the area of child welfare (generally a provincial responsibility), the provinces denied that they had any responsibility to "Indians." The federal government, which had the constitutional authority to legislate regarding "Indians," denied responsibility for child welfare. Children received no services beyond apprehension. From the Indian view, the federal government is our partner in the "nation to nation" relationship. Because of the failure of the federal government (and to a lesser degree provincial governments) to see Aboriginal nations as governments, we are left in the middle with no power or ability to resolve the problems that our communities face. This has been an effective state strategy for the avoidance of just resolution of the Aboriginal experience in this land since the advent of Canada.

The avoiding of personal and collective responsibility, such as evidenced by Chief Justice McEachern in the *Delgamuukw* trial, is doubly problematic when it is the supreme law of the land that is the focus of the judicial interpretation of Aboriginal (and treaty) rights. Judicial interpretation requires an awareness of how Aboriginal people have experienced our relationship with Canada, including the many ways colonialism is manifest (such as side-stepping, language, history and presumed European superiority). Accountability and responsibility for the protection of Aboriginal (and treaty) rights must be seen as personal, judicial and political. This seems like such a simple realization (and it is necessary to the solution). It is also elusive.

The solution requires that legal processes must come to embrace Aboriginal people's experience and the meaning that Aboriginal people attach to that experience. Chief Justice McEachern excused himself from any such personal responsibility in the early pages of his judgment:

> cases must be decided on admissible evidence, according to law. The plaintiffs carry the burden of proving by balance of probabilities not what they believe, although that is sometimes a relevant consideration, but rather facts which permit the application of the legal principles which they assert. The Court is not free to do whatever it wishes. Judges, like everyone else, must follow the law *as they understand it*. (*Delgamuukw* 1991:6, emphasis added)

At the same time that McEachern dismisses Aboriginal beliefs, he substantiates his own belief in Canadian law as both legitimate and unquestionable. Unfortunately, because Aboriginal people see Canadian law as oppressive (and colonial) we do not necessarily share these same beliefs. Courts, law and justices have continued to fail to recognize that the Aboriginal experience of Canadian legal relations is *not* the same as their own. McEachern's understanding is not subject to the same level of scrutiny that he seems to be requiring of the Gitksan and Wet'suwet'en peoples. The Gitksan and Wet'suwet'en have only belief, whereas McEachern's cultural beliefs are *the* law and legal principles. This is an unacceptable double standard which amounts to thinly disguised racism because it exercises colonial power silently. In *Delgamuukw*, this judicial power has been exercised against Aboriginal interests and is readily apparent for those who are willing to look.

Canadian law will continue to be seen as an unjust system if this form of double standard continues to be masqueraded as legal thought and reasoning. As it stands now, all too often legal pronouncements embrace only the Euro-Canadian worldview and cultural heritage, despite the efforts of individual members of the judiciary and legal profession. This reality, of course, is not surprising in that it is substantiated and prefaced upon a misplaced notion of Aboriginal inferiority. Also of note is the fact that within the present system there are no formal or informal mechanisms, beyond the appeal process, for judicial accountability when cultural (mis)interpretation underpins the resolution of legal issues. These inadequacies in Canadian law are serious impediments to Aboriginal Peoples' attempts to utilize legal institutions to secure just resolution of our claims. The inadequacies are exposed as Aboriginal people attempt to use a system that was never intended to be used to address the kinds of issues that are endemic to Aboriginal claims.

Given the utmost importance of the task of legally interpreting these three small words, "existing aboriginal rights," it is important to focus on their meaning before we try to apply them in any kind of specific setting, such as a case. My choice to focus on "existing aboriginal rights" to the exclusion of "existing treaty rights" is not an indication that treaty rights are not as significant or as important as Aboriginal rights. Treaty rights have a history which is similar but also unique from Aboriginal rights. One does not necessarily exclude the other, that is, a right could be both Aboriginal or treaty at the same time. I start with the concept of Aboriginal rights because it is a reflection of how my own thinking on these issues developed.

When I first came to the issues presented by section 35(1) and began considering the meaning of the phrase, "existing aboriginal rights," I found it essential to consider the effect of applying western constructions of "rights" to First Peoples, whose varied cultures do not necessarily embrace such an ideological construct. What I now understand is that rights discourse is not necessarily or automatically relevant to Aboriginal cultures.[10] A system of responsibility makes more sense to the Aboriginal being. Until the parties involved can come to some form of consensus on this question of the meaning of rights then I believe the possibility exists for the constitutional affirmation to be misconstrued by conventional legal interpretation systems. There is a dangerous potential for the judicial determination of rights to occur in such a way that the difference in meaning attached to this word by Aboriginal Peoples will be invisible and therefore excluded.

Noel Lyon suggests that the shape of what is has changed with the entrenchment of Aboriginal rights in the constitution:

> Section 35 is a solemn commitment to honour the just land claims of aboriginal peoples, fulfill treaty obligations, and respect those rights of aboriginal peoples which the *Charter* ... recognizes as their fundamental rights and freedoms. What else could it be? *Constitutional reform is not done to continue the status quo.* (1988:101, emphasis added)

This passage was quoted by the Supreme Court of Canada in the *Sparrow* decision (at page 178). Constitutional scholars and lawyers (Aboriginal and Canadian) in conjunction with Aboriginal Peoples must articulate their understanding of what the status quo is before anything new can be constructed. Until we clearly understand what has been forced on Aboriginal Peoples (or what we need reject) we cannot understand what exactly requires renewing. This means that we have a lot of work to do before we can hope to interpret to its full potential the meaning of section 35 in specific cases. As the conventional legal system is absolutely not geared to this kind of analysis or process, I am fearful that the analysis which is essential to any future progress on Aboriginal rights will get lost in the rush to both prepare for litigation and keep court dockets moving. The opportunity that exists in section 35(1) for us, both as Aboriginal Peoples as well as to Canadians, may not again soon be presented.

In contemplating the meaning of section 35, I began to read about the history of rights (predominantly the liberal view), but was never satisfied. What I was reading did not fit the way that I had been brought up and the way that the Elders had taught me. I could not situate my Aboriginal self within the discourse about rights (Monture-Angus 1995:152–168). The result was a tension that I could not initially resolve (and it continues to perplex me). It is this tension and how I have come to understand it, that I want to speak about.

What I want to avoid is constructing a competing theory of rights. I do not want to displace the western or liberal theory of rights with an

Aboriginal theory of rights (particularly not a single theory, as Aboriginal Peoples are very diverse). But, at the same time I do not want a liberal or western theory forced upon me or my people. Let my people choose to pick it up if we decide that it is able to work for us.

Not belonging to the western culture, which spawned the existing theory of rights, I am not the appropriate actor to redefine the parameters of liberal rights theory. All the guidance that I can appropriately provide is to point to the fact that the theory is excluding my voice. My voice represents a separate culture and tradition; it is one of many voices within that culture, which in turn is one of the many cultures and traditions of Aboriginal Peoples. My dissatisfaction with the liberal theory of rights is probably also filtered by the fact that I am a woman.[11] The liberal theory of rights must recognize and affirm that it is possible for another theory of "rights" (in this case, more accurately, responsibilities) to exist within Aboriginal people's cultures, and that this other theory is legitimate. Equally important is the realization that these theories of rights can co-exist, as opposed to being competitive or combative.

Theoretically, we have to understand and accept that a right, to Aboriginal people, means something fundamentally different than it does within the sphere of Canadian legal relations. Recognition consists of different acts and understandings. Aboriginal people, as a consequence of centuries of being forcefully told we are inferior, must continue to remind ourselves that our experience and understanding are equally legitimate and encompass complete authority. Others have the difficult task of opening their eyes and ears for the first time. My objective here is to begin constructing, in a language that can be understood by people who have not been educated to our ways, what a theory of Aboriginal rights looks like from one Aboriginal location. Unfortunately, this is a formidable task, and more frequently I find myself articulating what the rights do not look like.

Examining the history of rights accorded to Aboriginal Peoples in Canadian jurisprudence, what I first came to understand was that it is a history bounded solely by Canadian law. The term Aboriginal rights is a term with a specific legal meaning and one that only expresses claims that have currently been accepted within Canadian law. Canadian legal process is therefore the sole gatekeeper of this process. I am concerned with the rights that have been excluded and I also refer to these as Aboriginal rights. The source of the tension is that Aboriginal rights in Canadian law do not embrace the much broader notion of Aboriginal rights that exist within my Aboriginal understanding. In effect the same words mean very different things (and the pattern of exclusion in how legal concepts are defined has already been identified as problematic).

The first recognition that must be made about Aboriginal rights in Canadian law is that they developed almost exclusively around the right to property.[12] I would assert that this right to property is more appropriately described as a struggle for the ownership and control of the land. It is not the land in and of itself that is important, but the ownership of the land. Beginning with *St. Catherines Milling* (1888) and continuing through important cases such as *Guerin* (1984) and *Calder* (1970) this pattern of "ownership of land" can be seen to be at the heart of these disputes.

A property claim in Canadian law does not have the capacity to include the Aboriginal holistic view of the land, because ownership in Canadian law is based on the linear notion of the domination of land. A holistic view of landholding enshrines not only the linear concept of ownership but also, at a minimum, spirituality and responsibility:

> With respect to the lands they lived on, many Indians felt a strong religious duty to protect their territory. Future generations would need the lands to live on, many previous generations had migrated long distances to arrive finally at the place where the people were intended to live. One could sell neither the future nor the past, and land cessions represented the loss of both future and past to most Indians.
>
> … although Indians surrendered the physical occupation and ownership of their ancestral lands, they did not abandon the spiritual possession that had been a part of them. Even today most Indians regard their homeland as the area where the tribe originally lived. (Deloria and Lytle 1984:10–11)

The Aboriginal view of land rights encompasses both a notion of time as occupation (past, present and future) and a notion of spiritual occupation or connection. Both of these notions of Aboriginal occupation challenge the individualization of the common law system of property ownership. The relationship to land is seen not solely as a right but equally as a responsibility. In other words, the Aboriginal understanding of the relationship to land incorporates four separate (but integrated) ideas about land: individual rights and responsibilities, and collective rights and responsibilities.[13]

There have also been a number of important hunting and fishing cases heard by Canadian courts. The right to hunt or fish is one component, but not a nearly full articulation, of the right to use the land and in the case of Aboriginal people this right is one that was to exist forever—"as long as the grass grows and the rivers flow." It is often characterized in Canadian court decisions as a mere usufructuary right (a right of use, which is lesser than a right of ownership in Canadian law).[14] In Canadian law then, the history of Aboriginal rights is the history of the use and/or ownership of land rather than a relationship to be maintained to the law. Hunting and fishing rights are nothing larger, to date, than the further specification of the existing encapsulating structure of property relations as Canadian law understands them. As already indicated, this is a very narrow structure, which offends the holistic view of personal and collective relationships with the land held by Aboriginal Peoples.

It is precisely this relationship between Aboriginal rights and land that does not satisfy me. I do not think that the legally-based notion of property is a complete way of defining what Aboriginal right(s) are. The focus on property rights (or the squabble over ownership) has become misappropriately central in Canadian court decisions because it is the linear notion of ownership that is at the heart of the struggle between First Nations and Canada in the political realm. However, the consequence of dragging Canada's political inability to resolve the issue of the definition of land ownership, as well as the actual ownership rights, to the courtroom has been that Canadian law on Aboriginal rights has almost solely focused on the competing definitions of the relationship with land. This has happened with little attention paid to and little understanding of the Aboriginal intellectual tradition, which includes an understanding of land relationships as a foundational principle.

We must recognize that the competition of worldviews results in the failure to legally construct a compelling and complete theory of Aboriginal rights. Imagine the outcome if a series of contract, criminal or tort cases proceeded to adjudication without the benefit of a sound theoretical framework in which to resolve the issues. For a lawyer, this is unthinkable. The theoretical framework is in fact equally the role and *duty* of the court and not just of the legislatures.

Encapsulated in this recognition is a smaller theoretical conundrum. The larger concept of land rights is just a small portion of what must be talked about. In the common law history and the case law that we have to rely on, property is the almost exclusive place where attempts to characterize Aboriginal rights coalesce. I am not suggesting that a focus on property/land is or was wrong or even unnecessary. It was essential, as both the environment and Aboriginal Peoples' economic futures were fundamentally threatened by the loss of land. My point is simply that to locate a theory of Aboriginal rights on a borrowed construction of land rights is overly narrow, limiting, unfairly constraining and lacks vision.

When the legal analysis focuses on the framework in which individual decisions are embedded, further areas of contradiction with Aboriginal worldviews are exposed. (Legal academics are as equally responsible as the courts for this portion of the theoretical vacuum that has been created.) One such example is the way in which Canadian law is bounded by the important distinctions between matters public and private.[15] Public matters are generally matters in which one of the various arms of government is involved. Private matters on the other hand tend to involve individuals. Matters of family law between individuals are private, but matters of family law that involve the state (such as child protection hearings) are public. Aboriginal Peoples have had some success in having their traditional or customary laws regarding private-law matters, such as adoption and marriages, recognized in Canadian law.[16] Much has been made of this alleged accomplishment. However, the fact that Canadian law has recognized Aboriginal family relations only in the private-law sphere must be viewed as problematic.[17] Recent Canadian decisions where state removal of children has been the issue have not been as successful as the private-law cases. This location in the private sphere is a marginalization of Aboriginal rights and therefore is another way in which the legal structure embraces the notion of European superiority. From an Aboriginal point of view, family relations would not be seen as private-law rights. In fact, the public/private law distinction as an organizational principle of social order makes little sense to the Aboriginal mind.

Feminist writing and research, on the other hand, has pointed to the fact that so-called women's concerns tend to vest almost solely within the private sphere, and this has propagated discrimination against women in law. Care must be taken when constructing theories of Aboriginal rights to ensure that the same pattern of trivialization of women's concerns are *not* followed for Aboriginal systems of rights.

It is naive to think that Aboriginal Peoples will stop bringing their claims to court whilst this issue of the lack of a viable framework is addressed. Therefore, concurrently with continued adjudication, courts and legal academics must begin to significantly address the theoretical shortcomings and the structural obstacles in Canadian legal process and practice, and the myths (such as the myth of European superiority) which Canadian law continues to propagate.

I am more concerned about the exclusions than the inclusions (which is why a review of the case law is not central to the discussion I first wish to provoke). Interestingly enough, the case law method of Canadian law is a central problem for the kind of theoretical development that I am proposing. By wedding ourselves to the decisions of the past, we continue to entrench in present-day form, the oppressive relations of Canadian, British and French history. I understand that I am asking lawyers, judges and to a lesser degree lawmakers to do a remarkable thing, something they have never had to do in the past (as evidenced in Justice McEachern's words cited earlier in this chapter). I would hope that the legal profession looks upon it as a marvelous challenge and not a threat to the dominant legal system. After all, what we are talking about is defining and interpreting the supreme law of this land. It ought to challenge our collective and varied cultural legal imaginations.

It is very important that both the parallels and contradictions which exist between the Canadian system and the Aboriginal process of law are discussed before we go any further in interpreting section 35(1). First, such an analysis would dispel the myth that incorporating Aboriginal

Peoples within Canadian legal structures (perhaps through separate systems) will somehow ghettoize the Canadian system as opposed to improv-
ing it (Monture-Okanee 1994:222–232). Second, it would alleviate the
necessity of devoting (as now) the majority of our energy to telling you
how different we are (which is really a discussion about why removing the
boot of oppression from our necks is a good thing to do).

The recognition that the Canadian legal rights of Aboriginal Peoples
are thus far merely rights about property enables one to recognize what
has been excluded. As much of my work has been focused around the
rights of Aboriginal offenders and the criminal justice system as it is
experienced by Aboriginal people, and particularly Aboriginal women, it
was easy for me to recognize what was glaringly absent from the case law
on Aboriginal rights. We have not even begun to discuss what "human
rights"[18] Aboriginal Peoples may have under section 35(1).

There are several reasons why this omission was fairly easy for me
(and other Aboriginal people) to recognize. It is very much part of my
culture to look at the history of any phenomenon to understand what it has
come to mean today. The history of the development of human rights
shows that it was not until 1985 and the *Bhinder* (1985) and *O'Malley*
(1985) decisions, that the courts in Canada came to articulate that intent
does not have anything to do with discrimination (Monture 1990:351–36).
In Great Britain and to a lesser degree in the United States, intent was
removed from the purview of the courts some fifteen years before the
recognition was made in Canada (Vizkelety 1987:14–36). It is no wonder
that sometimes it feels like it is taking us a very long time to get anywhere.

I want to tie the notion of human rights to the broader Aboriginal
notion of land rights. As already discussed, the relationship that First
Nations have to land is much broader than rights associated with the
ownership of land. The relationship to land is spiritual and sacred. The
relationship to land reaches beyond and behind individual ownership,
recognizing both past generations (the bones of my ancestors in the land)
and future generations (which we refer to as "the faces in the sand"). Earth
is Mother. Land is seen as part of the "human" family. It is part of all that
is natural. Human rights in an Aboriginal frame of reference seem to me to
include the relationship with the land. What I think human rights means in
this context is the right to be self-governing or self-determining or sovereign. This right is essentially the right to be responsible. This is the most
fundamental of all human rights (or responsibilities).

In attempting to understand the difficulties that arise from the failure
to articulate a cohesive and complete theory of Aboriginal rights in Canadian law, I have identified three "eras" of Aboriginal rights litigation.
During each of these eras, the case law developed differently. The first era
is best characterized as a period where a string of small, random victories

were embedded against a backdrop of political non-will. The lack of a cohesive and complete theory is most apparent in this period. This is the pre-1990 period and is fully discussed in chapter three. The second period covers the years 1990–1995. This period can best be characterized as the early years of constitutional negotiation. The Supreme Court in this period, particularly in the *Sparrow* case, took some brave, bold and new steps forward, the analysis of which is presented in chapter four. Finally, the Supreme Court in 1996 released several decisions which pulled back from the broad and solemn language of the *Sparrow* decision. The discussion in chapter five considers the *Delgamuukw* decision with a view to determining how much progress is being made. Chapter five also considers the degree to which the Supreme Court's articulation of Aboriginal rights can embrace Aboriginal demands for self-determination.

Notes

1. Again, my thanks to Tom Porter for sharing this teaching.
2. Paul A. Wallace first published the *White Roots of Peace* in January of 1946 (see Wallace 1994).
3. The contributions of the Haudenosaunee to ideas about democracy can be found in: Jose Barreiro 1992, Laurence M. Hauptman 1986, Bruce E. Johansen 1982 and Oren Lyons et al. 1992.
4. This is Robert Warrior's phrase.
5. I also discussed this in my first book, *Thunder in my Soul*, in chapters 7 and 8 (Monture-Angus 1995).
6. Under the heading of the "Rights of the Aboriginal Peoples of Canada" a single section appears which addresses these rights:

   > 35. (1) The existing aboriginal and treaty rights of the aboriginal peoples of Canada are hereby recognized and affirmed.
   > (2) In this Act, "Aboriginal peoples of Canada" includes the Indian Inuit and Métis peoples of Canada.
   > (3) For greater certainty, in subsection (1) "treaty rights" includes rights that now exist by way of land claims agreements or may be so acquired.
   > (4) Notwithstanding any other provision of this Act, the aboriginal and treaty rights referred to in subsection (1) are guaranteed equally to male and female persons.

7. Equality is a tricky word and it has many meanings. I use the word to simply mean respect for all peoples and traditions.
8. Section 35(2) provides that the Aboriginal Peoples includes the "Indian, Inuit and Métis."

   It is curious to note that the word "aboriginal" is not capitalized in the text of the constitution. This may be picking at small points but in my mind it is exemplary of the failure to respect Aboriginal Peoples that has permeated Canadian history. For this reason, I have chosen to capitalize the words in the text whenever I am not directly quoting another source.

9. I am not suggesting that this is the only problem that can be found within the reasoning of the trial court in the *Delgamuukw* case (also referred to in this discussion as the Gitksan and Wet'suwet'en case).

10. I am grateful to many Elders for helping me understand my confusion. In particular, I am grateful to Chief Jacob E. Thomas, Cayuga, Six Nations Territory.
See also the discussion in Mary Ellen Turpel, "Aboriginal Peoples and the Canadian *Charter*: Interpretive Monopolies, Cultural Differences" (1989–90), 6 *Canadian Human Rights Yearbook*, 3–45.

11. In the view of John Locke, man's freedom is a measure of man's natural right to have equal access to the fruits of his labour. The subjection of women within the family, on the other hand, is seen by Locke as a necessary and legitimate means to ensure that private property relations are maintained. Women do not have a natural right to the fruits of their labour. Not only is this Lockean definition of equality problematic for women but it demonstrates the relationship of freedom and equality rights to relations of property ownership (or man's domination of the land). See John Locke 1980:39–42.

12. There is a relationship here between the evolution of Aboriginal rights and treaty rights. The development of specific treaty rights has also and unnecessarily been tied to the question of ownership of the land. Prior to the case of *R. v. Sioui* [1990], the federal government asserted that a treaty must involve a surrender of land. Cases such as *Sioui* and *Simon*, [1986] demonstrate that fundamental change within Canadian law is possible.

13. A similar conclusion is reached by Leroy Little Bear 1976:30–34.

14. Aboriginal rights were first characterized as usufructuary rights of a personal nature (that is they are alienable only to the Crown) in the *St. Catherines Milling Case*. This view was rejected in *Guerin* where Justice Dickson stated:

> The nature of the Indians' interest is therefore best characterized by its general inalienability, coupled with the fact that the Crown is under an obligation to deal with the land on the Indians' behalf when the interest is surrendered. *Any description of Indian title which goes beyond these two features is both unnecessary and potentially misleading.* (136, emphasis added)

In an earlier case (*Calder*), Justice Judson opined:

> ... it does not help one in the solution of this problem to call it [Indian title] a "personal and usufructuary right." (156)

Scholars and judges who continue to rely on the usufruct as descriptive of Aboriginal rights rely on legal principles which Canadian courts have rejected in favour of a *sui generis* view of Aboriginal (land) rights.

15. The most famous case here is *Retail, Wholesale and Department Store Union, Local 580 v. Dolphin Deliver Ltd.* (1986).

16. See for example the following custom adoption cases: *Re Beaulieu* (1969), *Re Katie's Adoption Petition* (1961), *Re Tagornak* (1984) and the discussion

in Norman Zlotkin (1984). For marriage cases please see *Connolly* v. *Woolrich* (1867) and the discussion in Constance Backhouse 1991:9–28; *Re Wah-Shee* (1975).

17. Although a lengthy discussion of several of the cases that respect Aboriginal customs in relation to adoption and marriage are discussed in *Partners in Confederation: Aboriginal People, Self-Government and the Constitution* by the Royal Commission on Aboriginal Peoples, 1993, pp. 5–8, this particular concern is oddly never mentioned. Of further concern is the fact that the brilliant feminist discussion pursued by Professor Constance Backhouse (1991) in her text, *Petticoats and Prejudice*, is also overlooked by the Royal Commission on Aboriginal Peoples. Neither of these oversights are acceptable as the exclusion is gender based.

18. I do not intend to limit the discussion of human rights protected under section 35(1) by defining human rights in the manner that Canada is presently accustomed to in its statutory framework. It is also ironic to note that the *Canadian Human Rights Code* section 67 provides an exception for the federal *Indian Act* regime and any regulations made thereunder. The result is that the *Indian Act* is not subject to the federal Human Rights Code.

Chapter Three

The Crown's Ability
To Deny Responsibility
The First Era—Judicial Decisions
Before 1990

The attempt to justly resolve Aboriginal claims within the parameters of the Canadian state, including Canadian courts, challenges the basic presumptions on which the state (and the courts) lay claim to their legitimacy. Concepts such as the division of powers, parliamentary supremacy, the independence of the judiciary and the rule of law are seen by Canadian governments as absolutes to which Aboriginal people must conform their visions for governance. This difficulty has been brought to our attention before, as Kent McNeil notes:

> The Eurocentric vision of two founding nations, and the constitutional dogma of exhaustive division of legislative powers in our federal system, simply left no place for Aboriginal governments in the minds of most non-Aboriginal politicians and jurists. (1993:96)

Justly resolving Aboriginal claims, therefore, requires a measure of creativity and a break with past policies, laws and practices, both of which are hard for Canadian governments to imagine. This conclusion is easily reached by many Aboriginal people who have considered the impact of colonialism on our lives. All of our experience demonstrates the obvious nature of this recognition. For many others, however, it is not so apparent and requires a demonstration of the many reasons why Aboriginal people reach this conclusion.

Canada's political history demonstrates that since the time of the signing of the numbered treaties, the will to resolve outstanding Aboriginal claims has most often been non-existent. Perhaps this pattern is now beginning to be broken. For example, the Federation of Saskatchewan

Indian Nations and Canada, with the assistance of the Office of the Treaty Commissioner, have commenced a process which, after more than 120 years of a treaty relationship, seeks to implement the treaties (Treaty Commissioner 1998:7). This is one small sign that things might be done differently in the future.

The well documented lack of political will on the part of all levels of Canadian government has left Aboriginal people little option but to turn to the courts to resolve outstanding issues. These efforts have never been fully successful. For example, prior to the 1997 Supreme Court of Canada decision in *Delgamuukw*, courts have been reluctant to clearly define the concept of Aboriginal title (not that the *Delgamuukw* decision is a complete or final articulation of this concept), and Aboriginal title is the pivotal point in many Aboriginal claims. Litigation has sometimes resulted in a positive outcome by forcing Canadian governments to at least recognize that there are outstanding legal issues. At most, the Canadian history of adjudicating Aboriginal claims can be viewed as a string of narrow victories, secured at great cost to both Aboriginal nations and individual citizens of those nations, each no more meaningful than a single stroke of a pen. Because these legal victories are viewed against a backdrop of political non-will, the illusion is created that their magnitude is great. After all, Aboriginal people do need something to cheer about.

However, our celebration has been used to cloud the truth that very little has been accomplished through litigation.[1] The experiences of Aboriginal people and the legal system must be placed in a larger social context and brought back into a realistic perspective.

By agreeing to the litigation process to resolve a claim, Aboriginal Peoples agree implicitly to the terms on which the non-Aboriginal dispute resolution system is based, regardless of the consequences or biases that process affirms. Certainly, as these structural obstacles are identified, they can be challenged. However, this incremental case-by-case approach to resolution of Aboriginal claims fates Aboriginal people to generation upon generation of legal challenge. This cannot be seen as significant or meaningful advancement.

There is an insurmountable problem in taking Aboriginal claims to territory before the courts. Courts owe their creation to the fact of Canadian sovereignty. They cannot question that sovereignty because, to find it wanting would in fact dis-establish their own legitimacy. Without legitimate claim and control over territory, the international definition of sovereignty collapses.[2] Aboriginal people must be acutely aware of this limitation when they prepare their cases for litigation.

The best example of the phenomenon of nominal gain through legal victory is the 1973 decision of the Supreme Court in the Nishga land litigation case (*Calder*). Despite the fact that the *Calder* case was lost on a legal technicality, it was a victory for the Nishga nation. In *Calder*, six of the seven Supreme Court Justices found that there was a pre-existing Aboriginal title which was not exclusively sourced in the *Royal Proclamation of 1763* or in any other enactment of a non-Aboriginal government. This decision is important because its release became a major turning point in Indian/Canadian political relations.

After the Calder decision the Canadian government was forced to recognize the existence of *legal* rights to land held by Indian nations. Prior to *Calder*, Canada had recognized these claims as only moral or political rights, neither of which are legally enforceable. Michael Asch describes the impact the Calder decision had:

> Prior to the Calder case, the government regarded Aboriginal rights as a transitional issue, for Aboriginal societies would presumably assimilate eventually into the Canadian mainstream. Given such an ideology, the notion that Native peoples could possess permanent constitutional rights, including the perpetual right to self-government, was unthinkable. Immediately after the Calder decision, government took the position that the transition had already taken place. But within five years this was replaced by a new perspective: that Aboriginal society was not a transitional phenomenon and its survival should be recognized. Initially, the political component of this continuity, based on legislative authority, was not to be entertained, but this also may be reconsidered. In sum, government on Aboriginal rights has evolved, even on the question of political rights, from a position of resistance to one of reluctance. (1984:71–72)

The result of the *Calder* litigation was the establishment of a land claims process by the Trudeau government to resolve both specific and comprehensive claims (*Sparrow* 1990:179–180). Unfortunately, this new approach to land claims was not successful in finalizing the many outstanding land issues.

The problem with solely viewing the decision in *Calder* as progress is in the fact that Indian people were required to go to court to attempt to force Canada to step up to its responsibilities to the Nishga people. Having to force Canada to pick up its moral, political and legal responsibilities is not celebration because this is what Canada was obligated to do in the first place. These small legal successes often mask the larger reality and context. The relevant question must be: How has this successful court action changed things in the community and for the average Indian person?

It is not just the substantive conclusions reached by courts that impact adversely on Aboriginal people who seek to secure through litigation just resolutions to their claims. The court process contains a number of difficulties which, by their very nature, are problematic for Aboriginal claimants and for the just resolution of their claims. For example, the rules of the judiciary often ensure that Aboriginal Peoples cannot overcome the historical biases that form the basis of the Canadian legal legacy.

One such rule is the system within the legal process called precedent (and there are many more examples that could be offered). By establishing a system which relies on previous court decisions (that is, precedent), the judiciary is backward looking. Since there is little in the history of the legal resolution of Aboriginal claims that could be characterized as beneficial to Aboriginal Peoples, such a process, unless it is vigilant to cultural differences, ensures that historic Canadian beliefs about Aboriginal people are continually affirmed, unquestioned, in future resolutions. Its effect is to unconsciously and perhaps unintentionally entrench the beliefs of historical times, such as that of European superiority, in present day decisions. In this first era of judicial resolutions of Aboriginal claims, the problem of precedent is glaring.

One of the earliest cases on the rights of Aboriginal people living in the territory that became known as Canada offers clear examples of the problems associated with the rule of precedent. In 1888, the Judicial Committee of the Privy Council in England handed down its decision in the case of *St. Catherines Milling and Lumber Company* v. *The Attorney General of Ontario*. To fully appreciate the consequences of this decision it is necessary to understand that the strength of the precedent is partially determined by the level of court making the decision. As the Judicial Committee of the Privy Council was the highest court then hearing appeals from the Canadian courts, the precedent set in *St. Catherines* was significant. This decision set the tone and provided the legal parameters for Aboriginal land litigation until the decision of the Supreme Court in the *Calder* case in 1973. *St. Catherines* was the first significant Canadian case to take the issue of Indian[3] title before the courts.

The dispute between the lumber company and the Ontario government arose as the result of the signing of Treaty Three in northern Ontario in 1873. The lumber company, which was closely connected to the federal government led by John A. Macdonald, had received a licence to cut timber in the area of Wabigoon Lake (Cottam 1991:247). It had cut two million feet of lumber and was preparing to remove it from the area. In this particular case, the province took issue with the right of the federal government to issue the timber licences (and the company's right to remove the timber). The dispute had been simmering between the two levels of government since the Dominion acquired the territory from the Hudson's Bay Company in 1870 (Cottam 1991:247–48). The province decided it was time to litigate. Wishing to affirm its beneficial interest[4] in the land by virtue of section 109 of the *British North America Act* (BNA Act), the province brought action against the lumber company seeking an injunction to stop it from removing the timber. The federal government intervened in the appeal as a co-defendant.

Lord Watson, writing for the Privy Council, upheld the province's view that although title to the land vested in the Crown, the beneficial interest vested in the province. Based solely on the constitutional provision found in section 109[5] the Privy Council reasoning was in fact correct. I also have no dispute with the fact that federal and provincial governments can legitimately order their relationships according to the agreements reflected in the constitutional provisions. The federal government had no authority to issue a timber licence and the lumber company had been unlawfully carrying out its economic pursuits. Damages and an injunction lay against the company. The sound constitutional reasoning of the case eclipses the impact that this decision soon had on Indian nations.[6] In fact, only by examining the context does it become clear why the interests of Indians ever became an issue in this case.

The constitutional provisions in the BNA Act reflect an agreement between only the federal and provincial governments. The process to resolve any disputes between these two levels of government is also part of that constitutional agreement. Indian nations are fully outside this agreement, never having consented to the imposition of Canadian constitutional law. No process or practice exists in Canadian or British law to go behind a constitutional document that is being litigated to remedy the shortcomings (exclusions), regardless of the degree of devastation that the omissions create for an enclaved people. In fact, the very idea is contrary to the Canadian legal imagination. Nonetheless, the Indians' interests were drawn fully into the dispute resolution process in the St. Catherines case.

In the face of the rather clear statement of provincial interest contained in section 109, the only hope the federal government possessed to claim the land was to argue that the result of the extinguishment of the Indian interest by treaty[7] created a complete vesting of the land interest in the federal government. The federal government saw nothing wrong with using the Indian population and their rights in this manner. The federal government's hopes in this case rested squarely on the backs of Indian people and the hope that the Court would recognize that Indian title was a recognizable legal interest. Writing in detail about the politics surrounding the *St. Catherines* case, Barry Cottam describes:

> The Dominion argued, through John A. Macdonald, who was both the Prime Minister of Canada and the Superintendent General of Indian Affairs, that the Indians had owned the land and passed it to the Dominion through the treaty; thus the Dominion owned the land and its resources even though they lay within the boundaries of Ontario as established by the JCPC in 1884. The

Ontario government had to produce an alternate view; Indian title
had to be established as something less than full ownership for
Ontario's counter claim to stand. The Ontario government met
the Dominion argument with assertions that the Indians had no
concept of property recognizable in law, and that, whether they
did or not, the title to the lands of North America lay in the Crown
of England by virtue of the processes of discovery, conquest and
settlement. If the Indians had any rights at all they came through
the generosity of the Crown. (1991:248)

The federal government attempted to stand in the place of Indian people
solely for the purpose of increasing its own interest in lands that under
simple constitutional interpretation belonged to the province. The federal
attempt failed. The result of the federal action was the legal diminishing
of the Indian interest in land.

Indian people were neither parties in the action nor were they represented at any stage in the court process. Yet, Indians have been living with
the consequences of this decision for more than a century. Not only were
the Ojibwe people, or any other Indian nation, unrepresented at the hearing, nowhere was any concern expressed by Lord Watson (or those judges
who, in later years, relying on precedent, have cited Lord Watson's decision) regarding the fact that the Indian position and Indian people were
not parties to the case and therefore were not heard. This failure to hear
Indian concerns may have been typical of the times but it was nonetheless
a complete breach of the principles of fundamental justice, which the
Euro-Canadian system alleges it reveres. Subsequent court application of
the Privy Council decision in this case determined the interests of all
Indian Peoples (not just those signatory to Treaty Three) for nearly a
century before it was successfully challenged.

The decision of Lord Watson has percolated through the great majority of court cases on Indian title since 1888. In rendering his judgment,
Lord Watson noted:

> there was a great deal of learned discussion at the Bar with
> respect to the precise quality of the Indian right, but their Lord-
> ships do not consider it necessary to express any opinion upon the
> point. (*St. Catherines Milling* 1888:55)

Presenting yet another illogical shortcoming in its reasoning, the Court
continued by offering its comments on the nature of Indian title, regardless of whether or not this was necessary for the decision. It was held that
the Indian interest in land was a "mere burden" on the absolute Crown
title. Lord Watson characterized the Indian interest as a "personal and
usufructuary right" (*St. Catherines Milling* 1888:55). This is legalese for

the right to merely use the land. Usufructuary rights are less than estates[8] or interests in land on which the British (and later Canadian) system of landholding is based. The legal interest of the Crown in the land, therefore, was found to be greater than the interest of Indian Peoples. Apparently, the obvious superiority of European peoples is the underlying reason why a greater legal interest vests in the Crown.

Following the reasoning of Lord Watson an interesting and disturbing observation is made. Nowhere in the decision does the Court identify and fully explain the source of Crown title. The same imprecision does not surround the source for the Indian interest in land, which Lord Watson carefully sources in the *Royal Proclamation of 1763*. If Indian title comes about by virtue of *Royal Proclamation,* then Crown action is seen by the Court to be required before the Indian interest legally exists. This is contrary to Aboriginal understandings about the source of our rights which pre-exist contact with European nations. This was the burden left to litigators of Indian claims, who in the future would be required to displace these findings before they could even attempt to successfully articulate their legal claims to the land. The judicial reasoning in *St. Catherines* can only be seen as a colonial gesture of great magnitude and must be viewed as an untenable construction of the history of this land and the relationship of Indian nations to it.

Immediately after 1888, it would have been fairly simple to argue that the aspects of the definition of Indian title found in the decision of the Privy Council in St. Catherines were obiter[9] as, in fact, Lord Watson noted. However, as Aboriginal people were not involved in judicial processes at this time the opportunity was missed to stop the obiter comments from being entrenched, through the process of precedent, in later cases. The consequences of the exclusionary history, structure and practice of courts must be acknowledged. The publication of cases, even today, is not accomplished in such a way that Aboriginal communities have great access to this information (and in my view this is another serious problem with the legal process as a means to resolve Aboriginal claims). As the cases immediately following the Privy Council decision embraced and affirmed fully the reasoning of Lord Watson, the faulty reasoning became binding on future decisions. This required subsequent courts to follow the definition of Indian rights to land as "mere burden" and owing their existence to Crown action, or to break with precedent.

From 1888 to 1973 when the *Calder* decision was handed down by the Supreme Court of Canada, little progress was made in the courts toward justly resolving Aboriginal claims. John Borrows and Leonard Rotman summarize this period:

> For close to one hundred years the majority of judicial decisions concerning Aboriginal rights primarily involved the competing

legislative and commercial interests of the federal and provincial governments, rather than the laws and interests of Native peoples. The preponderance of these decisions held that Aboriginal rights were premised entirely upon the benevolence of the Crown. (1997:17)

In many of these decisions the Aboriginal title was seen as a "mere burde-" ~-own title. This rule was more and more forcefully applied ~e more entrenched in Canadian law. Indian nations 'ire consequences of a rule definition process that

'ls of difficulty in the *St. Catherines* case from mework. First, the process offered no protec- lly outside of either constitutionalism, the The denial of the rights of the Indian people ce was compounded over time. The fact that ard, even though their rights as collectives ndamentally affected, must be seen as highly . only is the process problematic, but substantively, ,sion is also unacceptable. It is based on ethnocen- u. ,ws about Canada, the land, the ownership of the land, and history. It is an exclusionary judgment and its value as a legal precedent must be fully surrendered.[11]

These two difficulties expose a third concern. The judicial process on which we rely to resolve Indian claims is not accountable to the people whose future it determines. Canada (either federal or provincial governments), on the other hand, can by the authority vested in its legislative powers, circumvent judicial decisions by passing or amending the statutory provisions. This forces courts to at least acknowledge seriously the position the various Canadian legislatures take on certain issues. No such deference to Aboriginal governments exists in the present balance between judicial and legislative powers. This problem of accountability must be taken seriously because it fundamentally affects the way courts make decisions, particularly in cases that involve inherent Indian jurisdiction. This jurisdiction is a significant function of self-determination.

For nearly a century after 1888, little if any progress was made before the judiciary, but certain changes did occur on the political front which directly impacted on the change to occur in the judicial decisions on Indian rights during the 1970s. In 1951, the prohibition on retaining counsel or raising money for litigating Indian claims was removed from the *Indian Act*.[12] There is no question that this section affected the type of Indian rights litigation that was brought before domestic courts. It was one important reason why few, if any, comprehensive claims were found in the courts prior to the *Calder* decision.[13] Before the 1950s the Aboriginal rights litigation was comprised predominantly of claims regarding the right to hunt or fish. The prohibition most likely explains this preponderance of individualized hunting and fishing rights cases, which are still the most popular form of Indian litigation.

Most hunting and fishing rights cases are individualized claims, which, despite the intention of the First Nations' citizens who brought these cases to court, do not necessarily advance self-governing interests. Within the court structure they are quasi-criminal in nature. This fact did not escape the attention of the Court in *Sparrow,* where it was noted that:

> the trial for a violation of penal prohibition may not be the most appropriate setting in which to determine the existence of an aboriginal right.... (at page 172)

Such an arena is clearly not the best for providing sound judicial articulation of the principles of Indian rights. The removal of this section which effectively prohibited Indian litigation follows the post-World War II sensitivity to human rights as the result of wartime atrocities and not necessarily any particular sensitivity to Aboriginal concerns.

During the post-war period, international human rights protections also began to appear. In 1960, the federal government introduced the *Canadian Bill of Rights,* which guaranteed anti-discrimination protections.[14] During this same period (1960), the federal franchise was granted to registered Indians. All of these factors produced a greater awareness amongst both the Canadian public and the judiciary regarding Canada's history and its discriminatory treatment of Indian people. In fact, the judiciary is not unaware of these facts and in 1990 they stated:

> For many years, the rights of the Indians to their aboriginal lands—certainly as *legal* rights—were virtually ignored. The leading cases defining Indian rights in the early part of the century were directed at claims supported by the Royal Proclamation or other legal instruments and even these cases were essentially concerned with settling legislative jurisdiction or the rights of commercial enterprises. For fifty years after the publication of Clement's *The Law of the Canadian Constitution* (3d ed., 1916), there was a virtual absence of discussion of any kind of Indian rights to land even in academic literature. By the late 1960s aboriginal claims were not even recognized by the federal government as having any legal status. Thus the *Statement of the Government of Canada on Indian Policy* 1969, although well meaning, contained the assertion (at p. 11) that "aboriginal claims to land ... are so general and undefined that it is not realistic to think of them as specific claims capable of remedy except through a policy and

> program that will end injustice to the Indians as members of the
> Canadian community." ... It took a number of judicial decisions
> and notably the *Calder* case in this Court (1973) to prompt a
> reassessment of the position being taken by government. (*Spar-
> row* 1990:177)

By the 1970s, the time was right for a partial break with the judicial past.
How substantial this break has been remains open to question.

The change in the outcomes of Aboriginal litigation in the post-war
period from decisions that protected government or commercial interests
can be first noted in the British Columbia Court of Appeal decision in the
White and *Bob* case (*R. v. White* 1964). This case marks the "re-emergence
of Aboriginal rights interpretations according to indigenous legal conceptions" (Borrows and Rotman 1997:18). Here Norris J.A. held that treaties
should "be given their widest meaning in favour of the Indians" (1964:635).
This reason is then furthered by the Supreme Court of Canada case in the
Nishga decision.

The importance of the *Calder* case has already been noted and it may
come as a surprise to some that the Nishga were not successful in their
claim. Based on the technical decision of Justice Pigeon, the Nishga lost
their suit for a declaration that their title to the land had never been
extinguished.[15] The Nishga had failed to secure a fiat (the permission of
the province to go ahead and sue them) prior to commencing their litigation, as was then required by the British Columbia statutes (*Crown Procedure Act* 1960). Judson agreed with the opinion of Pigeon on the result of
the failure to secure a fiat prior to litigating. Tallying up the opinions, the
Nishga narrowly lost their bid to secure a declaration stating their title
was unextinguished by a split decision of four to three.

Looking beyond the technicality that decided the case, Justice Judson
and two other Supreme Court justices held that Aboriginal title had been
extinguished indirectly through a series of legislative and Crown procla-
mations. Two justices concurred with Justice Hall who insisted that extinguishment can only be demonstrated by the "clear and plain" expression
of the Crown. The fact that the Nishga lost their case on the fiat technicality, however, does not diminish the success of six of the seven Supreme
Court of Canada justices agreeing that the concept "Indian title" was a
valid legal concept.

The way in which the Nishga drafted their litigation is an important
issue in and of itself. The remedy sought was a declaration—a judicial
statement—and nothing more. The Nishga did not ask the Court to define
the broad concept of Indian title or the more specific question of Nishga
title, merely to note that it had not been extinguished. The question was
purposefully a narrow one that averted the real question of land ownership
which underpinned this case. The Nishga themselves ensured that both

remedially and substantively the issue before the courts could cause them as little harm as possible. This is an important lesson regarding the care which must be given to the way an Aboriginal claim is framed before it is taken to court.

Two comments can be substantiated from the recognition of the narrow scope of the Nishga claim. First, the Nishga did not trust the courts with the larger question of Indian title.[16] Second, by seeking only declarative relief, the Nishga understood that the real solution lay outside the judicial process and that the court action was just the first step[17] to securing a political negotiation process that had evaded the Nishga since shortly after their contact with the settler nations.

I do not dispute the fact that the Nishga case was a victory. It is the magnitude that I question. In fact, I believe the need to characterize this victory as great is partially explained by understanding the colonial process. Colonialism breeds negative expectations in the hearts of the colonized. Therefore, a small victory feels much larger. However, by recognizing clearly the magnitude of the 1973 victory the true nature of Canada's history becomes exposed. More than a hundred years after confederation, Canada was forced by the courts to stop denying its legal responsibility and deferring it to moral or political arenas.

The fact that six of the seven justices clearly expressed the view that Aboriginal title does in fact exist and that it exists independently of the *Royal Proclamation* is an accomplishment. The establishment in Canadian law of the Aboriginal view that sees Aboriginal rights as inherent, or coming from within Aboriginal nations, is significant and long awaited. It was this judicial recognition that persuaded politicians that a land claims process was overdue. Unfortunately, *Calder* only partially resolves the substantive concerns articulated in the *St. Catherines* case, as Indian title is still viewed by Judson as a lesser interest. Although some justice is done to the history of this land prior to 1763, the Indian interest is still viewed by the majority of the *Calder* Court as a lesser interest. As I view the *St. Catherines* statements on Indian title to not only be wrong in law but wrong in fact, it is difficult to fully celebrate the partial reversal of a wrong decision, which made bad law, that took Canadian courts almost a hundred years to reconsider and begin to step away from.

Little attention has been paid over the years to a serious legal inconsistency in the *Calder* case. In concluding his judgment, Justice Judson stated:

> There is a further point raised by the respondent that the Court did not have jurisdiction to make a declaratory order requested because the granting of a fiat under the *Crown Procedure Act*, R.S.B.C. 1960, c.89, was a necessary prerequisite to bringing the action and it had not been obtained. *While it is not necessary, in*

view of my conclusions as to the disposition of this appeal, to determine this point, I am in agreement with the reasons of my brother Pigeon dealing with it. (1973:168, emphasis added)

Every court is required to have jurisdiction before it can take hold of a matter. This is an elementary rule in Canadian law. If Crown fiat was required and not secured then the court was not properly charged with the matter. To be overly technical, without jurisdiction, the courts have no authority to speak to an issue. Yet, Justice Judson—a justice of the highest Court in the land—spoke at some length regarding the scope of Indian title and the test to be applied to the extinguishment question. All of the reasons of Justice Judson sit in the air (or in legal talk, his comments are obiter).

This presents an interesting problem, quite like a double standard. Indians are expected to respect the Canadian system of laws, despite the fact that it has been unilaterally forced on us. However, when that system side-steps its own rules on occasion, this does nothing to foster Aboriginal respect for Canada's cultural (and legal) difference.

This criticism may be seen as extreme and certainly in breach of the protocol respect owed to any high court. However, the concern is grounded in a desire to see Aboriginal "perspectives" on justice and judicial practice taken seriously. It is ironic that Aboriginal people are expected to have *prima facie* faith in the judicial process when the judiciary so easily overlooks basic procedure rules, practices and beliefs in Indian claims (and I quibble even though the overlooking is in this case beneficial or done in the interest of advancing Aboriginal rights.)

Although the bulk of Justice Judson's comments in Calder are technically made without jurisdiction, this is not the status that the Canadian judicial process has accredited to them. Justice Judson's comments have often been reproduced at length in subsequent cases (and they do respect the Indian point of view that Indian title is independent to British or Canadian Crown action). Justice Judson stated:

Although I think that it is clear that Indian title in British Columbia *cannot owe its origin to the Royal Proclamation of 1763*, the fact is that when the settlers came, the Indians were there, organized in societies and occupying the land as their forefathers had done for centuries. That is what Indian title means and it does not help one in the solution of this problem to call it a "personal or usufructuary right." What they are asserting in this action is that they had a right to continue to live on their lands as their forefathers had lived and that this right has never been lawfully extinguished. (1973:156, emphasis added)

As progressive as Judson's statement may seem, the impact of his position is immediately diminished as he asserts "there can be no question that this right was dependent on the goodwill of the Sovereign." This establishes a familiar pattern of "slight of pen" which emerges in the majority of Indian rights cases. The courts frequently make sweeping statements that affirm Indian views, which are next abruptly diminished. This pattern of flowing Aboriginal rights language masks the colonial aspects (often one-liners) of most decisions.

Although Justices Hall and Judson agree that the source of Aboriginal title is in historical occupancy (that is prior to contact), they disagree on the test required by the Crown to demonstrate extinguishment. Judson constructed from a variety of documents an argument that was based on *implied* Crown extinguishment (because no words expressly stated this). On the other side of the issue, Justice Hall's test is strict, requiring the Crown to demonstrate a "clear and plain" intention on the face of any Crown enactment. Justice Hall stated:

> It would, accordingly appear to be beyond question that the onus of proving that the sovereign intended to extinguish the Indian title lies on the respondent and that intention must be "clear and plain." There is no such proof in the case at bar; no legislation to that effect. (*Calder* 1973:210)

The Court is evenly split (three to three) on this issue as Justice Pigeon makes no comment on the issues of substance. It is not until the *Sparrow* decision in 1990, some seventeen years later, that this issue of a test for extinguishment is resolved when Justices Dickson and LaForest affirm the Hall view in *Calder* (*Sparrow* 1990:174).

It is important to remember that it was not just a seventeen-year wait for a clear rule. Since contact governments have been arguing various themes of extinguishment from discovery to conquest. The lack of legal clarity on extinguishment (and other legal concepts unique to Indian rights jurisprudence) has allowed the governments of Canada to benefit. This must be acknowledged. Although the extinguishment rule offers clear benefit to the Indian position on this issue, the amount of time where there was no legal clarity was not beneficial to Indian interests. As well as being a clear demonstration of the snail's pace at which legal resolution of Indian claims is occurring, this offers further example of the disadvantage inherent in the time consuming litigation process.

Eleven years following the Calder decision, the Supreme Court handed down its decision in the *Guerin* case (1984). Before this decision[18] the federal government had no recognized legal responsibility for the way in which reserve lands were administered by the Department of Indian Affairs. In the case that created a revolution, the Musqueam Indian Reserve had leased land to the Shaugnessy Golf Club. The terms of this lease were misrepresented to the band, and the terms they had directed the Department to secure were ignored. Unable to secure a copy of the lease for a number of years,[19] the band was frustrated in its attempts to resolve the inequity in a satisfactory manner.

All eight judges of the Supreme Court of Canada were unanimous in awarding relief to the Musqueam Band in this case. The most interesting of the three judgments in *Guerin* is penned by Justice Dickson with Beetz, Chouinard and Lamer concurring.[20] All three judgments present a different legal theory which allows the court to impose liability on the federal Crown. Writing shortly after the decision was released, McMurtry and Pratt concluded:

> It is our argument that, properly understood, all three judgments in the *Guerin* case may be seen as partial outlines of a complete constitutional theory of mutual rights and obligations subsisting between the Indian people and the Crown. It is our further suggestion that this theory can be acceptable both to governments and Indian people and it is our hope that this theory can form a blueprint for future political initiatives to enhance Indian self-government, as well as a theoretical framework for the legal assessment and resolution of past, present and future disputes between the Indian people and the Crown. (1986:20)

I concur with their conclusion that *Guerin* offered a first and unique legal opportunity to focus judicial (and scholarly) attention on the uncertainty (which in my opinion is closer to a vacuum) that exists beneath the theory of Aboriginal rights. The authors assert that one "must use a properly grounded constitutional theory of the relationship between the Indians and the Crown" (McMurtry 1986:23, emphasis added). I am less convinced of these authors' abilities to speak responsibly for all Indian people. In my mind such an assertion of Indian concurrence requires demonstration. This is not a comment motivated by a desire to quibble with a simple introductory comment of two lawyers. It is rather a systemic concern about the degree to which Aboriginal analysis and criticism are excluded from legal process. From Lord Watson to the scholars of the 1990s, many still believe they can speak for us (even though some have never met "us"). Much of this debate is incredibly privileged and passes by the average Aboriginal person (contrary to the rules of process at least among the Haudenosaunee).

In order for the Musqueam Band to secure a remedy, it had to demonstrate that a legal obligation existed that prohibited the Department from procuring less favourable lease terms. A problem arose in the litigation of this case because the Band was not a party to the lease. Rather, because the *Indian Act* and *the Royal Proclamation of 1763* provides that land can only be surrendered to the Crown, they had agreed to a conditional surrender of their land in a separate and distinct legal document to the Department for the purposes of the lease. The surrender document was so generally worded that no lawful violation of the document had occurred. The lease terms were also not violated. As the Musqueam Band was not a party to the lease, and the golf club was not a party to the surrender, the First Nation appeared to be stopped from securing a remedy. This is the general rule regarding privity of contract, and it forced the Band to seek an unconventional legal remedy. This is a familiar situation confronting First Nations, as law and the structure of law were not shaped in an inclusive way that addressed the nature of First Nation's concerns and claims or the uniqueness of the Aboriginal legal situation in Canada. This is both an historical problem and one that continues to manifest itself in present times.

The relationship created in Dickson's judgment to resolve the legal obstacles in this case was the fiduciary relationship. This legal concept had never before figured so significantly in Indian litigation.[21] The fiduciary relationship, although similar to trust, is not a trust according to the Court (*Guerin* 1973:131). It is emphasized by the Court in this case that all "Indian" law is *sui generis*, meaning simply that it is unlike anything else (*Guerin* 1973:136). It is the concept of *sui generis* first developed in *Calder* that facilitates the reasoning of Justice Dickson in *Guerin* (Borrows and Rotman 1997:19). Despite the fact that *Guerin* is most frequently cited as the judicial source of the fiduciary doctrine, the Court equally refined the *sui generis* nature of Aboriginal rights. The Court found that the fiduciary relationship arises in the historical occupation of the land by Indian nations, jointly with the fact that the Crown has assumed that the land is only alienable to them. This last point is a fundamental component of both the *Indian Act* regime and the *Royal Proclamation*.[22]

There is confusion about the source of the fiduciary duty because courts have chosen to redefine existing Crown/Indian relationships based on a current understanding of legal duties. One scholar suggests: "It is the fiduciary duty assumed by the Crown which gives rise to the surrender requirement, not vice versa" (Rotman 1996:108). Another group of lawyers note:

> The first general observation to be made on the matter of when fiduciary obligations arise is that there should be a presumption as to the existence of those obligations in any situation where an Aboriginal collectivity is constrained in its action in the exercise of rights to lands or resources or the exercise of its internal or external sovereignty. After all, those constraints either result from

> historical concessions made in return for promises or from unjus-
> tifiable unilateral action by the Crown. (Hutchins 1995:104)

It is the exercise by the Crown of its discretion that triggers the fiduciary relationship. This discretion is exercised both by framing the general statutory scheme which provides that land can be surrendered only to the Crown and by making individual decisions within the statutory frame-work. The Court affirms that "the hallmark of the fiduciary relationship is that the relative legal positions are such that one party is at the mercy of the other's discretion."[23] It is important to note well that this encapsulates both general and specific (or incident based) duties.

In determining the results of the Crown's breach, the court clearly points out that the Crown acted unconscionably. Dickson stated:

> The oral representations form the backdrop against which the Crown's conduct in discharging its fiduciary obligation must be measured. They inform and confine the field of discretion within which the Crown was free to act. After the Crown's agents had induced the band to surrender its land on the understanding that the land would be leased on certain terms, it would be uncon-scionable to permit the Crown simply to ignore those terms.... The existence of such unconscionability is the key to a conclu-sion that the Crown breached its fiduciary duty. Equity will not continence unconscionable behaviour in a fiduciary, whose duty is that of utmost loyalty to his principal. (1984:129)

The unconscionable action by the Crown is crucial, as the remedy is characterized as an equitable one and provides an example of the specific nature of the duty owed. The remedy is dependent on the irregularities in the surrender process during the exercise of the Crown's discretion. It is this Crown action the Court found to be unconscionable and a violation of the honour required by the person who exercises discretion. The Court also emphasized the fact that the Crown acted without consultation with the Band in the negotiation of the lease.

The reasoning of the Court provides a clear test for litigants to follow in the future although few have yet chosen to follow this fiduciary path. Leonard Rotman summarizes the content of the fiduciary relationship as follows:

> The evidentiary requirements for demonstrating a fiduciary rela-tionship are substantially lower than those necessary to prove a trust. There are no 'certainties' in fiduciary law as there are in trust law. Moreover, the existence of a fiduciary relationship is not dependent on the existence of a property interest, or *res*, as is

a trust relationship. *It is the nature and scope of a relationship* which renders it fiduciary, not the actors involved or the subscription to particular rules or regulations. (1996:104–105, emphasis added)

I think that the fiduciary path is one that holds much hope for Aboriginal people. What is novel about this approach is that it focuses attention on the actions of the Crown (or the relationship) rather than on Aboriginal people or their Aboriginal rights. In my opinion, Canadian law can only bind Canadians. Canadian courts are more appropriately suited to defining Canadian duties than Aboriginal rights. Courts have demonstrated a tremendous difficulty in understanding two significant components of these rights, namely Aboriginal history(s) and Aboriginal culture(s). Aboriginal Peoples are bound only by their traditional laws until such a time that they freely consent to the application of Canadian laws. Perhaps unfortunately, there has been little litigation of the fiduciary relationship subsequent to Guerin.[24]

Litigation under the fiduciary duty is problematic because the basis of this duty rests on the dependent status of Indian nations, communities and citizens. This may seem contradictory given the concerns I have repeatedly raised about entrenched and ongoing ideas of Aboriginal inferiority (or Euro-Canadian superiority). However, the fact is that the result of colonial impositions has been to create dependency. I do not believe that the relationship of dependency can be evolved until it is acknowledged and addressed, and litigation under the fiduciary duty allows for just that possibility. As other scholars have noted, it is essential to start at the beginning, with the history of this land, if the task is to understand relations between Aboriginal Peoples and the Crown (Hutchins 1995:100; Slattery 1991:701). Colonialism and its impacts will not simply disappear because we wish them away. I, therefore, remain convinced that the fiduciary relationship as a legal duty holds some potential as a litigation strategy and requires further examination.

A second concern which is also about the failure to reach the potential that exists in section 35(1) requires further consideration. Recognition of the dependent quality of the relationship between Aboriginal Peoples and the Crown which has resulted from colonial impositions does not deny Aboriginal aspirations for self-determination. There is noting contradictory in asserting both the fiduciary duty and rights of self-determination. The fiduciary relationship as it acknowledges dependency is a recognition of the historical origins of the relationship *but* that is not all the fiduciary relationship is. The fiduciary relationship is also about the honour of the Crown (*Sparrow* 1990:183–184). Therefore the fiduciary duty of the Crown and the Aboriginal desire to reclaim powers of self-determination are fully reconcilable. Alan Pratt makes further distinctions which demonstrate why there is no difficulty in resolving federal duty with the Aboriginal right to self-determination:

> Self-government has so far been a product of political processes, although there has been a great deal of speculation as to extent of the right in law. The fiduciary relationship, and the Crown's fiduciary duties that derive from that relationship, have, by contrast, been the product of the judicial process. In considering the legal and political aspects of the special relationship between the Crown and aboriginal peoples, this is in my view entirely appropriate.
>
> Both are perspectives on a relationship between the Crown and aboriginal peoples that is usually described as special, or in legalese "sui generis." Fiduciary law is the mechanism whereby the legal components of the special relationship has been given expression. By contrast, self-government is by its very nature the political aspect of the special relationship. (1992:166)

The task is not about reconciling contradictory concepts; rather the task is about reconciling responsibility between the standards the judiciary has created and the failure of Canadian governments to fully embrace these standards.

To suggest that the fiduciary obligation can be full and thereby final, say as a result of the realization of self-government, is also to mischaracterize the Crown's commitment to Indian nations. The fiduciary relationship is not just historical. It is not an umbilical cord to be cut (Pratt 1992:169). The Crown's relationship with Aboriginal nations must be viewed from both the colonial perspective and the Aboriginal perspective. After discussing the importance of the Two-Row Wampum (a document that I would assert provides important instruction on the implementation of treaty relationships), James Tully notes:

> The convention of continuity through relations of *protection and interdependency* is also a common feature of Aboriginal constitutionalism. Article 84 of the constitution of the Haudenosaunee confederacy of six nations, for example, states that, 'whenever a foreign nation has been conquered or has by their own will accepted the Great Peace [confederated with the other nations], their own system of internal government may continue but they must cease all warfare against other nations'. True to form, each of the six nations of the confederacy has its own language, customs and government. The confederation itself was founded by the mediation of Deganawidah, who brought the original five warring nations together and guided them to reach agreement

81

through dialogue on a form of association to protect their differences and similarities. (1995:128–129, emphasis added)

When taken seriously the difference between dependency and interdependence is more than just semantics. The fiduciary relationship, stripped of the offensive notion of one party's natural inferiority, is not a problematic concept. Getting rid of this notion of Aboriginal inferiority is the task that will breath life into the relationship between the Crown and First Nations.

Adopting the fiduciary relationship as a litigation strategy will not be simple. The significance and content of the concept remains unclear. One view of the decision in the *Guerin* case is very narrow and this is generally the view reflected by the Crown (McMurtry 1986:20). Some have suggested that the fiduciary relationship will only apply to unconditional land surrenders and not other Crown actions, although this view cannot be substantiated by any comments made by the court.

To the contrary, the court and various scholars describe the legal relationship that results from *Guerin* in very broad terms. In the most comprehensive work on the fiduciary relationship which exists between First Nations and the Crown, Leonard Rotman concludes:

> The duty which arose from this undertaking was not initially restricted to the protection of aboriginal lands. It extended to a protection of the aboriginal peoples in the enjoyment of their pre-existing rights *in rem*, such as the right to hunt, trap, and fish, as well as to exercise religious, cultural and linguistic freedom, and to practice self-government. To limit the application of the legally enforceable Crown duty affirmed by *Guerin* to something less than the initial intention behind the Crown's undertaking of that duty is inappropriate. Consequently, the Crown's fiduciary obligation found in *Guerin* cannot be restricted in its application to Indian land interests, but extends to all aboriginal interests; in its broadest form, it is a general, all encompassing duty. (1996:109–110)

The narrow view can only be substantiated in overly technical terms by relying on the principle of interpretation that suggests no precedent can be larger than the facts it is decided upon. I have already clearly stated that I believe it is time to get beyond the consistent use of either technical legal arguments (such as the relying on Crown fiat) or after-the-fact narrowing of decisions which courts intend to be broad and future looking, as these techniques are clearly intended to be biased against the Aboriginal claimant. Such strategies result in the compromising of our ability to address the serious theoretical vacuum that exists beneath the idea of Aboriginal rights.

Another significant result of the *Guerin* decision, because of the economic disadvantage most Indian nations in Canada face, is the remedy awarded for the breach by the Crown of its fiduciary responsibility. As a breach of all legal rights, of which the fiduciary relationship is but one, requires a complementary remedy, the Department was required to pay damages in the amount of $11 million dollars to the Musqueam First Nation. Although financial remedy is not necessarily the primary purpose of litigation, it is a consequence of significance as Aboriginal people continue to seek ways to resource economic development in their communities.

In the same way that political attitudes changed after *Calder*, the winds that swirled following the release of the *Guerin* judgment also brought change. The Department of Indian Affairs began to actively follow a policy of "devolution,"[25] the process whereby Indian bands are facilitated in assuming greater administrative control over their affairs. Without commenting fully on the merits of the devolution process, it must be noted that greater administrative control is obviously not tantamount to self-determination. Self-determination requires the recognition of law-making powers in Indian nations. Assuming greater administrative control at the band level frequently only amounts to agreeing to control our own misery. Furthermore, in such a circumstance, the Crown is released from any direct, visible and immediate (but not legal) responsibility for the misery created by its past and present laws and policies. I am concerned that devolution will operate to further mystify the colonial source of the continued oppression in First Nations communities, at least in some communities and for some Indian leaders. Failure to take responsibility is not a step toward a brighter future but just a new lesson in a continuing tale of victim blaming. The irony is that, as devolution is an act of government discretion, it cannot escape Justice Dickson's definition of the fiduciary duty and the corresponding judicial review of any wrongdoings under such a policy.

The governmental justifications for the devolution process are suspicious. As already pointed out, devolution is a federal exercise in responsibility shifting which is sometimes paid for by a nominal increase in dollars directly available to the band. As such, devolution is yet another potential unconscionable act on the part of federal authorities. The interesting question remains. Can an unconscionable act protect the same federal authorities from their earlier unconscionable acts that would be subject to the fiduciary standard? To conclude in the affirmative defies logic; two wrongs cannot make a right.

The placement of the *Guerin* case in this chapter may seem unusual and perhaps even inappropriate. *Guerin* is clearly one of the largest successes Aboriginal people have secured from the Supreme Court, perhaps the largest. My concern is that the potential in this case has not been reached. Subsequent judicial decisions have not lived up to expectations (*Sparrow, Van der Peet, Adams, Cote,* or *Delgamuukw,* for example), even though the manner in which these cases were structured and argued (all are fishing rights cases with the exception of *Delgamuukw*) accomplished the potential that was implicitly promised by *Guerin.* Despite the recognition that *Guerin* from within the four corners of the case is a great victory (of a magnitude contingent on future Supreme Court decisions), the opportunity to begin structuring a comprehensive and respectful theory of Aboriginal rights has been missed. It is this larger realization that precipitates my classifying *Guerin* alongside other cases which are nominal legal victories.

Litigators who represent Aboriginal nations need to give serious consideration to the degree to which courts can resolve or more accurately cannot resolve Aboriginal claims. Alan Pratt offers this observation:

> It is my view that it would be politically unjustifiable for self-government to be defined as an aboriginal right through judicial decisions for the very reason that the Courts are an agency of the Euro-Canadian legal and political order. The courts can of course declare the *existence* of the right of aboriginal self-government, and indeed can indicate the extent and nature of the legal protections and immunities which are implied by that right, but in delving further into definition they encounter a conundrum in that they cannot define the *content* of the right without acting in fundamental disrespect to the right itself. (1992:167)

The right to Aboriginal independence only makes sense when that right is self-defining.

The recognition that the courts can never be the final resting place of the power to define Aboriginal rights may not be clearly understood by the Supreme Court. In *Guerin,* Justice Dickson embraces the American Marshall trilogy, three cases which stand for the principle that Indian nations domiciled in what is now the United States have been recognized as "dependent domestic nations." This recognition in *Guerin* steps over the power that can be legitimately placed in the courts as it crosses the line which Alan Pratt identifies for us. An acceptance (particularly an unquestioned acceptance) of the American stance, a stance developed in the early 1800s, denies some of the substantive areas in which some First Nations believe they maintain self-determining powers. The acceptance of the American standard has been accomplished without consultation, negotiation and consent.

In the wake of the *Calder* and *Guerin* cases, another familiar pattern emerges, the impact of these decisions on the political realm. Although the impact initially appears to be progressive, closer scrutiny raises questions about the level of success that was actually attained in each case. Simply put, these cases have only forced Canada to take seriously that which ought to have always been central in its responsibilities. The year 1982 brought significant changes to the Canadian constitution, and the next required analysis is a determination of those constitutional provisions and of the ability of courts to break with the past and the attitudes that fostered decisions such as the one in *St. Catherines Milling*.

The courts have been the vehicle by which Aboriginal people have successfully forced governments to come to terms with outstanding land issues. This success is, however, not complete. In and of themselves, the court decisions are narrow victories and the cases only partially address the difficulties which confront Aboriginal nations today. In all of the cases, the courts reserve to the Canadian Crown a "present proprietary estate" or recognize that the underlying Crown title is absolute. It is therefore accurate to conclude that this string of narrow victories sits under a heavy ceiling of the Euro-Canadian presumption of superiority. This presumption was first embroidered into the *St. Catherines Milling* case and, to date, we still see the threads of belief in Indian inferiority woven through current judicial decree.

Despite the nominal successes of the cases at the end of this era, it remains important to remember that most of the attempts to destroy cultures and peoples have been implemented through law, and when not implemented under lawful authority, have been done under such a guise. Although Aboriginal people have forced the truth about their experiences to be told in louder voices these last few decades, little mention is yet made about the tool—the law—through which our oppression has flowed. This recognition must now come to include the realization that the Canadian judicial system is equally part of the law and the problem. This second silence must also be broken. Understanding the source of as well as the tools used to enforce our oppression allows us to see clearly the pathway to the decolonization of our lives. I urge this because I am interested in more than economic resolutions to the taking of our land and our lives. My goal is eloquently stated by Maori scholar, Sidney Moko Mead: "Liberation is the opposite of cultural death" (1997:28).

Notes

1. I am not suggesting that Aboriginal litigation ought to be fully abandoned. My preference would be to see more creatively structured litigation strategies. This would require an opportunity to overcome the isolation in which most lawyers are required to work. To support such an endeavour Aboriginal people require institutional space. The creation of a litigation centre, to offer one possible solution, would go a long way to fulfilling this need.
2. Kanien'kehaka scholar Gerald (Taiaiake) Alfred disputes the usefulness of

the concept "sovereignty" when applied to First Nations (1999:55–58).

3. Until 1982, the term Indian was used to describe the Indians, Inuit and Métis. Since its first use in the *Royal Proclamation of 1763* the word Indian has subsequently acquired a very narrow meaning. As *Re Eskimos,* [1939] demonstrates, Indians once included at least Inuit peoples. The Métis can also make sound and convincing arguments that they were included in the historical usage of the word Indians. Please refer to Clem Chartier 1978–9:37–69.

4. A beneficial interest is an interest in land which is not based on the ownership of that land. It is generally only a right to use the land which means it is a lesser interest than an estate (ownership).

5. Section 109 reads:

> All Lands, Mines, Minerals, and Royalties belonging to the several Provinces of Canada, Nova Scotia, and New Brunswick at the Union, and all Sums then due or payable for such Lands, Mines, Minerals, or Royalties, shall belong to the several Provinces of Ontario, Quebec, Nova Scotia, and New Brunswick in which the same are situate or arise subject to any Trust existing in respect thereof, and to any Interest other than that of the Province in the same.

6. I am here adopting the language of the times and intend to create no disrespect to Métis and Inuit nations. As previously discussed, I firmly believe that the Métis and Inuit were included in this historic term.

7. I am not suggesting that this is in fact the legal consequence of the treaty process. I do not believe it is.

8. An estate describes the interest (degree, quantity, nature and extent) that an individual has in land. An estate can be considered synonymous to "ownership."

9. This is a legal term that means the point is not relevant or necessary to the determination of the issue in a particular case and therefore is not binding on future courts.

10. There is no such right that accrues to an individual not party to a case.

11. Common law principles (that is law made by judges) can be set aside by legislative action. It was unnecessary to have left Aboriginal Peoples in the position to have to challenge the "mere burden" principle.

12. This section was included in the *Indian Act* of 1927.

13. The decision in *Logan* v. *Styres* 1959 is but one example of this lesson.

14. *The Queen* v. *Drybones* 1970 struck down section 94(b) of the Indian Act which prohibited Indians from being intoxicated off a reserve.

15. In summarizing the Nishga position, Justice Judson provided:

> The Nishga Nation did not agree to or accept the creation of these reserves. The Nishgas claim that their title arises out of aboriginal occupation; that recognition of such a title is a concept well embedded in English law; that it is not dependent on treaty, executive order or legislative enactment. In the alternative they say that if executive or legislative recognition ever was needed, it is to be found in the Royal Proclamation of 1763, in Imperial statutes acknowledging that what is now

British Columbia was "Indian Territory," and in Royal instructions to the Governor of British Columbia. Finally, they say that their title has never been extinguished (*Calder* 1973:149).

16. Personal conversations with Frank Calder, 1990.
17. This strategy can also be found in other cases such as *Dumont et al. v. Attorney General of Canada and Attorney General of Manitoba* 1990.
18. *Guerin* was decided after the entrenchment of Aboriginal rights in the Canadian constitution. Although the court does not rely on the new constitutional provisions in its decision, it is nevertheless aware of the new legal relationship in section 35(1). The court in *Guerin* was not acting in an unpredictable way. See also the discussion in *Sparrow* 1990:178.
19. The federal government tried to shield itself behind the Musqueam delay in bringing the action. The statute setting out limitation periods indicated a seven year limit. The court chastised the Crown, as the delay was a result of failure to provide the band with a copy of the lease, despite the numerous attempts of the band to secure it.
20. Madame Justice Wilson also provides a judgment which locates a trust relationship in the nature of Aboriginal title as evidenced by section 18 of the *Indian Act*. Estey provided a judgment that focused on agency.
21. As Richard Bartlett points out, two cases, *Canada (A.G.) v. Giroux* (1916) and *Dreaver* v. *The King* (1935) rely on the concept of "trust" and fiduciary to resolve issues of dependency of the Indians on Crown decisions (1989:304–305).
22. Justice Wilson writes a concurring opinion that sources the "trust" relationship within a statutory framework.
23. *Guerin* 1984:137, citing Professor Ernest Weinrib 1975:7.
24. Please see *Kruger* v. *R.* (1985), *Apassin* v. *Canada (Department of Indian Affairs and Northern Development)*, and *Blueberry River Indian Band* v. *Canada*, (1995). Since 1995, there have been a number of lower court decisions which are based on the fiduciary doctrine.
25. The process of devolution first began in the 1970s as a response to Indian demands for greater control over the education of our children.

Chapter Four

The Supreme Court Speaks To Aboriginal Rights
Colonial Reminders

In May of 1990, eight years after the entrenchment of section 35(1) in the Constitution, the Supreme Court of Canada released the decision in the fishing trial of one Ronald Edward Sparrow. The response to this first pronouncement by the highest court of the land on the meaning of section 35(1) was immediate. In a media flurry, it was hailed as a breakthrough in the arena of Aboriginal rights.[1] It was in fact a victory of sorts: the conviction of Mr. Sparrow was quashed and a new trial was ordered.[2] But the *Sparrow* decision is no more than one small victory in a long history of Aboriginal struggle against colonial legal oppression.

Mr. Sparrow is both an "Indian" fisherman and a commercial fisherman. He fishes in the way of his ancestors as his father, great-uncle, grandfather and so on did before him. His son now fishes with him. He is a member of the Musqueam community. The Musqueam reserve is located within what is now the city limits of Vancouver. He was charged in May of 1984 with a violation of the British Columbia fishing regulations.[3] Mr. Sparrow acknowledged that he had been fishing in Canoe Passage with a drift net that was longer than the regulations provided. The facts of the case were never in dispute. In order to defend against the charge, he chose to assert that he was exercising an Aboriginal right to fish in that area as his people had for generation after generation (*Sparrow* 1990:164).

Life for the average Aboriginal person is precarious and the situation that Mr. Sparrow found himself in is but one example of the truth of this assertion. He supports himself and his family by fishing. This is not to suggest that the right asserted was merely economic, because fishing is a part of the way of life of Mr. Sparrow's people, the Salish. On one May day, drifting down the river behind his father, a portion of his life was taken from his control, as the next six years were to be spent defending his right to fish all the way to the highest court of the land. Legal costs are the obvious way in which the need to litigate can adversely affect an individual's life. I imagine that those were also stressful years of lawyer's appointments, band meetings and court hearings.[4] Court proceedings are adversarial and follow formal and often unexpressed rules. It is a process frequently foreign to Aboriginal Peoples. As he is both a commercial fisherman and an Indian fisherman, a conviction on an Aboriginal fishing charge could have resulted in the refusal of the Minister to renew his commercial licences.[5] Before discussing the legal impact of the *Sparrow* decision, I wish to pay my respects to the individual who carried the consequences that led to some legal gain for our people and communities. Too rarely is this considered in legal processes and academic commentaries on this case or others.[6]

My view of the law often differs from that of my legal colleagues as I see the entire process of law as one that centrally involves "stories" and the process of "storytelling." Stories of life are a key component in how law is done in the Aboriginal way. Although both Canadian and Aboriginal legal processes involve the telling of stories, the objectives of why those stories are told are very different; the results, as well, are not similar. My desire to deal first with the story aspect of the *Sparrow* case is my attempt to resolve the Aboriginal discomfort I always experience when trying to do Canadian law. It is a tool of survival for me. It is also an act of resistance. More so, it is an act of resistance that is calculated in an attempt to shift the experience of the power that law has over me into one that I can feel I participate willingly in. As Mary Ellen Turpel-Lafond notes:

> I often feel, particularly as a law teacher interacting with materials involving First Nations peoples, written by those without direct knowledge, that our problems have been studied enough, especially in the object mode of analysis. We need to turn our minds to a mutually-agreed-upon framework within which to resolve our relations with the state. We no longer need to be objects, nor do we need well-intentioned paternalism or projections of what we should become. (1993:74)

On a beautiful May morning in 1998, I sat with Bud Sparrow (as his family calls him) in his fishing shed alongside the Fraser River.[7] He was just about to go out on the boat for the day. We talked about the *Sparrow* case. Bud's view of the case is that he only did what he had to do. For me, this identified two things. First, I realized how much the case disappeared the real person and his story. Second, this identified the degree to which Mr. Sparrow respected tradition, as he did not see how what he had done made him any different from any of the other people. The community comes first and not the individual.

What I learned from the opportunity to discuss this case with several members of the Sparrow family was that the charges against Bud were part of a larger community resistance. One scholar suggests that "the events leading to *Sparrow* had been preceded by increasing acrimony and hostility between the DFO and the Musqueam Indian Band" (Sharma 1998:37). None of this is apparent from reading the decision. It points to a question that has not yet been addressed by research, legal or otherwise. As someone legally trained, I have been taught to only read between the four textual corners of legal decisions. Until recently I never realized that perhaps the real story lives outside the reported judgments. Very early on in my visits to Musqueam and with members of the Sparrow family, before I developed a "research" interest in this case, I realized that the real success of this case is the impact it has had on the community. Musqueam has revitalized its fisheries, and the *Sparrow* case is, in my opinion, a part of this revitalization.[8]

It is through my efforts to understand this one single case that I stumbled onto a much more important realization. The Canadian legal process is a process of fragmentation. I had known this since my law school days. However, the full impact of this on First Nations communities had not registered with me. Legal processes take the stories[9] of people and transform them into discussions about the meaning of words and phrases like "existing," "Aboriginal rights," "recognized and affirmed," and so on. This process is contrary to Aboriginal intellectual traditions (including Aboriginal legal processes) as it removes the stories from individuals, families, communities and nations. This is a primary violation of Aboriginal law as I understand it. Further, there is no mechanism in Canadian law, formal or informal, that ensures the stories will be returned to the people and their communities. I know that legal education and legal practice do not prepare lawyers for this consequence or the offence that Aboriginal clients might take to this outcome. In my opinion, it is a glaring insufficiency in Canadian legal process which operates to disrupt Aboriginal traditions, beliefs and values. It is not only a significant structural obstacle but it is also a colonial edifice.

The action that Mr. Sparrow took to defend himself against the charge of breaching the fishing regulation was political action, and the fact that this action was located in the judicial process must not be seen to minimize the political dimensions. In other words, Mr. Sparrow is one of the outstanding legal warriors of the 1990s. On the day he was charged, Mr. Sparrow was just one of many fishermen out on the water. Because of the activities of fisheries officers in the preceding few years, the community knew that further charging would indeed be a possibility. The fisheries officers passed by many boats, including Mr. Sparrow's father's, before stopping at Ronald's boat. By choosing to assert his Aboriginal right[10] to fish as his defence, he chose to characterize his actions in a bolder manner. But this choice also carried with it a serious responsibility. What if his case were not successful? What if the courts said there was no Aboriginal right to fish? His actions carried with them the serious risk of grave consequences for his family, his community and many other Aboriginal nations that depend on the fishery. This is a position into which *only* an Aboriginal fisherman can be thrust.

Mr. Sparrow was therefore put into a role much larger than merely defending himself against a charge of a breach of a fishing regulation.[11] Concern must be raised about the way in which the Aboriginal culture is put on trial, especially in hunting and fishing cases, which comprise the majority of litigation in the area of Aboriginal rights. Fish are not commodities in the Aboriginal way of thinking. All life that has spirit is sacred. The testimony of Dr. Suttles (an anthropologist) confirmed this tradition:

> Dr. Suttles described the special position occupied by the salmon fishery in that society. The salmon was not only an important source of food but played an important part in the system of beliefs of the Salish people, and in their ceremonies. The salmon were held to be a race of beings that had, in "myth times," established a bond with human beings requiring the salmon to come each year to give their bodies to the humans who, in turn, treated them with respect shown by performance of the proper ritual. Towards the salmon, as toward other creatures, there was an attitude of caution and respect which resulted in effective conservation of the various species. (*Sparrow* 1990:172)

It is an onerous responsibility to be the individual who chooses to put his culture on trial in an institution that belongs to another culture. In a related way, it is interesting to note that the testimony of a non-Aboriginal anthropologist is the required standard of proof in order to have recognized in court facts which are apparent to just about any individual living in the Musqueam community. The standard to which courts hold Aboriginal people accountable regarding cultural facts is unacceptable.[12]

The context which surrounds the *Sparrow* decision is not widely discussed by Canadian courts, the legal profession or by legal academics. The Supreme Court did make one notable but brief comment which minimally indicated it was aware of the impact its articulation of Aboriginal rights has. The Court recognized that a "trial for the violation of a penal prohibition may not be the most appropriate setting in which to determine the existence of an aboriginal right...." (1990:172). Unfortunately, the Court did not expand on its reasons for asserting its dissatisfaction. This reality of Aboriginal litigation must be seen as a factor in future governmental decision making.[13] When Canadian politicians fail to negotiate satisfactory remedies to outstanding issues with Aboriginal Peoples, the responsibility of the Canadian government, including its fiduciary duties is transferred to individual Aboriginal people such as Mr. Sparrow. This is one of the invisible impacts of colonialism. With the possibility of self-government negotiations on the table, this issue of responsibility is of particular importance.

The Court recognized that the issue in the *Sparrow* case was much larger than Mr. Sparrow's ability to defend himself against a fishing regulation infraction. "The issue is whether Parliament's power to regulate fishing is now limited by section 35(1)...." (1990:164). The Court adopted a pragmatic approach to this question, turning to the text of section 35(1) which states:

> The existing aboriginal and treaty rights of the aboriginal peoples of Canada are hereby recognized and affirmed.[14]

The decision of the Supreme Court focused on the definition of the words and phrases, "existing," "Aboriginal rights" and "recognized and affirmed." It is followed by the Court's application of the definitions it prescribed to the facts in this single case. It is this pragmatic and definitional approach to the issue at the heart of the case that contributes significantly to the importance of the case as a legal model for the resolution of future disputes. The *Sparrow* case is the Supreme Court of Canada's first pronouncement on the meaning of section 35(1).[15] Whether or not this pragmatic and definitional approach creates a constitutional space for the future development of Aboriginal rights is open to question.

The first step in the Court's journey was to define the word "existing." The entrenchment of section 35(1) created a flurry of both litigation and academic activity.[16] One of the central debates in this literature and in lower court decisions[17] was the definition of this word. As a starting point, the Court immediately concluded that the entrenchment of section 35 did not have as a purpose the revival of Aboriginal rights which had already been extinguished (1990:169–70). This legal conclusion is easily reached and should be self-evident. The meaning of the word extinguishment or the test to reach such a conclusion is less readily discernible and was not approached by the Court in this section of the case.

An important distinction is made in the case between rights which have not been extinguished and the manner in which rights are exercised. This distinction is a subtle one that may not be easily discerned by those not accustomed to reading legal text. In the Canadian articulation of a right it is not necessary for the right to be acted upon for it to exist. Rights that lie dormant are not rights without meaning; nor are they rights that have ceased to be. These dormant rights can be picked up and used again; they are "existing" Aboriginal rights within the meaning of section 35.

This distinction is a very important one for Aboriginal people to consider.

It is absolute that the purpose of section 35(1) was not to re-enforce the myriad of differing regulatory systems which existed in 1982. That would have granted new powers of limitation to the Crown under the heading of "Aboriginal rights." Such an outcome would logically defy the purpose of section 35(1). The purpose of section 35(1) is obviously about recognizing rights that Aboriginal Peoples and Aboriginal people possess. It is interesting to note that much more of the *Sparrow* decision is about articulating the relationship between existing constitutional powers possessed by the Crown *and* interfering with these powers as little as possible than it is about affirmatively articulating the content of Aboriginal rights. Issues such as the meaning of section 91(24) and the realignment of federal and provincial powers to include a sphere of jurisdiction for Aboriginal nations should have been open to discussion and a new interpretation in this decision. Although the court asserts that the analysis is "purposive," (*Sparrow* 1990:179) it is difficult to demonstrate that the court has met this standard.

Much of the Court discusses and affirms in *Sparrow* when it is not granting new powers to the Crown (or reaffirming the supremacy of the existing relationships of constitutional federalism), is merely the obvious. For example, it is obvious that the constitution is the supreme law of the land. Equally, it is well known and established that statutes are subordinate to constitutional provisions and protections. Regulations are subordinate to statutes. Nothing in section 35(1) warrants or requires a discussion of these basic constitutional tenets. These tenets of constitutional supremacy do not contain an implicit and negative impact on the relationship between Aboriginal nations and Canada, unlike the parameters of constitutional federalism. Much of what the Court affirms in *Sparrow* is an affirmation of the self-evident. It is legal simplicity to conclude that regulations cannot alter constitutional rights (even though the Crown chose to argue this very point). This is not progress. This does not advance the position of Aboriginal Peoples in Canadian society and I would assert that this is the basic element of the "promise" that section 35(1) made to Aboriginal nations. These recognitions demonstrate one of the major difficulties in litigating Aboriginal rights.[18]

A second issue the Court deals with under the heading of "existing" is the manner in which Aboriginal rights previously held only at common law have been regulated. This distinction between common law Aboriginal rights and constitutional ones is important. Any common law rights can be replaced by statute. This is a general principle of law. This is not so for constitutional rights. These rights cannot be altered by statutory enactments. This is the significance of 1982. Aboriginal rights existed only at common law prior to 1982 and could lawfully and unilaterally be altered by the Crown. The question in the *Sparrow* case is simple: Do existing provincial and federal regulatory schemes in any way impact the content of constitutionally protected Aboriginal rights? The answer is obvious based on the general principles of the status of constitutional laws.

There are several consequences beyond the ability of regulatory schemes to alter common law rights that the Court was concerned with. This regulatory process[19] that many Aboriginal rights have been subject to, and especially hunting and fishing rights, results in a "crazy patchwork" of systems that vary from one jurisdiction to the next. Blair J.A. in the *Agawa* case commented on this structure:

> Some academic commentators have raised a further problem which cannot be ignored. The Ontario Fishery Regulations contain detailed rules which vary for different regions in the province. Among other things, the Regulations specify season and methods of fishing, species of fish which can be caught and catch limits. Similar detailed provisions apply under the comparable fisheries Regulations in force in other provinces. These detailed provisions might be constitutionalized if it were decided that the existing treaty rights referred to in section 35(1) were those remaining after regulation at the time of the proclamation of the *Constitution Act, 1982*. (1988:87 and also affirmed in *Sparrow* 1990:170)

Generally, a system that creates vastly different rules in different domestic jurisdictions is not viewed as positive. This view must be balanced against the need for flexibility as local circumstances, such as particular conservation or environmental concerns, vary from place to place. However, such a system can breed confusion if there is a need for a clear national standard on Aboriginal fishing rights. Canadian law operates on the premise that such confusion leads to chaos and disorder. Notwithstanding, the multitude of hunting and fishing regulations (many of which are provincial and not federal) regarding Aboriginal and treaty rights (a matter of national dimensions) has stood unchallenged for many years. As the need for a national standard is indeed a legislative task and not a judicial one, the failure of Canada's parliament to fulfill its obligations to Aboriginal people is exposed.

The manner in which Aboriginal hunting and fishing rights have been regulated has serious consequences as well. The Supreme Court cited with approval this passage from an article written by Professor Brian Slattery:

> This approach reads into the Constitution the myriad of regulations affecting the exercise of aboriginal rights, regulations that differed considerably from place to place across the country. It does not permit differentiation between regulations of long-term significance and those enacted to deal with temporary conditions,

or between reasonable and unreasonable restrictions. Moreover, it might require that a constitutional amendment be enacted to implement regulations more stringent than those in existence on 17 April 1982. This solution seems unsatisfactory. (1990:170)

This conclusion is obvious and should have required little academic or judicial discussion. At the same time it is also clear that Professor Slattery understands that section 35(1) has not fully closed the possibility that Aboriginal rights will require regulation and believes that some limits do adhere to Aboriginal rights. Slattery's question is not if Aboriginal rights should be regulated but rather when and how this can be accomplished.

The Court's preoccupation with discussing the obvious is a matter of some curiosity, especially in the face of the great number of issues that remain unresolved in the area of Aboriginal rights. In fact, the Court in *Sparrow* did not articulate a clear theory of Aboriginal rights. I recognize that I have the benefit of hindsight; I had not yet reached law school when the Aboriginal and treaty rights provision became part of Canadian constitutional law. However, one must recognize that the gap that exists between Aboriginal expectations and Canadian ones is the cause for much of the litigation in this area.

A more fundamental problem is not referred to by the courts. The rights of Aboriginal Peoples do not flow from the Crown; neither can their source be found in provincial, territorial or federal statutory regimes. Aboriginal rights are originated in the historical occupation of Aboriginal nations of the territory that became Canada (*Calder* 1973:156). The presumption that provincial, territorial or federal jurisdictions have the authority to regulate Aboriginal rights—rights which do not owe their origin to any Crown enactment or action—is presumed. The right to regulate Aboriginal lives is therefore without clear foundation in Canadian law. Asch and Macklem conclude:

the Court *unquestioningly* accepted that the British Crown, and thereafter Canada, obtained territorial sovereignty over the land mass that is now Canada by the mere fact of European settlement. The Court's acceptance of the settlement thesis appears to exclude any possibility of the recognition and affirmation of a constitutional right to aboriginal sovereignty. (1991:507)

The difficulty with the Court's position is that the settlement thesis only secures for the "discovering" Crown sovereignty over the territory if that land is unoccupied (or occupied by uncivilized people). Canada was not unoccupied at the time Europeans arrived here. If, the assertion is that Aboriginal Peoples were not civilized enough to "control" the territory, the time has come to release this myth.

The Court, before discussing the scope and definition of an Aboriginal right, dealt with an issue that arose because of the Crown's position. The Crown asserted that the Aboriginal right to fish was not demonstrated by Mr. Sparrow at trial. This failure to meet the evidentiary burden, contended the Crown, was fatal to the action. There was evidence presented at trial to suggest that the right to fish had been scantily exercised by the community during some periods between 1867 and 1961 (*Sparrow* 1990:172). The Court, however, pointed to the misconception that such an argument is prefaced on—rights that are not exercised are not extinguished due to lack of use (172).

The Court provided a long historical account of the regulation of the British Columbia fishery. This brought the Court face to face with a legal controversy left unresolved in the *Calder* decision. There, Mr. Justice Judson asserted that the extinguishment of an Aboriginal right need not be express. Extinguishment took place when the Crown acted in a manner that was "necessarily inconsistent" with the continued enjoyment of an Aboriginal right.[20] In *Calder*, Mr. Justice Hall took another view. He asserted that the Crown's intention must be "clear and plain" for an extinguishment of Aboriginal title to take effect. In the seventeen years since Calder was decided, the issue of extinguishment remained unresolved. This is another example of the marginal progress that is made through the litigation route.

The indecision in resolving the issue of extinguishment had some serious consequences. The federal government continues to rely on a "soft" definition of extinguishment as it did during the years of legal ambiguity. The Crown has not held itself to an onerous standard regarding extinguishment (a mere collateral intention would do) and there is little evidence post-*Sparrow* that there has been a significant shift in the Crown's position. Further, Canadian governments still force Aboriginal people to extinguish their pre-existing rights in order to access present-day land settlements. The vagueness which often cloaks the legal concepts integral to Aboriginal rights in all likelihood benefits the Crown, most frequently strengthening the already more powerful position it occupies. Legal vagueness not only clearly benefits the Crown, it also offers clear disadvantage to Aboriginal nations pursuing claims. This fact necessitates the recognition that in Aboriginal affairs the legal and judicial processes are not fully independent but interconnected. The processes can only appear independent and separate if a particular cultural paradigm is embraced by the observer.

The polarized opinion on extinguishment left by the judiciary after *Calder* is finally set aside in the *Sparrow* decision. Justices Dickson and LaForest in *Sparrow* stated:

> The test of extinguishment to be adopted, in our opinion, is that
> the Sovereign's intentions must be clear and plain if it is to
> extinguish an aboriginal right. (1990:174–75)

It is indisputable that the affirmation of the Hall view of extinguishment is
an advantage to Aboriginal Peoples. It requires the government to meet a
more onerous test. When this test of extinguishment is applied to the facts
in the *Sparrow* case, the Court easily concludes that the Crown "has failed
to discharge its burden of proving extinguishment" (1990:175).

Beyond the embrace of the settlement theory, the courts' ability to
presume regulatory powers over Aboriginal rights rests on an overly
narrow interpretation of the powers divided between federal and provincial governments in sections 91 and 92 of the *Constitution Act*, 1867. It is
presumed that the sovereign powers of government are fully exhausted
between the two levels of government. James Youngblood Henderson
briefly describes the Aboriginal criticism of this debate:

> While the division of powers in the criminal justice system was
> an existing constitutional fact at the time the Victorians were
> making treaties with First Nations, none of the prerogative trea-
> ties ratify this division. Indeed, as was made clear by First Na-
> tions ... in the Victorian treaties, the Crown and the First Nations
> established an alternate system—the peace and good order sys-
> tem—that is separate and distinct from the 1867 system. (1994:424)

There is no reason why the systems that Professor Henderson refers to
should be limited to criminal justice matters; this is merely the context in
which he discusses the self-governing powers of Aboriginal people. It is
also a view that is not uniquely applicable to the numbered treaties.

The Supreme Court's conclusion in *Sparrow* leaves no room for the
creation of a constitutionally recognized Aboriginal jurisdiction. This
defies the position advanced and understood as fundamental by Aboriginal Peoples. By skipping over such an essential issue, the Canadian courts
covertly affirm the existing self-governing powers of Canada as both
complete and absolute. They implicitly accept the idea that there is no
space for the self-governing powers of Aboriginal Peoples in the Canadian federation. This is the heart of my criticism of the *Sparrow* case.[21] If
section 35(1) is the solution, then it must fundamentally disrupt the
historical interpretation of section 91(24). This is an error that is repeated
throughout the decision.

In fact, "counsel for the appellant *(the federal Crown)* argued that the
effect of section 35(1) is to deny Parliament's power to restrictively
regulate fishing rights under s. 91(24)...." (1990:176). This, in the Crown's
view, is an unacceptable infringement on federal power. The federal

Crown's position demonstrates the degree to which section 35(1) can be seen to have a disruptive quality. It also identifies that the Crown lawyers resist this outcome. This is a realization which holds a contradiction as Canadian legislatures intended to entrench section 35(1) in the constitution.

In closing its discussion of the meaning of the word "existing," the Supreme Court stated:

> the phrase "existing aboriginal rights" must be *interpreted flexibly so as to permit their evolution over time.* (1990:171, emphasis added)

Or in the words of Professor Slattery, the Court affirms that the word existing means that Aboriginal rights are "affirmed in a contemporary form rather than in their primeval simplicity and vigour." (1990:171). These statements are very important because one of the characteristics of colonialism is to deny Aboriginal Peoples and our cultures the opportunity to change and adapt to the advancing world around us. These statements acknowledge that Aboriginal Peoples and cultures are not to be frozen in historical times.

The Court next turned its attention to defining the scope of the concept of Aboriginal rights and, as noted by Justices Dickson and LaForest, its strength as a promise made to Aboriginal people (*Sparrow* 1990:63). It should be noted that this decision speaks only to the issue of Aboriginal rights as the Musqueam, like many other "British Columbia" First Nations, have not taken treaty. The first step in this definitional exercise is to ascertain that the Musqueam did indeed have a right to fish in the area of Canoe Passage and that the right existed from time immemorial. The Court stated:

> The evidence reveals that the Musqueam have lived in the area as an organized society long before the coming of European settlers, and that the taking of salmon was an integral part of their lives and remains so to this day. (1990:171)

On the facts of this case, the requirement to source the Aboriginal right to fish in the culture of the Salish was not a difficult one to demonstrate. This was the first test articulated by the Court. The person asserting an Aboriginal right must show that such a right exists.

"Mr. Sparrow was fishing in ancient tribal territory where his ancestors had fished from time immemorial" (1990:172), and that this was not contested results in a situation where the Aboriginal right asserted was easily demonstrated and accepted. This meant that it was unnecessary for the Court to turn its full attention to delineating the meaning of Aboriginal rights in a comprehensive way. The Court did note that an Aboriginal right is a right which is "an integral part of their distinctive culture" (1990:175). The idea that Aboriginal rights are integral becomes very important in subsequent cases, such as *Gladstone, Van der Peet* and *NTC Smokehouse*. Aboriginal rights which are merely incidental do not receive constitutional protection (*Gladstone* 1996:78). The integral idea suggests that the court sees Aboriginal rights as "the totality of powers and responsibilities *necessary* to maintain and reproduce Aboriginal identity and Aboriginal social organization (Asch and Macklem 1991:506, emphasis added). Aboriginal rights are about the distinctiveness of Aboriginal people and presumably then, Aboriginal rights have as their purpose preventing the end of this distinctiveness. This principle needs to be cast alongside a general understanding of the space that is occupied by other constitutional rights.

A constitution is one source of a nation's autonomy (Hogg 1985:49). This has been particularly true for Canada since the repatriation of the constitution in 1982. Constitutions prescribe the powers, including legislative, executive and judicial, of government. Civil liberties, or the limits on government powers over individuals, also are found in Canada's constitution. Constitutions not only establish rights and powers but also "recognize and protect the values of a nation" (Hogg:1985:1). Granted, Canada's constitution does not contain any grand statements of purpose or principle. Elsewhere, Canada's constitution has been described as:

> a rather technical document, providing Canada with a federal system of government with legislative powers divided between Parliament and the provincial legislatures, without any of the high-sounding rhetoric commonly found in other constitutions. (McNeil 1993:114)

The scope and purpose of a constitution is the context in which the meaning the Court in *Sparrow* has given to Aboriginal rights must be understood. There is no reason, if the rights of Aboriginal Peoples are being taken seriously, to presume that section 35(1) does not accomplish for Aboriginal Peoples what the constitution accomplishes for other Canadians. In fact, the language used by the courts, such as "promises" and "solemn commitments," substantiates the conclusion that what section 35(1) accomplishes is significant. This recognition does not hold up to a careful scrutiny of the principles embedded in the *Sparrow* decision. In *Sparrow*, the Court has upheld the supremacy of the federal parliament over Indian nations because Parliament may limit Aboriginal rights if there is a pressing legislative objective and if the infringement respects the "honour of the Crown" (1990:182). The court will examine in the second step of the test if the infringement imposes "undue hardship" or denies the "preferred means of exercising the right" (1990:182).

The answer to the question, "Why did the Supreme Court decide that those rights are still subject to justifiable federal legislation?" (McNeil 1993:110) is not cohesively argued by the Court. Kent McNeil suggests that the simple answer is that the Court choose to protect federal legislative powers under section 91(24) because: "s. 91(24) would have no work to do if Parliament could no longer legislate regarding Aboriginal rights" (1993:111). Professor McNeil is not persuaded by this notion as:

> on a closer examination, this explanation is insufficient. Nothing in s. 35(1) prevents Parliament from enacting legislation involving aboriginal rights. Instead, it can be interpreted as barring Parliament from *infringing* Aboriginal rights, while leaving intact Parliament's jurisdiction to enact legislation *protecting or enhancing* Aboriginal rights." (1993:111)

Professor McNeil continues his analysis of the deficiency in the Court's position:

> Lack of faith in the capacity of Aboriginal Peoples to govern the exercise of their rights is also implicit in the Supreme Court's decision. (1993:112)

To simply state the purpose of section 35(1): It was more likely intended to end colonial relationships that have been forced on Aboriginal nations for more than a century than it was to perpetuate colonial powers that can be disguised as legitimate legislative authority under section 91(24). However, as the courts remained tied to this colonial philosophy, this very purpose is undermined.

There are other qualities which the Court ascribed to Aboriginal rights. In order to establish an Aboriginal right, a litigant must demonstrate the continuity of the right (1990:172). Continuity does not have to be absolute. There can be gaps in the timeframe. The essence of the continuity requirement (and why absolute continuity is not required) is that Aboriginal rights must be sourced to "time immemorial" or, more simply put, Aboriginal rights must have existed before European contact. This is a troublesome requirement and exposes the degree to which colonialism is embedded in the Court's decision. The rule does not allow Aboriginal Peoples and cultures to adapt to European influences but rather sees anything that results from or after contact, as European. This is difficult to fully reconcile with the Court's statement that Aboriginal rights can be "exercised in a contemporary manner" (1990:175). Despite the rejection of the "frozen rights" approach (1990:170) to the constitutional recognition of Aboriginal rights, the Court introduces a form of frozen-rights theory when it delineates the meaning of Aboriginal rights.

Although the decision in *Sparrow* is held as landmark, it is difficult to conclude that the Court provided a clear and progressive definition of Aboriginal rights.

The idea that Aboriginal people must connect their present rights to the far distant past creates the likelihood that Aboriginal Peoples and cultures are being denied one of the fundamental characteristics of self-determination. Cultures and peoples do change over time. In Kanien'kehaka law, the concept "adding to the rafters" is present in what is known as a constitution.[22] Second, the idea that Aboriginal rights must arise pre-contact turns the reality of contact, that is, the sharing of diverse cultures formerly separated by an ocean, into a story *only* about the impact Europeans had on Aboriginal people (and in such a way that it appears that Aboriginal people had no choice but to accept those new people and ways). This is not the truth. The third concern is the manner in which contact disrupted Aboriginal relationships with their territories. Relocation has been a colonial strategy to control Indian people. To hold Aboriginal people to this time immemorial standard without understanding the history of interference entrenches historical and colonial patterns by their consequence into current Canadian legal results. Not only does the Court's analysis fail to fully consider colonial impacts, it develops a test that turns this colonial impact into a legal impasse that could have the result of denying constitutional protection to some Aboriginal nations.

What disturbs me is a familiar pattern of avoidance that emerges in the Aboriginal rights cases. Courts created the time immemorial requirement. It is a legal fact (or fiction depending on your view). Aboriginal recognition that we occupied this territory prior to the arrival of Europeans and others does not necessitate the precise and narrow way the courts have constructed the continuity argument. It is a vast misunderstanding of the Aboriginal position. In some future case, rather than arguing the central issues important to an Aboriginal litigant, that litigant will be forced to argue around the legally created time immemorial requirement.

Equally troubling is the manner in which the Court constructed the time immemorial requirement, that is, that the Aboriginal society must have been organized. The language used to describe the concept is quite offensive. No one speaks of early Canadian society as being "organized."[23] In fact, early Canadian society was not so organized:

> In early Upper Canada, elections were tumultuous, often raucous affairs where cheers and catcalls were interspersed with flowing liquor and flying fists—as one government official put it, 'the more broken heads and bloody noses there is, the more election-like.' (O'Brien 1992:20)

This creates an interesting double standard in the way courts judge Aboriginal people, our cultures, our histories and our societies. Further, such language is a throwback to the days when people believed that Aboriginal people were not civilized and were lesser forms of humanity. The reliance on stereotypes of Aboriginal inferiority (or Euro-Canadian superiority) can be frequently cited in this (and most other) court decisions. All of this kind of thinking and talking must disappear from Canadian court decisions if the goal of the courts can be assumed to be about inspiring the trust and faith of Aboriginal people (and Canadian laws and courts do recognize that bias and the perception of bias is a particular fault to be guarded against). Trust and faith, perhaps, are the forerunners to the creation of a system of justice that people believe is just.

There is also a third concern regarding the way in which the Court defined Aboriginal rights. The Court indicated that the right which Aboriginal people seek to protect must have been integral to their community. Further into the decision, the Court provided this description:

> The anthropological evidence relied on to establish the existence of the right suggests that, for the Musqueam, the salmon fishery has always constituted an *integral part* of their distinctive culture. Its significant role involved not only consumption for subsistence purposes, but also consumption of salmon on ceremonial and social occasions. The Musqueam have always fished for reasons connected to their cultural and physical survival. As we stated earlier, the right to do so may be exercised in a contemporary manner. (1990:175, emphasis added)

Precisely the scope of the integral requirement is unknown. Rights which are not integral do not have constitutional protection. If the courts understand an Aboriginal right as merely incidental to distinctive Aboriginal cultures then it is potentially a way in which that right could be limited and constitutional protection denied (*Gladstone* 1996:78). As it has been demonstrated that the courts do not possess adequate skills for identifying and correcting cultural bias, such a standard must be viewed as troublesome.

Interestingly enough, the Court paid more attention to limiting Aboriginal rights than to positively defining or affirming the nature of the constitutionally protected Aboriginal rights. This is again demonstrated by the Court's discussion of the next question that had to be determined—the scope of the existing Musqueam right to fish. This question required the Court to apply the general definition of Aboriginal rights to the specific facts of this case. The Court again emphasized that an "aboriginal right should not be defined by incorporating the ways in which it has been regulated in the past" (*Sparrow* 1990:175). Again, there should have been no debate. This only creates an acceptable minimum standard. To have decided otherwise would have allowed governments by regulation to establish constitutional standards. This result would have been absolutely contrary to principles of Canadian constitutional law.

This right to fish must be seen as only one component, perhaps a small component, of the rights that may be classified as Aboriginal (or treaty) rights. Within the given terms of legal analysis, the narrowing of the discussion to only the right to fish, although predictable, raises some concerns regarding the future application of the *Sparrow* decision. The right to fish is not fully, or even expansively, detailed in the *Sparrow* decision. The Court narrowed its discussion even further, addressing only the Musqueam right to fish *for food*.[24] Sometimes this right referred to the right to fish for subsistence purposes only. The Court, therefore, concentrated on specifying the purpose of the Aboriginal right to fish rather than on considering the content of the right. In this way the Court continued to allow the box named Aboriginal rights to remain close to empty. This space leaves ambiguous the issue of whether or not the Aboriginal right to fish includes the right to self-regulation.

The Court's application of the law to the facts also included a resolution of an issue that should have been viewed as rudimentary. Does fishing for food include fishing for social and ceremonial purposes? This is also an issue that is raised as a result of the simplistic and limiting way that the Crown continues to insist on characterizing Aboriginal rights in its factums and arguments.[25] The Supreme Court summarized the Court of Appeal findings as follows:

> the aboriginal right was to fish for food purposes, but that purpose was not to be confined to mere subsistence. Rather, the right was found to extend to fish consumed for social and ceremonial activities. (1990:175)

The language used by the Courts—"mere subsistence," "fish for food"— is also distressing. It again entrenches the notion of European superiority in the present day definition of Aboriginal rights. The use of superiority language and concepts which diminish the position of Aboriginal rights is a common theme in this case as well as in others. Even though the Court resolved this issue in a way that encompassed the Aboriginal view, the fact that an overly simplistic Crown argument was disturbed is not cause for celebration.

The Crown's relationship with Aboriginal people requires a higher standard of conduct even when they are adversaries. To allow litigation and the adversarial nature of this process to exempt the Crown from their obligations to Aboriginal people serves only one purpose and that is to continue to entrench colonial relations. In fact, the Court noted:

> Government regulations governing the exercise of the Musqueam
> right to fish ... have only recognized the right to fish *for food* for
> over a hundred years. This may have reflected the existing posi-
> tion. *However, historical policy on the part of the Crown is not
> only incapable of extinguishing the existing aboriginal right without
> clear intention, but it is also incapable of, in itself, delineating
> that right.* (1990:176, emphasis added)

Given that the government is required to act in a fiduciary capacity[26]
towards Aboriginal Peoples, it is hoped that in future its arguments will
not be so demeaning to the concept of Aboriginal rights. If this cannot be
accomplished, then the gains that can be made in the courts with regard to
defining "existing Aboriginal rights" will be minimal.

This contradiction, that the government must defend Canada's interest at the same time as protecting the Aboriginal interest, is one of the
central problems in Aboriginal people's quest to successfully secure satisfactory litigation outcomes. It seems that the government is consistently
willing to put the interest of the Crown ahead of its fiduciary responsibilities to Aboriginal Peoples. This recognition leads to a simple conclusion.
Perhaps future litigation should not focus on the definition or assertion of
Aboriginal rights but on strictly holding governments accountable to their
fiduciary responsibilities and the subsequent liabilities[27] for the breach of
those responsibilities.

The phrase "fish for food" arises in the regulatory regime instituted
by British Columbia. It is, therefore, an externally imposed characterization of the right to fish. The 1878 fishing regulations were the first to
specifically mention Indians. By adopting the language of the late 1800s,
the Court allows the philosophy of the time (that is, the belief in European
superiority) to seep into the case. The regulations allowed Indians to fish
for food for themselves, but not for sale or barter.[28] The present-day
regulations provide for the issuing of an "Indian food fish licence" on the
approval of the Minister.[29] There is no compelling reason why the definition of this term in the 1984 regulatory scheme needs to have the 1878
regulatory exclusions of "sale and barter" read into it. In fact, as Aboriginal understandings of the world are holistic, separating fishing activities
into distinct spheres such as economic, sacred or sustenance disrespects
the Aboriginal cultural framework. The logical extension of this kind of
reasoning will result in the complete grounding of Aboriginal rights
outside of Aboriginal cultural beliefs. There will be little Aboriginal left
about such rights.

It is also an important observation that the regulatory regime in place
in British Columbia and elsewhere was instituted unilaterally without
consultation with Aboriginal nations or people.[30] Courts must be not only
aware of this exclusive history but also accountable to the impacts. By

adopting a standard of language that is borrowed from legislative frameworks, such as the concept "fish for food," the Court has sanctioned (albeit covertly) the exclusionary development of such concepts. Again, as this is a constitutional standard, it must be seen as unacceptable.

The definition of the right to "fish for food" in and of itself was quite controversial. The Crown argued before the Supreme Court that the right to take fish did not include "the ceremonial and social activities of the Band." Mr. Sparrow argued that the way in which an Aboriginal right is exercised is discretionary in the holder of the right (1990:175). The Court concluded its discussion of the Aboriginal right to fish with this statement:

> In the Courts below, the case at bar was not presented on the footing of an aboriginal right to fish for commercial or livelihood purposes. Rather, the focus was and continues to be on the validity of a net length restriction affecting the appellant's *food fishing licence*. We therefore adopt the Court of Appeal's characterization of the right for the purpose of this appeal, and confine our reasons to the meaning of the constitutional recognition and affirmation of the existing aboriginal right to fish for food and social and ceremonial purposes. (1990:176)

Following the Court's reasoning, it can be concluded that a food fishing licence also includes the right to fish for social and ceremonial purposes. This clarity is of assistance to Aboriginal Peoples, although the lengthy and costly process required to achieve such a rudimentary victory is certainly not a cause for celebration.

It is worth emphasizing that the right to fish for commercial purposes is recognized as a more essential right in terms of the Aboriginal desire for self-sufficiency. However, it appears that the courts do not see this issue in this way. In various cases the "presumption that 'aboriginality' is ordinarily incompatible with profit" (Barsh and Henderson 1997:1005) prevails. It is clearly disappointing that this right is excluded from Supreme Court review in this case. This is another one of the ways to demonstrate that the decision in *Sparrow* was not as complete a statement on Aboriginal rights as it could have been. In *Sparrow*, the delineation of rights is consistently narrowed in such a fashion that valuable Aboriginal time and energy must be repeatedly expended to secure narrow victory upon narrow victory with the great consequence of failure looming around every judicial corner. This is the core of the frustration with Canadian law that I carry.

What is absent from the Court's reasons is any discussion of the commercial fishery.[31] The Court fails to look at this question as it was not part of the representations made before the lower courts. The right to establish commercial practices in the fisheries is essential to the livelihood of many Aboriginal nations. For the Musqueam people, not only was the right to fish essential to their culture but also to their economy. Therefore, the right to fish for sustenance or commercially should have been seen as the exercise of an Aboriginal right in a *contemporary manner*.

The failure to resolve this issue in the *Sparrow* case may be seen as one of the weaknesses of the court process, inherent in the very nature of the process. Issues are drafted as narrowly as possible. The outstanding issues in Aboriginal claims are both broad and multifaceted. To rely on the courts to resolve these issues will continue to be a long and tedious process as every little detail must be litigated in a series of cases. I am not convinced that, even after years of litigation, the collection of narrow and detailed Supreme Court of Canada decisions will ever be able to fully articulate the meaning of Aboriginal rights in a way that respects Aboriginal understandings. *Sparrow* is purported by the courts and many legal scholars to be a broadly reasoned case; however, that reasoning is not yet broad enough to embrace a comprehensive theory of Aboriginal rights.

The most expansive part of the Courts reasons is the discussion of the definition of the phrase "recognized and affirmed." It is in this portion of the judgment that the Court more fully identified and defined a theme that was introduced earlier in the case. The resolution of Aboriginal claims requires an articulation of the "appropriate interpretive framework for section 35(1)" (1990:177). The starting point advanced by the Court to articulate the appropriate interpretive framework is the *Royal Proclamation of 1763*. The Court recalled that the British policy towards the Indian population "was based on respect for their right to occupy their traditional lands" (1990:177). The Court confirmed that this honourable standard must again be adopted. In this discussion, the Court was at last able to acknowledge the colonialism, at least the historical colonialism, embedded in state relations with First Nations.

It is from within this "interpretive framework" that the delineation of Aboriginal rights must be approached. Quoting from an essay written by Professor Noel Lyon, the Court affirmed this view of the change that was introduced in 1982, with the passing of section 35(1):

> the context of 1982 is surely enough to tell us that this is not just a codification of the case law on aboriginal rights that had accumulated by 1982. Section 35 calls for a just settlement for aboriginal peoples. It renounces the old rules of the game under which the Crown established Courts of law and denied those Courts the authority to question sovereign claims made by the Crown. (1990:178)

Whether the Court itself can adhere to this high standard poses an interesting question. The Court does not seem to be aware that it, that is, the institution of the judiciary, is part of the colonial experience of Aboriginal Peoples in this country. The Court's failure to consider its place in the colonial experience determines just how little of a break with the past is to be found in the *Sparrow* decision and, from this point forward, its ability to fairly resolve disputes Aboriginal Peoples bring to it must be suspect.

The Supreme Court clearly emphasizes the interpretive process as a key to resolving Aboriginal claims. This is seen by the Court as a central issue. However, the Court fails to take its analysis to a full conclusion—instead drawing the section 35(1) protections of Aboriginal rights into the existing law of constitutional interpretation. With this quote borrowed from the *Manitoba Language Reference* (1985):

> The Constitution of a country is a statement of the will of the people to be governed in accordance with certain principles held as fundamental and certain prescriptions restrictive of the powers of the legislature and government. It is, as s. 52 of the *Constitution Act, 1982* declares, the "supreme law" of the nation, unalterable by the normal legislative process, and unsuffering of laws inconsistent with it. The duty of the judiciary is to interpret and apply the laws of Canada and each of the provinces, and it is thus our duty to ensure that the constitutional law prevails. (*Sparrow* 1990:179)

The Court fails to observe or understand that the problem underpinning many Aboriginal rights claims is one of competing values and principles between Aboriginal Peoples and Canada.

The question of remedies is also central in trying to justly resolve Aboriginal claims. In *Sparrow*, the Court ordered a new trial. This is a familiar pattern. Yet in other areas of constitutional litigation, more creative remedies have been used. Kent McNeil explains that the remedy awarded in the *Manitoba Language Reference,* based on the Court's concern about leaving a statutory vacuum, "was to invoke the rule of law as a fundamental constitutional principle to maintain the application of invalid statutes until they could be translated into French" (1993:121). Professor McNeil parallels this reasoning to the *Sparrow* case in order to offer an explanation of why the Court chose to create out of the air a right of infringement in the federal Crown:

> This section could have been interpreted as placing those rights outside federal and provincial jurisdiction. This would have created a jurisdictional vacuum which could have been filled by Aboriginal governments, terminating the constitutional colonial-

ism under which the Aboriginal Peoples have suffered since 1867.
(1993:119)

Again, we see that the theoretical principle underpinning the judicial
interpretation of section 35(1) is colonialism (McNeil 1993:114; Turpel
1991:17).

In a similar way, the arguments made by the Court to advance a
progressive interpretative framework actually operate to disguise the colonialism that is embedded in the decision. Not all of the colonialism is
embedded. One of the most damning statements in the case followed the
progressive interpretation talk:

> there was from the outset never any doubt that sovereignty and
> legislative power, and indeed the underlying title, to such lands
> vested in the Crown. (1990:177)

For this principle, the Court relies on both the *Royal Proclamation* and the
American case *Johnson* v. *Mc'Intosh* (1823). This principle of underlying
sovereignty and Crown title is not as universally accepted as Canadian
courts lead us to believe. It would be heatedly disputed by most Aboriginal people. Canadian courts must begin to consider this. In fact, Aboriginal litigation has largely been successful only because Aboriginal people
have carefully drafted their litigation matters to avoid running into this
presumption of Canadian law. In the same paragraph, the Court asserted:
"We cannot recount with much pride the treatment accorded to the native
people of this country" (1990:177). Perhaps *Sparrow* should not be noted
as a progressive decision but one that is wrought with so many contradictions that its future application will necessarily be problematic.

Other writers have also noted these difficulties. Michael Asch and
Patrick Macklem note that the decision in *Sparrow* embraces both a
contingent theory[32] of Aboriginal rights as well as an inherent rights
approach. They emphasize:

> the commitment to a right of aboriginal self-government in *Spar-
> row*, initiated by the adoption of an inherent theory of aboriginal
> rights, is ultimately rendered fragile and tentative by the Court's
> subsequent embrace of the competing contingent rights approach
> and the Court's unquestioned acceptance of Canadian sovereignty.
> (1991:508)

Despite all the Court's warnings about the fact that section 35(1) is
removed from the ambit of the *Charter*, the Court relied on a *Charter*-type
justification test to determine if this specific regulation of the fisheries
was constitutional. It is very interesting that the court did not provide any

convincing explanation for the creation of this limitation. This should cause extreme concern as section 35(1) is not part of the *Charter*.[33] In establishing the rationale for the justification test the Court later provided in its judgment:

> There *is no explicit language* in the provision that authorizes this Court or any Court to assess the legitimacy of any government legislation that restricts aboriginal rights. Yet, we find the words "recognition and affirmation" incorporate the fiduciary relationship referred to earlier and so import some restraint on the exercise of sovereign power. *Rights that are recognized and affirmed are not absolute.* Federal legislative powers continue, including, of course the right to legislate with respect to Indians pursuant to s.91(24) of the *Constitution Act, 1867*. These powers must, however, now be read together with s.35(1). In other words, *federal power must be reconciled with federal duty and the best way to achieve that reconciliation is to demand the justification of any government regulation that infringes upon or denies aboriginal rights. (Sparrow* 1990:181, emphasis added)

There are a number of troubling pronouncements contained within this partial paragraph. First, the Court opens the door for a justification test similar to that found in section 1 of the *Charter*.[34] Second, the Court is again assuming that the legislative authority found in sections 91 and 92 are fully spent and that those powers have not been altered by section 35. This conclusion is less difficult to assert than it is to purport that section 35(1) contains an obvious and logical limitation. Following the suggestion of Professor Noel Lyon, surely section 35 changes the rules of the constitutional game. I see little truly "new" in the way the Court has decided the *Sparrow* case. In fact, the decision follows very neatly the pattern that was established in early Aboriginal rights litigation. It is not revolutionary nor does it create significant constitutional space for Aboriginal aspirations to flourish. In fact, *Sparrow* creates more space for Canadian governments to continue to interfere with both constitutionally protected rights and Aboriginal aspirations.

Sparrow sets out a test which focuses not on affirming or enhancing Aboriginal rights but rather on entrenching the powers of the Canadian government over Indians under section 91(24). This is accomplished under the guise of articulating the words "recognized and affirmed." Almost incredibly, it is the fiduciary relationship that is used to justify this approach. In my opinion, this finding does little to alter the "rules of the game," nor does it disturb the familiar pattern of colonialism that Aboriginal nations have survived since the coming of the Europeans. The potential in *Sparrow* is more likely to be used to harm Aboriginal aspirations of self-determination than it is to advance them.

The most pressing determination for me is the degree to which the *Sparrow* decision allows Aboriginal aspirations to flourish. I was born into a time when Aboriginal nations were strongly asserting their rights to be self-determining. This remains paramount. Unfortunately, the conclusion I reach regarding the *Sparrow* decision is that, despite the fact that the constitutionalization of Aboriginal rights was of potential, the Court's interpretation is unnecessarily restrictive. This analysis shows clearly that the courts do not possess any trust in the belief that Aboriginal nationhood and Canadian sovereignty can co-exist.

Kent McNeil's conclusion is more encouraging. He notes that, despite the Supreme Court's decision and the embedded colonial values of the Court, *Sparrow* does identify some ways in which Aboriginal Peoples can use the decision to inform their next moves. He notes:

> The key is to meet the Court's unarticulated, but evident, concern that a jurisdictional and legal vacuum would result if federal authority over Aboriginal and treaty rights was excluded by s. 35(1). (1993:133)

This would be accomplished by filling the constitutional space with Aboriginal laws. If these laws are already in place, then it is just a matter of demonstrating their existence. If they are not in place, then the option exists to make them (McNeil 1993:134). This reinforces a message that I have been delivering for years, one that the Elders shared with me: Sovereignty is not something you talk about. It is simply something you do!

Although I agree with Professor McNeil's conclusion, the decision in *R. v. Pamajewon* must serve as further warning. As Bradford Morse notes: "nowhere is a missed opportunity more apparent than in *Pamajewon*" (1997:1015). There, members of the Shawanaga First Nation and the Eagle Lake First Nation asserted their right to host various gambling activities. They asserted there was no need to obtain a provincial licence because the bands had an inherent right of self-government over gambling (*R. v. Pamajewon* 1996:167). The Court noted: "assuming without deciding that s.35(1) includes self-government claims, the applicable legal standard is nonetheless that laid out in *Van der Peet*" (1996:171). There the Court emphasized: "in order to be an aboriginal right an *activity* must be an element of a tradition, custom or practice *integral* to the *distinctive culture* of the Aboriginal group claiming the right" (*Van der Peet* 1996:201, emphasis added). Ironically, it appears that the Court is willing to use Aboriginal "distinctiveness" as a limit on the scope and nature of Aboriginal rights. If what is asserted as an Aboriginal right, such as gambling, appears too "mainstream," then clearly it is not distinctive and not an

Aboriginal right. *Pamajewon* does not offer encouragement that a right to self-government is embraced in the constitutional protection of Aboriginal rights.

At least one notable scholar concerned with the issues of Aboriginal and treaty rights believes that the section 35 process was doomed from the outset. Menno Boldt suggests:

> While entrenchment may have given a small measure of legal and political legitimacy to aboriginal rights, a strong case can be made that entrenchment has placed aboriginal rights in a legal and political quicksand. As a consequence of entrenchment, Indians have essentially forfeited their prerogative to define these rights. Because entrenched aboriginal rights can be constitutionally defined only by amendment, if and when there is a constitutional amendment that defines aboriginal rights it will say what the eleven governments of Canada want it to say. If there is no constitutional amendment, then Canadian Courts will define aboriginal rights. Either way, whether the definition is made by political process or by judicial process, Indians will be spectators (euphemistically termed 'consultants'), not decision makers or arbitrators. (1993:28–29)

This is not dissimilar to the point made by Alan Pratt and discussed in chapter three. Courts cannot define Aboriginal rights without disrespecting Aboriginal understandings that these rights are inherent.

The power to define our own experience is essential to the survival of oppressed and colonized peoples. If the purpose of the political negotiations which led up to the entrenchment of section 35(1) in the new constitutional arrangements was to create space for Aboriginal Peoples, then it is fairly obvious that these efforts have failed. Section 35(1) presents a new and interesting option in the legal arsenal of Aboriginal Peoples, but it does not yet represent a fundamental change. If we are to hold out hope for fundamental change, then we must find ways to persuade courts that they must look at our relationships in a truly new way. This is a monumental task but I have little doubt that Aboriginal Peoples will rise to the challenge.

Notes

1. I am not the first person to note dissatisfaction with the construction of the *Sparrow* decision as progressive. See for example, Menno Boldt 1993. The best discussion I have seen on the negative implications of the *Sparrow* decision is written by Kent McNeil 1993.
2. In fact Mr. Sparrow was never forced to trial the second time on this charge.

3. He has also twice since this infraction been charged with fishing offences under Aboriginal-specific regulations. No convictions have yet been registered but the harassment must seem unending.

4. These are my thoughts and feelings. I am not certain Mr. Sparrow would agree.
   It is also important to note that Mr. Sparrow was supported by the Musqueam government in his efforts. See the preliminary discussion in Parnesh Sharma 1998:37–41.

5. Mr. Sparrow has four licences, both commercial and Indian. The discretion rests with the Minister to issue both types of licences. A conviction on this charge could have resulted in a denial to renew any one of Mr. Sparrow's licences. His ability to remain in his chosen profession is conditional on his ability to maintain his licences.

6. A notable exception may be the literature which has been inspired by the decision in *Delgamuukw* v. *B.C.* The reader is referred to an inspirational piece by Dara Culhane 1992.

7. I wish to here acknowledge the financial support of the Canada Council. This discussion is the first sharing of my research, and further work on the impact of this litigation on the community is forthcoming.

8. I pay my respects to Leona Sparrow who has not only taught me much but always welcomes me into her home.

9. For a fuller discussion, please see Patricia Monture Angus 1999b.

10. It is important to note that this case does not speak directly to the important question of defining the meaning in Canadian law of the concept of treaty rights. Within the legal process only findings that are essential to the resolution of the specific case at issue will be commented on by the courts. As the Musqueam First Nation has never been party to any treaty with the Crown, the question of treaty rights does not arise in this case.

11. Section 61(1) of the *Fisheries Act* makes it an offence to contravene either the Act or the regulations.

12. Another good example of evidentiary burdens impacting negatively on Aboriginal claimants are the comments of Steele in the *Bear Island Foundation* trial. Of particular importance are the difficulties that Aboriginal claimants face when an historical context that respects the Indian understanding is also required of the judiciary. Steele J. states:

> Chief Potts, who is 38 years old, has a white mother and a father who is not of pure Indian ancestry, and whose Indian ancestry descended from persons who arrived on the lands about 1901, long after most of the issues in dispute had occurred. It could not be said that his own ancestors had any direct *oral knowledge* of the events in question. He was therefore merely giving evidence of oral history he had accumulated from other members of the band. He cannot speak the native language and therefore has difficulty communicating fully with some of the oldest members, although they speak English. (1984:337–338)

13. The decision to charge is made within the bureaucracy of Canadian government. Who is making these decisions is often shielded from public view and

in particular the information is not readily available to Aboriginal people. It is difficult to imagine litigation that would open this question regarding the bureaucratic decision to charge. It is at this place—the decision to charge—that much is going wrong with the litigation of Aboriginal rights. Aboriginal people are left in a defensive (as contrasted with affirmative) position battling powers that have the ability to limit the delineation of our rights. Perhaps a national moratorium on the quasi-criminal prosecution of Aboriginal people for hunting and fishing infractions should be introduced and the use of a mediation process based on the inherency of Aboriginal rights initiated.

14. The Constitution Act, 1982, Part II. Section 35(1) appears under the heading of "Rights of Aboriginal Peoples of Canada."

15. The Court did have opportunities to examine the meaning of section 35(1) prior to this decision. The *Simon* decision (1986) is the most notable example. In that case the Court and the litigants chose not to enter the discussion on section 35(1). This also demonstrates my earlier comments on the necessity of examining the context.

16. See for example Brian Slattery (1987), Noel Lyon (1988), Kent McNeil (1982) and William Pentney (1987).

    Clearly these few articles are only examples of the academic literature that was generated. Of note, however, is the fact that these four articles are cited by the Supreme Court in the *Sparrow* decision. Also of note in a systematic analysis of the *Sparrow* pronouncements is the fact that all of the scholars whose work the Supreme Court relied upon are non-Aboriginal and all are men.

17. See for example *R.* v. *Eninew* (1984), *Attorney General of Ontario* v. *Bear Island Foundation* (1984),*R.* v. *Hare and Debassige* (1985), *Re Steinhauer* v. *The Queen* (1985) and *R.* v. *Agawa* (1988).

18. I want to recognize that I am not, by choice, a litigator, and all of my observations are made from a place outside of courtroom experience. I do not think this belittles my views. Rather, I am merely pointing to the fact that an experienced litigator would also be able to advance this critique in different directions. See for example, Louise Mandell 1987. In addition, some serious question must be raised by the fact that many (at least one half) of the Aboriginal people with law degrees make choices not to litigate.

19. The application of provincial regulatory systems is incompatible with the views that many Aboriginal nations hold regarding their hunting and fishing rights. This is one of the reasons for the large quantity of litigation in this area.

20. This view can also be found in the cases of *St. Catherine's Milling, Baker Lake* and *Bear Island Foundation.*

21. My view is echoed in the work of Michael Asch and Patrick Macklem 1991.

22. Source of Rafters.

23. A lengthy discussion of this requirement is found in *Hamlet of Baker Lake* v. *Minister of Indian Affairs and Northern Development* (1979). Mahoney J. states:

> While the existence of an organized society is a prerequisite to the existence of an aboriginal title, there appears no valid reason to demand

proof of the existence of a society more elaborately structured than is necessary to demonstrate that there existed among the aborigines a recognition of the claimed rights, sufficiently defined to permit their recognition by the common law upon its advent in the territory.

Again, the rights of Aboriginal Peoples are denigrated to the stature of the common law. Such pronouncements are unacceptable.

24. Although this is good legal practice, and the way the Court has structured its decision is predictable, it does nothing to advance a space in which the constitutional protection of Aboriginal rights can flourish (or grow like a "living tree" to use the appropriate constitutional parallel). Court practices must be examined and not presumed to be fair, just and right, despite the fact that such an examination would be controversial and without legal precedent. The failure to examine the process by which courts decided, by courts, leaves any historical presumptions intact and the benefit of those presumptions usually accrue to the Crown. The benefit which accrues to the Crown as a result of the legal process is not invisible to Aboriginal people. This is one point at which Aboriginal people see that the legal system repeatedly fails them.

25. In the factum of the Attorney General of British Columbia before the Supreme Court of Canada it was argued in *Sparrow* that:

> The specific aboriginal right here asserted is not the use of a fishery. Use of the fishery of the Fraser estuary is open to all. The right asserted is regulatory immunity from the *Fisheries Act* and regulations thereunder. *It is conceded the Musqueam had no aboriginal system of regulations whatsoever. They exercised no aboriginal jurisdiction.* Accordingly, they can have no aboriginal right to regulatory immunity (*Sparrow* 1990:10).

What remains invisible to the government's lawyers is the fact that Aboriginal law might not appear in written form or as a system of regulations.

26. See the discussion in chapter three regarding the *Guerin* case.

27. It is worth remembering that in the *Guerin* case the Musqueam band received the significant sum of $11 million.

28. *Salmon Fishery Regulations for British Columbia*, 1878, as discussed in *Sparrow* (1990:173).

29. *British Columbia Fishery (General) Regulations*, SOR/84-248, s. 27(1).

30. Consultation must occur at both levels. Aboriginal nations have political understandings that Canada must learn to respect. Aboriginal people, who for example fish, have developed expertise in certain areas and should also be individually involved in the consultation process.

31. At least one lower court decision in Ontario looks at the matter of commercial fisheries and resolves the question in favour of the Indians. See *R. v. Jones and Nadjiwon*, [1993] 3 C.N.L.R. (O.C.J.). In *R. v. Gladstone* the Supreme Court found that as "for the Heiltsuk Band trading in herring spawn on kelp was not an activity taking place as an incident to the social and ceremonial activities of the community; rather, trading in herring spawn on kelp was, *in itself*, a central and significant feature of Heiltsuk society"

(1996:78). This distinguishes the *Gladstone* decision from two unfavourable commercial fishing decisions in *Van der Peet* and *N.T.C. Smokehouse*.

32. This is more justification than it is the kind of theory that I called for earlier in this work.

33. The Court in *Sparrow* is well aware of this fact and state:

> Section 35(1) is not subject to s.1 of the *Charter*, nor to legislative override under s. 33 (1990:176).

34. The test articulated in *Sparrow* is not as rigorous as the *Charter* justification test.

Chapter Five

Returning To Colonial Visions
The Supreme Court Speaks To
Delgamuukw[1]

Strictly speaking the Supreme Court of Canada case, *Delgamuukw*(1998), is not about either self-government or self-determination. The appeal raises a set of interrelated and novel questions which revolve around a single issue—"the nature and scope of the constitutional protection afforded by s. 35(1) to Common Law aboriginal title" (1998:21). Although the fragmentation of concepts central to Aboriginal ideas about traditional governance is problematic, Canadian law views Aboriginal title, treaty rights, Aboriginal rights and perhaps self-government as separate boxes whose meaning will be filled in on a case-by-case basis. My central interest in this chapter is not Aboriginal title but rather self-government[2] and the degree to which the Supreme Court of Canada's decision in *Delgamuukw* is a place where Aboriginal aspirations for self-government can find a home.

At trial, the Gitksan and Wet'suwet'en peoples argued the case as a claim for "ownership" and "jurisdiction" over 58,000 square kilometres in northern British Columbia. These lands are the traditional territories of the People. The trial judge understood that this claim to jurisdiction advanced by the people was a claim to the right of self-government. He rejected the possibility that such a claim could exist, stating: "all legislative jurisdiction was divided between Canada and the province and there was no room for aboriginal jurisdiction or sovereignty which would be recognized by the law or the Courts" (*Delgamuukw* 1991:210).[3] At the British Columbia Court of Appeal, MacFarlane affirmed the trial Court's decision (as summarized by the Supreme Court):

> the Gitksan and Wet'suwet'en people did not need a Court declaration to permit internal self-regulation, if they consent to be governed. However, the rights of self-government encompassing

the power to make general laws governing the land, resources, and people in the territory are legislative powers which cannot be awarded by the Courts. Such jurisdiction is inconsistent with the *Constitution Act, 1867* and its division of powers. When the Crown imposed English law on all the inhabitants of the colony and when British Columbia entered Confederation, the Aboriginal people became subject to Canadian (and provincial) legislative authority. For this reason, the claim to jurisdiction failed. (*Delgamuukw* 1998:32)

These reasons expose the space that courts might be willing to ascribe to self-government, that is, merely over the internal regulation of Aboriginal communities.

This conclusion is in essence the very same decision reached by the Marshall Court in the United States in the 1820s and 1830s, where Indian nations were viewed as "dependent domestic nations" (*Cherokee Nation* v. *Georgia*.[4] This recognition respected Indian nations' powers over internal (but not external) self-regulation. After a hundred years of dancing with the American conclusion, Canadian courts either lack the will, creativity or fortitude to arrive at a Canadian solution which involves Aboriginal people in the process. After all, the American answer is nearly two centuries old and can hardly continue to be viewed as progressive.

These two decisions of the courts in British Columbia in *Delgamuukw* demonstrate the degree to which courts have difficulty with any Aboriginal claim to jurisdiction over territory (or external issues of Indian sovereignty). It is unlikely claims for external power will ever be successful in Canadian courts, as jurisdiction powers are seen to have been fully spent in sections 91 and 92 of the constitution. This is a theme that is familiar and was seen in the analysis of the *Sparrow* case offered in the previous chapter. This conclusion, as it is based on the division of legislative powers, is unfortunate because it affirms Canada's powers to act in a colonial manner. There is nothing self-evident in Canadian law that suggests one section of the constitution cannot inform another. Rather, as constitution interpretation is intended to follow the doctrine of progressive interpretation (Hogg 1985:341), an opposite analysis would be warranted. Or to rely on Lord Sankey's metaphor: "The BNA Act planted in Canada a living tree capable of growth and expansion within its natural limits" (*Edwards* v. *A.-G. Can.* 1930:136). Therefore, there is not really any absolute legal impediment to suggesting that section 35(1) challenges the interpretation of the division of powers found in sections 91 and 92.[5] It was a colonial mistake of the past to exclude Indian nations from the legislative division of powers. As the courts have no ability to address this colonial error without exercising some creativity they are left to perpetuate it into the future.

Once before the Supreme Court of Canada on appeal, the parameters of the *Delgamuukw* case shifted. At trial and before the B.C. Court of Appeal, the case was argued on the basis of "ownership" and "jurisdiction." By the time the case reached the Supreme Court, this had evolved into "Aboriginal title" and "self-government" (1998:45). This shift recognizes the lesson about jurisdiction noted in the previous paragraph and was likely an effort to salvage the case. In my opinion, for the purposes of this litigation, there is logically little difference between ownership and Aboriginal title. Likewise, there is little difference between jurisdiction and self-government. The major difference is that self-government and Aboriginal title belong to the specific language that allows courts to address what is becoming the intersection of Aboriginal law and Canadian law which the courts call *sui generis*. Courts seem to be very comfortable, and only comfortable, with this characterization of Aboriginal rights. The concern that must be expressed is: Is the court's comfort with this special language a marginalization of Aboriginal rights, including Aboriginal title?

This is not the only way that the pleadings were changed before the Supreme Court. At trial, the case was argued as individual claims of certain chiefs with respect to the territory. Before the Supreme Court, the case was argued as one of communal interest. The Court found that this improper change in the pleadings caused prejudice to the Crown and as such was an irreversible error (1998:45–46). The Court based this conclusion on the general rule that "to frame the case in a different manner on appeal would retroactively deny the respondents the opportunity to know the appellant's case" (1998:46), and not on any specific, named disadvantage to Crown.

This issue of how to draft claims, either on behalf of individuals or communally, is a difficult one. Canadian law is accustomed to claims on behalf of corporations, government structures familiar to them (such as band councils but not traditional Aboriginal governments), or individuals. None of these forms fully encompass Aboriginal forms of traditional government or their relationships with individuals from their community. The pleadings problems reflect embedded structural obstacles to the just resolution of Aboriginal claims rather than difficulties with the plaintiffs' pleadings in this case. The outcome, however, of this structural difficulty is borne by the Aboriginal plaintiffs who are forced back to trial. I view this as an unacceptable outcome.

Despite this finding regarding the pleadings, the Court went on to provide an articulation of the meaning of Aboriginal title. On one hand this may appear as a benevolent act toward Aboriginal people by the Supreme Court. Lamer described his offerings on the meaning of Aboriginal title as an opportunity to give "guidance to the judge at the new trial" (1998:57). At the same time, as seen in the discussion of the *Sparrow* case, what the Court offered up as expansive was not necessarily a progressive acceptance of Aboriginal thought, practice and life. This is obvious in the way the court accepted the separation of issues of self-government (or jurisdiction) and Aboriginal title (or ownership).

A similar opportunity to provide guidance is not made with respect to the claim for self-government. Chief Justice Lamer held:

> the errors of fact made by the trial judge, and the resultant need for a new trial, make it impossible for this Court to determine whether the claim to self-government has been made out. Moreover, this is not the right case for the Court to lay down the legal principles to guide future litigation. (1997:80)

This is a curious finding. It is difficult to understand Aboriginal title and self-government as separate and distinct concepts (or relations). Kent McNeil indicates that "a careful reading of his decision reveals that, for theoretical and practical reasons, self-government is essential for his conception of Aboriginal title to work" (1998:13). Further, as seen in *Sparrow* and *Pamajewon*, it is more likely that the court is hesitant to approach the issue of self-government as a protected Aboriginal right. This avoidance cannot go on forever. However, it seems clear that when courts do get around to addressing the content of self-government rights protected by section 35(1), Aboriginal nations are not likely to be fully happy with those conclusions. The Supreme Court seems to view its task as mediating between the interests of the state and Aboriginal nations (in a way that is rather like sitting on the fence). Lamer noted that the meaning of Aboriginal title "lies somewhere between" the position of the Indian appellants and the Crown (1998:57).

I am concerned equally with the structure litigation forces on Aboriginal people as I am with the content of judicial decisions. In *Delgamuukw*, with respect to the issue of Aboriginal title, the Crown argued that:

> first, that Aboriginal title is no more than a bundle of rights to engage in activities which are themselves Aboriginal rights recognized and affirmed by s.35(1), and that the *Constitution Act, 1982*, merely constitutionalizes those individual rights, *not the bundle itself, because the latter has no independent content*; and second, that Aboriginal title, at most, encompasses the right to *exclusive use and occupation* of land in order to engage in those activities which are Aboriginal rights themselves, and that s.35(1) constitutionalizes this notion of exclusivity. (1998:57, emphasis added)

The failure of the Crown to put forward arguments in the adversarial process that honours its fiduciary obligation to Aboriginal Peoples must be a cause for significant concern. Its position is a rearticulation of the notion that Aboriginal rights in land are nothing more than rights to use the land and live on it. This is not a unique feature of the *Delgamuukw* case. In fact, in the majority (if not all) the Aboriginal rights cases, this is a serious issue. Until the Crown is moved away from such attempts to minimize Aboriginal interests and rights, it is difficult to continue to believe that there will be just resolutions to Aboriginal claims. In fact, the position taken by the Crown against Aboriginal interests is often the single most important reason why Aboriginal nations must commence litigation in the first place. Further, because of the Crown's attempts to minimize and narrow Aboriginal claims before the courts the potential for progressive decision making by the courts is harnessed and pulled back.

It is also important to understand my objection to what the Crown argued. The "bundle" the Crown refers to as having no independent content (which means the bundle is not a right as well) is, in part, self-government. The Crown sees Aboriginal rights as activities only, as Lamer suggested in *Van der Peet* (1996:201). Hunting, fishing, picking medicine and so on are all activities, but what about the ability to organize those activities in the communities? Or conduct the ceremonies related to those activities? This reliance on activities fillets Aboriginal society, culture and tradition into only the most visible top layer. This point is clearly demonstrated in these comments on the *Jack and Charlie* case, where two Indian men were convicted of killing a deer out of season for ceremonial purposes:

> Considering the practice by sole reference to the deer meat (and thus suggesting that frozen deer could be a substitute), misses the cultural and legal context within which the ceremony is performed. There is no appreciation of the matrix of family responsibilities and relationships that are triggered by the requirement of obtaining fresh deer meat for this ceremony. There is no understanding of how people plan for the trip, discuss its purpose, remember the great-grandfather, share their food and supplies, and experience nature together. There is no acknowledgment of the internal contractual and constitutional legal principles which govern the parties' conduct with Salish society. The event's narrow construction overlooks community participation that would accompany the preparation and dressing of a newly killed deer. The Court did not account for the people lifting the deer from the truck, taking it in the house or shed, skinning it, sitting around the table working at it, and discussing their routines and relationships in very specific ways. (Borrows and Rotman 1997:43)

This filleting of Aboriginal tradition is a serious consequence of litigation. Aboriginal people are expected to offer up our beliefs and ways in exchange for constitutional protection of rights.

In the analysis of the 1996 *Van der Peet* decision, Russel Barsh and Youngblood Henderson provide this insight:

> The fundamental issue is the identity of the decision-maker. The *Van der Peet* test entrenches European paternalism because the courts of the colonizer have assumed the authority to *define the nature and meaning of Aboriginal cultures.* The Supreme Court has declared to Aboriginal Peoples, in effect, "We shall decide which of your values and practices can be reconciled with our culture, and with our vision of Canada. It has done so evidently with the best of intentions—but we all know that best intentions alone can be dangerous. (1997:1002, emphasis added)

The splitting of Aboriginal tradition into parts is not simply fact specific but it is also central to the theoretical principles that the courts are articulating. It affects the manner in which courts interpret the constitutional provision and results in the requirement, as Barsh and Henderson so starkly declare, that Aboriginal Peoples change to fit into Canada, as Canada cannot be expected to do any changing. This systematic and structural fragmentation of Aboriginal cultures, which are by nature holistic, evidences the caution and care that must be taken when Aboriginal Peoples choose (if in fact such a real choice exists) to share their concerns and dilemmas with Canadian courts.

If indeed self-government is integrally related to Aboriginal title, and the Court has declined the opportunity to address self-government, then an examination of the Court's definition of Aboriginal title is the next logical step in this analysis. This examination must include the identification of the areas in which there is overlap with self-government. The Supreme Court defined Aboriginal title in the following way:

> Aboriginal title is a right in land and, as such, is more than the right to engage in specific activities which may be themselves Aboriginal rights. Rather, it confers the right to use land for a variety of activities, not all of which need be aspects of practices, customs and traditions which are integral to the distinctive cultures of Aboriginal societies. Those activities do not constitute the right *per se*; rather, they are parasitic on the underlying title. However, that range of uses is subject to the limitation that they must not be irreconcilable with the nature of the attachment to the land which forms the basis of the particular group's Aboriginal title. This inherent limit, to be explained more fully below, flows

from the definition of Aboriginal title as a *sui generis* interest in land, and is one way in which Aboriginal title is distinct from a fee simple. (1998:57)

The same requirements—"integral," "distinctive cultures"—that were troublesome in the *Sparrow* decision and were affirmed by subsequent cases such as the *Van der Peet* series of cases are again present in the *Delgamuukw* decision. A serious concern with respect to self-government must be whether the courts will be able to view self-government as integral to Aboriginal distinctiveness or if they will view this as incidental. If the "activity" is seen as incidental, then it acquires no constitutional protection.

There are several significant components of the Court's broad, preliminary definition of Aboriginal title. These are: "a right in land"; certain Aboriginal rights are "parasitic" on underlying title; the uses cannot "be irreconcilable" with Aboriginal title; and Aboriginal title is *sui generis* (and as such is distinct from fee simple). Kent McNeil summarizes the *Delgamuukw* findings as follows:

> The Supreme Court affirmed earlier characterizations of Aboriginal title as *sui generis*; that is, an interest in land that is in a class of its own. The fact that Aboriginal title cannot be sold or transferred is one aspect of the uniqueness. Another is the title's collective nature—it can only be held by a community of Aboriginal people, not by individuals. The source of Aboriginal title also distinguishes it from other land titles, which usually originate in Crown grants. Because the Aboriginal people were here before the Crown asserted sovereignty, their title is derived from the dual source of their prior occupation and their pre-existing systems of law. (1998:10)

The Court first notes that Aboriginal title is a right *in* land. This rejects, finally, the idea that Aboriginal uses of land are only personal and usufructory, such as the rights provided for in the 1888 decision in the *St Catherines* case, which allowed Aboriginal people to engage in activities on the land which were individual or personal. Those were rights *on* the land (or incidental to it), not *in* the land. It is clear from the two words, "in land," that the Supreme Court was providing that Aboriginal title is a property right in the tradition of Euro-Canadian common law. This of course is a positive aspect of the *Delgamuukw* judgment. However, I am concerned that this positive aspect not be used to cloud the other less helpful principles which the case presents. Again, the Court offers in flowing language a legal trinket to Aboriginal Peoples while at the same time subtly diminishing Aboriginal hopes and aspirations for an opportunity to co-exist in what is now known as Canada.

The Court also noted that some activities are parasitic on Aboriginal title but that those activities are not necessarily Aboriginal rights in and of themselves. Lamer said: "Aboriginal title ... is more than the right to engage in specific activities which may be themselves Aboriginal rights" (1998:57) (or may not be). Therefore, Aboriginal title is seen in this description to have a content that may be *different* from Aboriginal rights.

By describing Aboriginal title as *more* than Aboriginal rights, Lamer creates the illusion that he is adding something to the definition of Aboriginal title. The truth is that if Aboriginal title, which is not named in section 35(1), is more than (or outside of) Aboriginal rights, then it is not constitutionally protected. He also stated that Aboriginal title "confers the right to use land for a variety of activities, not all of which need be aspects of practices, customs and traditions which are integral to the distinctive cultures of Aboriginal societies" (1998:57). As previously explained, constitutional protection attaches only to rights that are integral (and not incidental) to distinctive Aboriginal cultures. What I fear is that Lamer was really articulating that not all aspects of Aboriginal title are constitutionally protected.

Later in the judgment Lamer opined:

> I addressed that question in *Adams*, where the Court had been presented with two radically different conceptions of this relationship. The first conceived of Aboriginal rights as being "inherently based in aboriginal title to the land," or as fragments of a broader claim to Aboriginal title. By implication, Aboriginal rights must rest either in a claim to title or the unextinguished remnants of title. Taken to its logical extreme, this suggests that Aboriginal title is merely the sum of a set of individual Aboriginal rights, and that it therefore has no independent content. However, I rejected this position for another—that Aboriginal title is "simply one manifestation of a broader-based conception of aboriginal rights." *Thus, although Aboriginal title is a species of Aboriginal right recognized and affirmed by s.35(1), it is distinct from other Aboriginal rights because it arises where the connection of a group with a piece of land "was of a central significance to their distinctive culture."* (1998:66–67, emphasis added)

This is difficult to reconcile with the previous finding that the rights are parasitic on underlying title, which infers that the source of Aboriginal rights is Aboriginal title. The confusion is likely the result of trying to force Aboriginal conceptions into linear legal frameworks, which can only operate to oversimplify Aboriginal knowledge about the relationship between territory and people (which is self-government in it's truest form). I understand that courts need to identify sources of Aboriginal rights because that is how that system works. What concerns me is the degree to which this forces constructions on Aboriginal (legal) relations which are not intrinsic in those cultures.

In discussing and defining Aboriginal title, Lamer did not fully separate the concept from that of Aboriginal rights. He stated:

> The picture that emerges from *Adams* is that the Aboriginal rights which are recognized and affirmed by s.35(1) fall along a spectrum with respect to their degree of connection with the land. At the one end, there are those Aboriginal rights which are practices, customs and traditions that are integral to the distinctive Aboriginal culture of the group claiming the right. However, the "occupation and use of the land" where the activity is taking place is not "sufficient to support a claim of title to the land." Nevertheless, those activities receive constitutional protection. In the middle there are activities which, out of necessity take place on land and indeed, might be intimately related to a particular piece of land. Although an Aboriginal group may not be able to demonstrate title to the land, it may nevertheless have a site-specific right to engage in a particular activity. (1997:67)

In this quotation it is clear that Lamer sees the demonstration of Aboriginal title to be more onerous than the demonstration of an existing Aboriginal right. What is not clear is whether any advantage attaches to securing the recognition that the "practice or activity" in question is sourced in Aboriginal title.

Undoubtedly Lamer's attempt to join Aboriginal rights and Aboriginal title was a well-intentioned effort to ensure that Aboriginal title is part of Canada's constitutional arrangements, that is, recognized and affirmed under section 35(1). It is worth noting that Aboriginal Peoples are the only people to have property rights recognized in the constitution (McNeil 1998:11). This raises the interesting question as to whether the title in Aboriginal title is equivalent to the title in Canadian law.[6]

The Court's attempt to connect Aboriginal title and Aboriginal rights raises another serious issue which does not seem to have been considered by the Court. Section 35(1) makes no mention of land or property. This is not surprising as "rights" in Canadian law are not generally connected to land. This is particularly true for what is known as civil liberties (and perhaps that suggests that Aboriginal rights are more than civil liberties). However, this alone should be a warning to Aboriginal people regarding the direction the Court has taken Aboriginal rights. It is one of the ways that the Court can be said to have demonstrated that Aboriginal rights are in fact truly *sui generis*. However, this *sui generis* construction of Aboriginal rights and Aboriginal title is not without issue:

> The *sui generis* concept is employed to discard those notions of the common law that have not been "sensitive to the Aboriginal perspective itself on the meaning of the rights at stake." As such, the doctrine can be characterized as part of the common law— that attempts to leave behind much of the common law. Such a selective invocation of the common law is a risk-laden speculation for Aboriginal Peoples. If they submit to even a part of the common law, it is inevitable that the other parts of this structure will continue to operate. A contextual shift in one doctrine does not mean that the accompanying legal blueprint will be redrafted to conform to the new principle. There is still an intricate system in place that supports the old design and architecture of the law. Since the past application of common law principles has restricted Aboriginal Peoples in the exercise of their original entitlements, its further use could represent the continuation of colonialism's design. (Borrows and Rotman 1997:26–27)

The fact that these rights (title or Aboriginal) are seen as self-government begs several questions: Whose concept of land is the Court relying upon? Is it the specific Aboriginal nation's understanding? Some collapsed pan-Aboriginal view? Or, of the most concern, a Euro-Canadian conceptualization?

In the Euro-Canadian view of land, control of territory is tied to the establishment and maintenance of sovereignty. Although Aboriginal Peoples maintain a close relationship with the land, and this is related to Aboriginal conceptions of sovereignty, it is not necessarily the same relationship Canadians understand. It is not about control of the land from my Aboriginal view. Earth is mother and she nurtures us all. If any hierarchy is attached to this view, it is the human race that is dependent on the earth and not vice versa. I remain concerned that the Court's efforts to tie Aboriginal rights to Aboriginal title is not just based on a desire to constitutionalize Aboriginal title. Further, a failure on the part of courts to get the relationship correct between title and rights, and therefore the constitution, will have vastly negative consequences for Aboriginal aspirations toward self-government.

I am cautious regarding the hopes that I will allow myself to attach to the ability of courts to advance Aboriginal aspirations of self-determination. This grows out of the degree to which being Kanien'kehaka or First Nation matters to me. It also attaches to the degree to which I see myself and my family as part of the First Nations' community (either at Grand River or Thunderchild). However, others are able to maintain a greater degree of optimism about the judicial process and decisions such as

Delgamuukw. Kent McNeil, a scholar (and friend) whom I hold in great esteem, concludes:

> But the Chief Justice did not stop there—he declared as well that the right Aboriginal Peoples have to use and occupy their lands is an exclusive right. This means that Aboriginal Peoples are not just free to determine for themselves what uses they will make of their lands; they also have as much right as any other landholder to prevent others—and this includes governments—from intruding on and using their lands without their consent. Indeed, they should have even greater protection against government intrusion than other landholders because their Aboriginal rights have been recognized and affirmed by the Constitution. (1998:11)

In my opinion, the clearest danger to Aboriginal understandings of our self-government responsibilities lies in the "inherent limit" on the "range of uses" such that the use cannot be "irreconcilable with the nature of the attachment to the land" (1998:62). The interesting question, and it is a question which directly impacts on self-government, is *who* has the ability to decide that the use is not irreconcilable with the attachment to the land? There is no obvious answer to this question and several possibilities. Is this an articulation of the self-governing powers of First Nations? Is it a power of the federal Crown? The provincial Crown? And if so, what is the source of that power? If it is a power of the federal (or provincial) Crown, it is absolutely likely that this power will interfere with Aboriginally defined beliefs about self-government and internal community control. Or perhaps Lamer was articulating on behalf of the courts a new role for judicial scrutiny. If so, this is a very unusual role for courts, who would normally shy away from a responsibility that is ongoing and indefinite.

It is helpful to look further at Lamer's comments regarding this limitation:

> one of the critical elements in the determination of whether a particular Aboriginal group has Aboriginal title to certain lands is the matter of the occupancy of those lands. Occupancy is determined by reference to the activities that have taken place on the land and the uses to which the land has been put by the particular group. If lands are so occupied, *there will exist a special bond* between the group and the land in question such that the land will be part of the definition of the group's distinctive culture. It seems to me that these elements of Aboriginal title create an inherent limitation on the uses to which the land, over which title exists, may be put. (1998:63, emphasis added)

In Lamer's view then, it is the distinctiveness of Aboriginal Peoples' relationship with the land that grounds Aboriginal title. This is an interesting way of looking at the situation and not unlike the test, in *Sparrow* and *Van der Peet*, for when Aboriginal rights will be constitutionally protected. The "special bond" only looks special when it is viewed from the Euro-Canadian notion of ownership or control over land. Juxtaposing this view against Aboriginal understandings of the relationship between nations and territories creates a dichotomy which may not be helpful in resolving the constitutional question. This is not the way the "bond" looks from an Aboriginal "perspective." It is clear that the manner in which the Supreme Court has sourced Aboriginal title in a "special bond" is a Eurocentric fallacy.

Lamer provided two examples of the scope and need for this limitation: if land is used as a hunting ground it cannot be strip mined; or if the land has ceremonial or cultural significance it cannot be paved as a parking lot (1998:63–64). Not only are these two examples extreme, they are not realistic. The simple fact is that threats to Aboriginal lands have not historically been internal but rather external (from commercial interests such as mining and lumber companies or hydroelectric development, or from governments). It was not Haudenosaunee people at Oka who attempted to build nine more holes of a golf course over a burial ground. Lamer's limitation and the need for such a limitation must be realistically and not sensationally justified. Kent McNeil notes a concern of a similar nature:

> isn't it paternalistic for the Supreme Court to impose restrictions on Aboriginal title in the interests of cultural preservation— which seems to be what this is all about—if the Aboriginal community in question does not want them? (1998:13)

The extreme nature of Lamer's examples contributes to the insult that Aboriginal people themselves would treat sacred lands in such a manner. Again, the real question, as McNeil identifies, is *who* gets to determine to what use Aboriginal-title lands could be put. The manner in which the Court has imagined this limitation rule may in fact mean that there is little advantage for Aboriginal nations to hold their lands as Aboriginal-title lands—as it may mean becoming subject to yet another level of regulation over internal decision making. As a result, it is possible *Delgamuukw* operates to further oppress Aboriginal decision making and community accountability (that is to say, self-government). This is an absolute interference with the independence of First Nations. That such an outcome could arise in litigation brought forward in good faith by Aboriginal people must serve as a caution of the loudest variety regarding the faith we put in Canadian courts.

This is not the only way that *Delgamuukw* attacks the internal sovereignty of First Nations. Lamer, while still discussing the limitation Aboriginal-title lands are subject to, stated:

> If Aboriginal Peoples wish to use their lands in a way that Aboriginal title does not permit, then they must surrender those lands and convert them into non-title lands to do so. (1998:64)

This comment is a one-liner of the nature discussed earlier in this book. What Lamer offers as guidance is actually a threat. It says to First Nations that we must be frozen in our traditions or run the risk of being seen as too "modern." If we are too modern or economically advanced, then we risk being divested of our lands.

If nothing else, this is another familiar stereotype. If Aboriginal people become too successful in the "white" world we are no longer viewed as Aboriginal. As Kent McNeil noted:

> If ... [Aboriginal Peoples] try to adapt to meet the changes in circumstances caused by European colonization, as they must to survive, their activities are no longer "Aboriginal" and so are not encompassed by their Aboriginal rights. According to ... [this] approach, then, the Aboriginal Peoples are denied the opportunity to develop contemporary ways of life within their own communities on the basis of their Aboriginal rights. If sustained, this approach will probably result in the disappearance of Aboriginal cultures which make those communities distinct. (1997:135)

This is another version of the Euro-Canadian superiority myth. The variance implicit in this rendering is that Aboriginal people aspire to whiteness. This is also a demonstration of the sophistication of colonial strategies in present times.

Despite the nobility of the effort to include Aboriginal title in the definition of Aboriginal rights, thereby constitutionally protecting title, a tremendous contradiction exists in this case. The constitution is Canada's supreme law. Yet if Lamer's reasoning regarding the limitation on Aboriginal issues in land is correct, two occurrences result. First, Aboriginal people are being encouraged in the name of economic development to opt out of hard won constitutional arrangements and protections. Surrendered lands are likely no longer legally Aboriginal-title lands and are therefore not constitutionally protected. This is an alternative that does not exist in the same form for any other individual or government in Canada. Second, if the federal government is able to introduce and enforce a statutory mechanism to ensure Lamer's limitation of use is respected, the federal government has the potential ability to unilaterally amend and alter section 35(1) rights. It appears that many of the encumbrances of Lamer's limitation test have not been considered in this backwards attempt to protect Aboriginal lands from intrusion.

Yet again, this is a familiar theme. Litigation in the area of Aboriginal rights and Aboriginal title proceeds without a grounding in a solid, coherent theory of the relationship between Aboriginal people and the state (which is really the essence of the problem with Aboriginal-rights litigation). Without the theory, the direction in which we are headed is unclear. It creates the opportunity to focus on limiting Aboriginal rights rather than enhancing those rights. This latter task should be the ambition of the Court, as constitutionally protected rights should be taken seriously.

In *Delgamuukw*, the Supreme Court of Canada clearly affirmed that Aboriginal title is of a *sui generis* nature. This simply means that these rights are not like any other rights. This conceptualization "of Aboriginal rights will respect the existence within Canada of two vastly different legal cultures, European and Aboriginal, and will incorporate both legal perspectives" (Borrows and Rotman 97:25). In *Van der Peet*, Aboriginal rights are characterized as "intersocietal law" (1996:199 quoting Slattery 1992:121–22 and discussed in Borrows and Rotman 1997:25). It is clear that the *sui generis* doctrine holds potential for the litigation of Aboriginal rights including Aboriginal title, however not without certain dangers. As W.I.C. Binnie notes:

> At least some of those who control the federal and provincial treasuries may welcome *Sparrow's* ringing affirmation of *sui generis* Aboriginal and treaty rights in terms of iron clad guarantees of mere economic subsistence. (1990:241)

This is one of the clear dangers.

The *sui generis* nature of Aboriginal rights allows courts to respect the source of Aboriginal rights as originating in Aboriginal legal systems, customs and practices. This is the potential. Canadian courts have now repeatedly recognized and respected the Aboriginal view of our difference as independence, but only with reference to the source of our difference. If Courts continue to limit the logical extension of this difference, it is unclear if the *sui generis* construction holds any more potential. If the right to our different legal systems is truly inherent then obviously there must be a way of protecting the exercise of this difference. To allow otherwise is to deny the right. To expect and accept less is to acknowledge that our colonization is complete.

As Borrows and Rotman enumerate:

> while the doctrine [*sui generis*] may avoid hammering the square pegs of indigenous laws into the round holes of conventional

legal categories, its use reinforces the larger common law system with all of its associated improprieties. (1997:28)

This paradox must be clear in our minds as it holds the potential either to offer a bridge away from colonialism (Borrows and Rotman 1997:28) *or* to recreate colonial relations which are disguised by judicial robes. It is not just Aboriginal people who have to vigorously guard these boundaries but Canadian courts as well. Therefore, the real potential of the theory of self-governing rights lies in the hands of the judiciary. As Borrows and Rotman conclude:

> The interpretation of *sui generis* rights without reference to clearer standards leaves judges with too much discretion, especially when most do not understand indigenous legal principles and perspectives. As such, the real extent of the protection afforded by descriptions of Aboriginal rights as *sui generis* may be rendered entirely dependent upon the goodwill of the judiciary. Being dependent on the goodwill of the judiciary is likely no better protection than being "dependent on the goodwill of the Sovereign." (1997:32–33)

This analysis provides two obvious conclusions. Lamer's characterization of Aboriginal title as *sui generis* is insufficient and does not provide clarity regarding the content of Aboriginal title. Second, this is the familiar vacuum of the lack of theoretical foundation for section 35(1) and the jurisprudence on Aboriginal rights. It is this lack of theoretical foundation which fosters the contradictory nature of many of the Supreme Court of Canada's judgments.

There is a positive thread to the decision rendered in *Delgamuukw*. One of the essential components of self-determination is a recognition of Aboriginal law-making powers, including enforcement. Lamer recognized that prior occupation is relevant "because Aboriginal title originates in part for pre-existing systems of Aboriginal law" (1998:63). On the same point, later in the judgment, Lamer observed "the source of Aboriginal title appears to be grounded both in the common law and in the aboriginal perspective on land; the latter includes, but is not limited to, their systems of law" (1998:70). This recognition of Aboriginal systems of law affirms an essential aspect of self-government. These comments are the first significant and central acknowledgments by the highest Canadian court that Aboriginal Peoples did in fact have law. However, this recognition sits in the air within this judgment and is not directly related to any legal analysis of the right to self-government. It is a useful pronouncement but clearly not determinative of the question regarding the relationship between Aboriginal rights and self-government. This follows the familiar pattern of flowing rights language which casts little real light in terms of the content or exercise of the Aboriginal right at stake.

The meaning the Court ascribes to Aboriginal title is a mischaracterization of Aboriginal traditions. The Court suggests that irreconcilable uses "terminate" the continuity of the relationship with the land. It is important to remember the Court chose extreme examples of such uses, most likely for the purpose of insulating its creation of yet another limit on Aboriginal lives from criticism. This misinformed idea of continuity is being elevated to the level of legal doctrine, as it appears in a number of cases, including *Adams, Cote, Gladstone, N.T.C. Smokehouse,* and *Van der Peet,* which are all Lamer judgments. However, this doctrine is clearly Euro-Canadian based and shows no recognition of the fact that cultures and peoples change. This doctrine of continuity runs contrary to the *Sparrow* finding that Aboriginal rights shall be "affirmed in a contemporary form rather than in their primeval simplicity and vigour" (1990:171). If land is put to non-traditional uses (and building schools, roads, sewers and so on may not be seen as traditional uses), this may (or may not) in fact represent a change in cultural values. To propose and enforce such a test creates an opportunity for the Crown to use the courts to interfere with the local decision making process. It is the epitome of colonial relations as it vests the power outside of the community.

In *Sparrow*, it was demonstrated how the fiduciary relationship, supposedly a duty owed to the Indians, was used to potentially limit Aboriginal rights. It appears that the continuous relationship that Aboriginal Peoples have had with the land, which is the source not the character of the right, according to the Court, also flips the logical understanding of the relationship of continuity.

The diminishing of the solemn nature of the constitutional commitments to Aboriginal Peoples has been recognized by other scholars. Kent McNeil notes:

> in decisions since *Sparrow* the Supreme Court has watered down the protection accorded to Aboriginal rights to such an extent that, in my opinion, their constitutional status has been seriously undermined. It seemed clear from *Sparrow* that Aboriginal rights can only be overridden in exceptional circumstances, as one would expect where constitutional rights are concerned, and then only by means of or pursuant to legislation. (1998:17)

This solemn commitment is not the standard that Lamer established in *Delgamuukw,* and this is cause for concern:

> The general principles governing justification laid down in *Sparrow,* and embellished by *Gladstone,* operate with respect to in-

fringements of Aboriginal title. In the wake of *Gladstone*, the range of legislative objectives that can justify the infringement of Aboriginal title is fairly broad. *Most of these objectives can be traced to the reconciliation of the prior occupation of North America by Aboriginal Peoples with the assertion of Crown sovereignty*, which entails the recognition that "distinctive aboriginal societies exist within, and are a part of, a broader social, political and economic community." In my opinion, the development of agriculture, forestry, mining, and hydroelectric power, the general economic development of the interior of British Columbia, protection of the environment or endangered species, the building of infrastructure and the settlement of foreign populations to support those aims, are the kinds of objectives that are consistent with this purpose and, in principle, can justify the infringement of Aboriginal title. Whether a particular measure or government act can be explained by reference to one of those objectives, however, is ultimately a question of fact that will have to be examined on a case-by-case basis. (1998:78, emphasis added)

Lamer sees the solemn commitment as a reconciliation that requires Aboriginal people and Aboriginal nations to do the changing.

The question is then: What does this all mean in real terms regarding the rights of Aboriginal Peoples? It seems to me that what the Supreme Court is clearly saying is that it accepts that colonialism has been a vibrant and justified practice in the history of Canada. Further, because colonial practices (such as the taking of land to further hydroelectric development) enhance economic interests, then colonial practices can be overlooked. In other words, the ends justify the means. How the Court reconciles this with the *Sparrow* comments: "We cannot recount with much pride the treatment accorded to the native people of this country" (1990:177) remains a mystery.

I am also troubled by the fact that *Delgamuukw* was returned for trial. As a lawyer, I understand the procedural reasons for this. As an Indian person, I am horrified by the disrespect to the Elders. And in this returning to trial, another pattern emerges. *Sparrow, Gladstone* and *Blueberry Indian Band,* all of which are major Supreme Court of Canada decisions in the last few years, were all returned to trial. This does not resolve issues, despite all the flowing "rights" talk in the cases. In practical terms, the decisions mean little. Aboriginal people cannot turn to the courts with a certainty that our rights will be protected. And it is my experience that this is the essence of why Aboriginal Peoples turned to the courts in the first place.

Delgamuukw allows Aboriginal people the opportunity to sit back and consider how realistic our expectations of the Supreme Court are. I am not encouraged by the decision. It is clear that the Court has no difficulty in stepping over Aboriginal "perspectives" (as it calls them) if it is of benefit to the Crown's assertion of sovereignty. In other words, the Court expects Aboriginal people to change while Canadian federation has the right to remain the same, even when that interferes with Aboriginal people's rights—rights which are constitutionally protected. This clearly was not the intention of section 35(1). However, it is the consequence of section 35(1), after the Supreme Court has attached meaning to it.

I do not think this necessarily means that Aboriginal people should stop litigating. I do believe the courts can still be proactively used. However, Aboriginal people must take care to understand that claims to specific rights, such as hunting and fishing, may not be the most effective way to force the Supreme Court to advance Aboriginal rights. It appears that litigation framed around Aboriginal title may in fact be even more dangerous to Aboriginal interests. It seems that the practice of the Court is to give with one hand and take with the other. This is the familiar forked tongue of colonialism. As Aboriginal people have developed out of necessity a number of skills to deal with colonialism, some positive, some negative, I have confidence that the people have the knowledge and experience necessary to transgress the obstacles that the Supreme Court has aspired to mount in our path. However, this confidence is based on the need for Aboriginal people to understand that in the Canadian system law, justice and fairness are not "kissing cousins." Aboriginal communities need to be truly in control of their litigation efforts, and this requires community control over the decision making. The formal and technical legal decisions must be accessible to community members. It is clear that in many instances this has yet to occur. It requires a commitment from anyone representing Aboriginal communities to practice law in a different way than we were trained.

What is common between the decisions in *Sparrow* and *Delgamuukw* is the fact that the Supreme Court of Canada has used the opportunity to define Aboriginal rights as another occasion to introduce new limitations on the content and exercise of those rights. These limitations were not negotiated with Aboriginal Peoples and therefore share in common with other colonial experiences the quality of forcing rules, practices and ideas on Aboriginal nations. It is not just these two cases which erect colonial barriers that deny expression of self-determining relationships. Russel Barsh and Youngblood Henderson conclude after examining a number of recent Supreme Court cases:

> If all the hurdles announced by *Sparrow*, *Van der Peet* and *Gladstone* are assembled, they form a formidable and intimidating barrier: The Aboriginal practice at issue must be shown to be pre-existing and central; it must be shown never to have been extinguished by

the crown prior to 1982; it must have been infringed by government action after 1982; the government action must be shown to have lacked adequate justification; and it must be shown to go beyond the reasonable discretion enjoyed by the Crown as a "fiduciary" to determine whether the Aboriginal community concerned has been given an adequate "priority" in the enjoyment of the resources it has traditionally utilized. All of this translates into a heavier evidentiary burden at trial, more expense, and greater risk of an adverse ruling, amounting to a present-day extinguishment of the rights asserted. (1997:1004)

Section 35(1) might have had its successes but it has yet to live up to its promises. The way Lamer creates the balance between Aboriginal perspectives and Canadian sovereignty cuts the promise to almost nothing. Colonialism has not changed, just shifted, and it is now wearing judicial robes of respect for "perspective."

Notes

1. I have had the good fortune to be a member of the Assembly of First Nations' *Delgamuukw* Nation Review Research Group. This group is comprised of John Borrows, Frank Cassidy, Joanne Lysyk, Kent McNeil, Candice S. Metallic, Maria Morellato, Anita Gordon Murdoch, and Chris Robertson. This dynamic group has been a profound influence on my thoughts on the *Delgamuukw* case. Where possible I will attribute ideas to those who originated them.
2. In this chapter, I defer to the language of self-government as this is the language the Court used. It is not the language I prefer.
3. My friend and editor, Brenda Conroy, pointed out to me that the tenses in the quote were a little odd. Because she drew my attention to the verb tenses, I noticed that the one describing Aboriginal jurisdiction was future tense. I believe this subtly demonstrates the difficulty that the trial judge was having imagining that Aboriginal jurisdiction presently exists.
4. See also the discussion in Charles Wilkinson 1987:55–56 and John Borrows 1994:33–34.
5. Several other scholars have suggested such an interpretation, including Asch and Macklem (1991: 509–510), Barsh and Henderson (1997: 999) and McNeil (1993:111).
6. In a June 1999 conference call of the *Delgamuukw* Nation Review Research Committee, Kent McNeil suggested that the use of title is in fact different. The Court appears to mean "interest" when discussing Aboriginal title.

Chapter Six

Lessons In Rights Discourse
Charter Challenges
And Aboriginal Sovereignty

Rights philosophy and law in Canada[1] are now based in a liberal individualist ideology. It is the particular form of the individualist philosophy that is most difficult for me as an Aboriginal person (and as an Aboriginal woman) to accept. The judiciary and Canadian lawmakers envision two principle categories of rights: rights of individuals and rights of groups. Bryan Swartz notes: "Every person is inherently equal in legal dignity with every other. No special personal or ethnic history is necessary to entitle a person to equal respect from the state. The individual is to be free from restrictions in defining and pursuing his or her own ends in life...." (1986:1). From my point of view as an Aboriginal person, the legacy of taken lands, residential schools and child welfare practices are clear indications that, at least with respect to Aboriginal people domiciled in what is now known as Canada, law has not lived up to this vision.

Individual rights (obviously rights that belong to a single person) when bundled together are rights that can be best described as group rights. Examples of the need to bundle individual rights into a package called group rights are language rights and religious rights. The right to speak French (or Cree or Mohawk or any other Aboriginal language)[2] in an anglophone dominated state is utterly meaningless if it is understood only as an individual right. To be meaningful, the right to speak your own language must be exercised in combination with other individuals (the group). All people. including Aboriginal people, can and do hold both individual and group rights and in some circumstances choose to exercise those rights. There is a right to individual self-autonomy, which includes the right to live free of violence (physical, spiritual and emotional). As already mentioned, language rights also accrue to individual Aboriginal people as members of groups of Aboriginal people. This characterization of legal rights that Canada has adopted is not complete, but is, in fact, both overly and unnecessarily narrow.

Aboriginal people, when asserting their rights to political autonomy as nations (note, not states), most frequently borrow the language of collective rights. The problem with use of an ethnocentric language to express Aboriginal visions cannot be minimized; it is the central definitional problem discussed in chapters one and two. Collective rights are similar to group rights in the fact that to be meaningful they must be held by an identifiable group of individuals together. Despite this similarity in the numerical parameters of group and collective rights, these two categories of rights are not equivalents. Collective rights firstly belong to Aboriginal Peoples because of our distinct relationships with the territory that has become the Canadian state. Aboriginal Peoples rely on this notion to protect the exercise of rights which are unique to the way we order and organize our nations, communities, clans and families. Douglas Sanders provides this succinct description of the difference between group and collective:

> Groups that have goals that transcend the ending of discrimination against their members can be called collectivities, for their members are joined together not simply by external discrimination but by an *internal cohesiveness*. Collectivities seek to protect and develop their own particular cultural characteristics. (1991:369)

Collective rights are asserted by Aboriginal Peoples when we seek to protect our rights as nations (our internal cohesiveness) including but not limited to the right to cultural survival.

Canadian courts have had a very difficult time trying to conceptualize rights that are not individual or group based. This is one of the obstacles that Aboriginal people face in the Canadian Court system. It is an instrument of colonialism which we have not been able to banish from our lives. In the *Ontario Education Reference* the Supreme Court commented:

> Collective *or* group rights, such as those concerning languages and those concerning certain denominations of separate schools, are asserted by individuals or groups of individuals because of their membership in the protected group. *Individual rights are asserted equally by everyone despite membership in certain ascertainable groups.* To that extent, they are an exception from the equality rights provided to everyone. (1987:27, emphasis added)

Not only does the Supreme Court wrongly equate collective and group rights, its analysis of individual rights is also questionable. Group rights are seen as an exception to the principle that every individual shall be equally protected or treated in the same manner. In this particular case, the court fails to understand that treating unequals equally can result in discrimination.[3] This challenge to define equality in a meaningful way is the current "groove" the Court continues to revolve in.

In *R. v. Sundown*, the treaty right to hunt is described as a collective right of "the band as a whole and not to Mr. Sundown or any individual member of the Joseph Bighead First Nation" (1999:301). This division of individual and collective Aboriginal or treaty rights such that they are distinct and separate is troubling. It defies the Aboriginal understanding of rights. Not only is the separation of the individual from the collective unnecessary, it is also illogical. Individuals are the collective and the collective is the cumulative history, culture, governance traditions, ceremony and language of the people. This is not necessarily a right of the community but a right that flows around the individuals.

It is not a necessary fact of adjudication that rights need be characterized in a way that diminishes the unique qualities of collective rights. O'Sullivan J., in dissent in the Manitoba Métis land litigation case, in the first express reference to the rights of peoples that I am familiar with in Canadian case law, stated:

> Lawyers trained in the British tradition tend to look on rights as either private or public. If private, they must be asserted by persons who claim a property interest in the rights. If public, the rights must be asserted by an Attorney General or on the relation of the Attorney General. In extraordinary cases, it is conceded that individual persons may be granted special status to assert public rights...
>
> ... It was accepted that any individual who asserts a claim in himself, and who can show a claim of title or right of inheritance, may be able to secure relief by suing on his own behalf *but it is disputed whether anyone is capable of asserting in our municipal courts rights belonging to a people.*

It is difficult for common lawyers to understand what the rights of "a people" can mean. Indeed, at a hearing before a parliamentary committee on the 1987 Constitution Accord (of Meech Lake) held August 27, 1987, the distinguished constitutional expert, the Right Honourable Pierre Elliott Trudeau said:

> In my philosophy, the community, an institution itself, has no rights. It has right by delegation from the individuals. You give equality to the individuals. Then they will organize in societies to make sure those rights are respected.

This is an approach with deep roots in the British tradition...

But, as far as I can see, what we have before us in court at this time is not the assertion of bundles of individual rights but the assertion of the rights and status of the half-breed people of the western plains. (1988:47–48)

Rights in Canadian law do not necessarily include or reflect the understandings that Aboriginal Peoples have about our position in Canadian society. The mere acknowledgment of Aboriginal difference does not accomplish much unless it is accompanied by a legal acknowledgment, such as the one O'Sullivan provided, that the structure of existing legal relationships and concepts must evolve in a way that embraces and willingly includes this difference. This is not a departure from Canadian legal values about the equality of all peoples because equality is not about treating all individuals or peoples in the same way—(as the Supreme Court of Canada in fact acknowledged in *Andrews* (1989).

Kathleen Lahey points out that rights of anti-discrimination evolve from a system that was based on hierarchy in that it excluded some people from holding political rights (women, Aboriginal people and other racialized minorities).[4] As Lahey notes:

> As I read the history of the "Persons" case[5] in Canada and the history of constitutional and statutory human rights guarantees elsewhere, the original purposes of all human rights provisions have been quite simple: to nullify the age-old "civil incapacities" or "legal disabilities" that have been used to control and disadvantage selected groups throughout legal history. I have concluded that until human rights codes, international covenants, and Charter equality guarantees expressly give effect to this purpose, the roots of legal discrimination, which run much more deeply in Canadian jurisprudence than the roots of the "living tree" will remain beyond the reach of the legal system. (1998:403)

Furthermore, Professor Lahey suggests that the "concept of 'constitutional personhood' is still in the process of emerging in human rights discourse" (1998:403). Because equality as a concept is required to contradict and dispose hierarchy, in an oppositional way it really in fact operates to entrench that hierarchy and those beliefs. One definition of equality is therefore the eradication of rights assigned through any form of hierarchy. Equality, in such a system, is absence not presence. It is this ideological framework that predisposes an unfavourable outcome when Aboriginal people utilize rights discourse to advance our claims to difference. This can be seen in a number of the legal decisions which articulate meaning to the phrase "Aboriginal rights." In *Delgamuukw*, it means a right to self-government and not to jurisdiction. It means the right to *sui generis* legal status (which translated means relegated to the unending position of "other"). This ideological problem in rights discourse demonstrates the degree to which a culturally informed theory of Aboriginal rights is essential to securing just resolutions to Aboriginal claims in Canadian courts.

What is judicially required[6] is a third vision of the Canadian state, one which is open to the inclusion of Aboriginal Peoples and our understanding of how the universe is ordered. Rights as a construct is just one practical example of the reasons why Aboriginal people are repeatedly excluded from the institutions and benefits of Canadian society. I am not suggesting that the two worldviews are fundamentally and diametrically opposed, merely that Aboriginal people have not chosen to relinquish their distinct ways of being.

The notion of collective rights is not in and of itself sufficient to fully reflect Aboriginal traditions. Individual rights are embedded in the collective. The best parallel I know is what Elders have explained to me: it is self-disciplined (or in other words self-governing) individuals who ensure that self-determination is in fact a political reality. Self-determination is not possible without a society where the people understand what it means to be responsible (in an Aboriginal sense) concurrently to themselves, their communities and their nations. Courts have tended to understand individual and collective rights as capable of linear interpretations and conceptualizations. This misses the cumulative value of individual and collective rights which is identifiable when the thought processes are Aboriginally defined. As long as courts remain preoccupied with linear rights dialogue, then the potential to reach an inclusive theory of rights (including Aboriginal rights) will be illusive.

At least one Aboriginal scholar has suggested that individual-rights philosophies have benefitted discussions about Aboriginal rights, in particular the right to self-determination. John Borrows suggests in his analysis of recent cases on the political rights of Aboriginal women that:

> The ideology of the *Charter* stood as a backdrop in the development of this discourse and subtly helped to strengthen claims for equality. Tradition was brought forward, and its concepts were draped around the contemporary language of rights. The dialectical interaction of traditional practices and modern precepts forged a language that partook of two worlds. Rights talk could not overwhelm traditional convictions of symmetry in gender relationships while tradition could not ignore current concerns about equality in these same associations. Each discourse partook of the other and created an exchange of legitimacy. People who were concerned about their traditions could use the language of equality to preserve their interests, while people who sought for equality could use tradition to show that it sanctioned and justified the removal of gender discrimination. (1994:31)

Granted, the two dialogues, tradition and rights, may have begun to inform each other. However, without factoring domination into the analysis the conclusion might be misleading. Aboriginal people adopt rights talk as a conscious strategy to defend against our continued colonization and dispossession by the Canadian state. At the same time, Aboriginal people must assess if it is a strategy that is working for us. This assessment is an essential element of the "dialectical interaction" between Aboriginal Peoples and the Canadian legal system if representation of Aboriginal voices is to be taken seriously.

The commitments that must be made by Aboriginal Peoples and the Canadian state, including legal institutions, are further complicated by the need to also factor gender into the equation. In my experience this need is *not* prefaced in Aboriginal cultures and traditions but in the interaction of those ways with the Canadian state (in other words, patriarchy is a process that has been a fundamental part of the colonial legacy in Canada). Sherene Raczack demonstrates that this incorporation is a struggle:

> When women from non-dominant groups talk about culture, we are often heard to be articulating a false dichotomy between culture and gender; in articulating our difference, we inadvertently also confirm our relegation to the margins. Culture talk is clearly a double-edged sword. It packages difference as inferiority and obscures both gender-based and racial domination, yet cultural considerations are important for contextualizing oppressed groups' claims for justice, for improving their access to services, and for requiring dominant groups to examine the invisible cultural advantages they enjoy. (1998:58)

And with specific reference to Aboriginal women, Raczack notes:

> Aboriginal women's need to talk about culture in spite of these risks emerges out of different histories and present-day realities. Aboriginal women often confront sexual violence, beginning in residential schools. Harsh socioeconomic realities have followed the uprooting and displacement of Aboriginal peoples. The continued denial of Aboriginal sovereignty and the Canadian government's consistent refusal to honour treaties and resolve land claims maintain these profound injustices. These historical specificities mark an important difference between Aboriginal women and women of colour. While the cultures of women of colour are inferiorized whenever male violence in their communities is discussed, for Aboriginal women, their claim to existence as a community is itself imperiled. These important differences, notwithstanding, what I would suggest Aboriginal women and women of

> colour share *is the fact that we are both required to talk about culture and violence within the context of white supremacy, a context in which racism and sexism and their intersections are denied.* (1998:59, emphasis added)

It is this examination of the intersections that illuminates the way in which rights discourse can be a discourse of continued oppression (when equality is defined as sameness which is the counter position to hierarchy) rather than a path of freedom and independence.

I would never dispute that abuse—physical, psychological and sexual—of women and children in many Aboriginal communities does occur (as is also the case in Canadian society). Neither would I dispute that the treatment of Indian women by Indian men in some communities has been deplorable, especially around the issue of membership.[7] However, at a minimum, the abuse and treatment long suffered by Aboriginal women and our children is dissimilar to that suffered by Canadian women and children as the responsibility rests more absolutely at the foot of the federal *Indian Act* regime, as well as in criminal justice, child welfare and residential school experiences. Only a portion of the abuse has come from Aboriginal men, and only in recent times. Our men as well have not been insulated from abuse. Male children of women who "married out" were disenfranchised alongside their mothers. Indian men along with Indian women were defined in legislation as not being persons.[8] It is a senseless endeavour to try and characterize any of the forms of abuse that Aboriginal women and men have survived as worse than other forms. Abuse in Indian communities is not necessarily or always gender specific. Abuse is abuse. It is wrong. There is no dispute.

It is important to note that I am separating issues of violence against women in its physical forms and the systematic state violence done to the individual women who were disenfranchised. This is not the same phenomenon and nothing is gained (except for sympathy) by muddling the two experiences. Sympathetic responses to the violence that Aboriginal women currently survive in Canadian society will not change the fact that for many of us this is our predominant life experience. Speaking in clear terms about the kinds of violence that have been done to us is a responsibility that First Nations women must begin to assume.

The Canadian legal legacy that purports to share with Aboriginal people the granting of individualized equality rights is not a long one. In 1974, the Supreme Court of Canada handed down its decision in the *Lavell and Bedard* case.[9] Much has been written about this notorious decision and the exclusionary membership provisions of the *Indian Act*.[10] It was the first case to bring the discriminatory membership provisions applied to Indian women[11] since at least 1876 to national (and international) attention.[12] Five of the nine justices found that the stripping away of an Indian woman's status or right to be registered as an Indian under the *Indian Act* upon marriage did not violate the non-discrimination guarantees of the *Canadian Bill of Rights*.[13]

Ritchie J. applied the rule of law in such a manner that it limited the equality rights set out in the *Canadian Bill of Rights*. This rule, which Ritchie purported guaranteed only formal equality (that is equality as sameness), was applied so that the protections of equality before the law and the equal protection of the law were very narrowly defined. As Indian women were the group allegedly discriminated against, the two categories of comparison created by the courts were all women and all Indians. Against these two reference groups, no discrimination had occurred because all women were not discriminated against, only Indian women, and all Indians were not discriminated against, only Indian women. The result was, therefore, a finding that double discrimination amounted to no legal discrimination. Two lessons must be learned from this case. The reference groups chosen are essential components of the legal decision making process. As well, the rule of law is highlighted as a principle that Aboriginal nations must continue to be concerned with.[14]

The groupings in the *Lavell and Bedard* case (all women, all Indians) reflect the way courts saw (and see) rights of equality (or non-discrimination) as belonging to individuals. For Indian people the right to reside on the reserve *with other Indian people* and thereby have increased access to culture, tradition, ceremony, governance and language is not merely an individual right. This right is more fundamentally characterized as a collective right. It is the obscuring of the collective nature of the right that precipitated the court's ability to disappear the wrong that the *Indian Act* forced on Indian women.

Many times I have heard that the successful overturning of section 12(1)(b) was a great victory for women and Indian women. It is used as evidence of the positive nature of the interaction between Indian women and other Canadian women's groups (such as the National Action Committee for one example). This is not how I experience the legacy of 1985 and Bill C-31. Indian people now have a new membership and status system, one which continues to contain gender inequalities. The system still denies Indian women who marry out the right to register their grandchildren. Indian men who marry out do not suffer this same encumbrance (because their wives acquire Indian status, that is, they become legal Indians).[15]

A second example arises in the gaps within the legislation. Illegitimate girl children cannot be registered at local Indian Affairs offices as their registration is not automatic. These applications must be forwarded to Ottawa and I have heard that this process takes appropriately ten months. After the decision in *Martin* v. *Chapman* (1983) boy children can be registered locally. This is the description that appears in the Registration Manual of the Department of Indian Affairs:

> John Martin, the illegitimate son of a Non-Indian mother and
> Indian father, was denied membership in his father's band. At that
> time, the Registrar stated that he did not qualify under section
> 11(1)(c) on the grounds that it applied only to legitimate male
> children of male Indians.
>
> John Martin appealed the Registrar's decision to the courts.
> The Supreme Court ruled in John Martin's favour, stating that
> Indian status depends on proof of descent through the Indian
> male line and not on whether a child is legitimate or not. As a
> result of this decision, *all male children of entitled Indian males*
> *were eligible for registration whether they were legitimate or not.*
> (Unknown:2–12, emphasis added)

The gender inequality is just the tiniest factor in my list of grievances
with the 1985 *Indian Act* amendments. It is now more difficult to register
your children through the application of section 6(2) as the second generation cut-off is also future looking. Now all children of Indian/non-
Indian parentage receive a limited form of status which they cannot pass
on to their children. This causes a pressure toward a diminishing of the
registered Indian population in Canada. Whether intentional or not, the
gender equality amendment offered the federal government the opportunity to limit its future obligations to Indian people by limiting the number
of people who qualify for benefits (thus eradicating a certain amount of
the "Indian problem"). The government took it! Further, the separation of
status and band membership provided for in the amendments creates a
more complicated system to negotiate to secure registration for your
children. It is possible to be on the "status" list maintained by the Department and not be a band member (if the community has control of membership by virtue of a membership code under section 10). Being registered
(having status) is simply not enough as, without membership, there is no
guarantee that you can access any "special" rights, such as residing on the
reserve. This separation also operates to exclude even more Indian people
from benefits under the *Indian Act*.

The consequences of separating status from band membership are
seen acutely in the *Jacobs* decision *Peter and Trudy Jacobs* v. *Mohawk*
Council of Kahnawake 1998, first heard by a Canadian Human Rights
tribunal in 1995, with hearings that extended into 1996, 1997 and finally
1998. In this case Peter Jacobs, who after adoption was raised by Mohawk
parents, had his name removed from the band membership list when he
turned twenty-one.[16] This occurred despite the fact he was raised in the
community and spoke the language. His name still remains in the Indian
register in Ottawa (1998: paragraph 16). Peter married Trudy (who was

also a member of Kahnawake) in 1986 (1998: paragraph 11), and the *Indian Act* effective at that time did not strip women of their status for marrying out. However, Trudy was stripped of her status under the Mohawk Council of Kahnawake's membership code. This sounds very much like a re-enactment of section 12(1)(b) and not Mohawk laws (which are matrilineal and Trudy is the daughter of a Mohawk mother (1998: paragraph 11). Despite the fact that both partners of this couple were raised in the community and resided on reserve, they were systematically denied a number of services by the Band Council. Although I am sympathetic to the Council's position that there is a need to protect Mohawk culture, I am not convinced that this is what occurs by virtue of the operation of its membership laws. What I realized after reading the *Jacobs* decision is the amount of cunning it will require to weed the colonial roots out of what we now live as tradition. This task must be a community responsibility.

The disastrous results of the decision in *Lavell and Bedard* are still felt in Indian communities today whenever the issue of rights is discussed (and the *Jacobs* decision is but one example of the disconnections section 12(1)(b) has brought into our communities). The publicity surrounding the case highlighted the differences in political opinion held by groups of Indian women[17] and organizations that are represented as dominated by Indian men. In truth, the opinions on how to correct the gender discrimination in section 12(1)(b) do not neatly align into male and female camps (for one thing, Indian men who are the children of Indian women who were stricken from band lists are equally affected). In fact, most Indian people have always been in agreement on the need to remove the discriminatory provisions. In my experience, the views which led to the litigation in the *Sawridge* (Twinn 1986) case, which challenges women's entitlement to re-registration, are minority views in Indian communities.

The difference in opinion arises around the question of how to best achieve the result of gender equality in the membership provisions. Nonetheless, the artificial gender lines drawn by those outside the culture have surfaced in national debates ever since. The court is accountable for the flawed reasoning in *Lavell and Bedard* but in many circumstances this culpability has been transferred to Indian men. This familiar pattern was discussed in chapter three; responsibility does not always accrue to the party where it is warranted. Here, the lawmakers who created section 12(1)(b), (those who for decades before any national Indian political voices or organizations existed refused to see it removed), and the courts ought to carry the responsibility for the damage done in our communities. Even within our communities, the perspective on who has direct responsibility has become distorted (and that is confirmation of the degree to which we have swallowed colonialism).

Following the latest round of sizzling gender politics in Aboriginal communities, one Indian man notes the consequences of advocating a construction of gender politics that is polarized between men and women:

> A posture which recognizes, supports and promotes positive con-
> tributions from First Nations men does not excuse those who
> exercise oppressive authority, but it does require that people
> avoid making statements *that overreach merely to sustain their*
> *position.* There is a great temptation to make these expansive
> statements because they seem to make the point of sexism stand
> out in greater relief. I would argue *that such over-broad state-*
> *ments are dishonest and separate the person from the community*
> *and disconnect the individuals in the community from each other.*
> There is room in both law and politics for making interpretations
> of rights that do not have these adverse effects. Equality rights do
> not have to be applied to mean sameness. Individual and collec-
> tive rights do not have to be dichotomized. (Borrows 1994:47,
> emphasis added)

These overreaching statements are often cloaked attempts to garner sympathy for the levels of violence that Aboriginal women face, with hopes to
transfer that sympathy to another political position, which may or may not
have popular support among Aboriginal women. The continued muddling
of our experiences as a singular experience of oppression at the hands of
Indian men has created a direct and visible obstacle for Indian people (and
especially Indian women) to dismantle. The issue of violence in our
communities, violence primarily but not absolutely directed at women
and children as demonstrated by suicide statistics (violence toward self),
criminal charges of assault (often violence among men), and drug and
alcohol abuse (again self violence), is woven into an Aboriginally defined
rights talk. This is so because Aboriginal people seek to end the violence
we are presently surviving and this is one of several key factors that
motivates the quest for greater self-determination.

Two recent Supreme Court of Canada decisions are worthy of note
because they allow an opportunity to determine if the Supreme Court is
today better able to deal with issues of so-called double discrimination
than they were when *Lavell and Bedard* was handed down. In *Corbiere,*
voting rights in Band Council elections were extend to band members
living off-reserve. This distinction, on- or off-reserve, has long been a
source of division in Indian communities. Only on-reserve band members
are entitled to the majority of *Indian Act* "rights," including in most cases
the right to vote in Band Council elections. As Indian reserves are colonial
creations not Indian ones, I am pleased to see the distinction successfully
challenged.

As seen in previous case discussions, *Corbiere* (1999) too is really
not cause for celebration. Yes, the decision does provide some evidence

that the highest Canadian court is dealing with issues of intersectionality in a better way. However, one of the possible consequences of *Corbiere's* granting of voting rights to off-reserve residents[18] is that, with the greater trend toward urbanization, community residents could be denied control over their community. The most troubling consequence could be that individuals with no significant relationship with the community or the land could control the decision making, including, for example, in a decision to sell off the land or take a modern treaty "deal" that purports to absolutely extinguish all Aboriginal rights. In effect, it is like creating a political system where residents of Toronto will govern the city of Montreal (except for the fact that First Nations urbanization is more diverse and not necessarily coalesced in a single city).

The reasons of the Court for coming to the conclusion that off-reserve band members, by being denied the vote, had suffered a *Charter* violation under section 15 is worth examining. The ground was "race and place of residence" (1999: paragraph 62) or "Aboriginality-residence" (1999: paragraph 10). This demonstrates that the Supreme Court, unlike in the Indian/gender cases such as *Lavell and Bedard*, was finally able to get itself around the idea of intersectionality. This is the first scant evidence that the *Charter* may be of assistance in removing (or controlling) the amount of colonial damage that the *Indian Act* regime forces on Indian nations.

The second recent case that is informative is *Gladue* (April 1999, Court File No. 26300). Ms. Gladue was charged with second degree murder for the killing of her common-law partner. She pled guilty to a charge of manslaughter. At sentencing, the trial judge raised the issue of section 718.2(e) of the *Criminal Code*. This recent amendment recognizes that Canada has developed sentencing patterns that over-rely on incarceration. This section states: All available sanctions other than imprisonment that are reasonable in the circumstances should be considered for all offenders, *with particular attention to the circumstances of Aboriginal offenders*. The appeal of Ms. Gladue's sentence and the judge's reliance on section 718.2(e) took this matter all the way to the Supreme Court of Canada.

I sincerely applaud the Supreme Court's efforts to bring attention to and offer a solution to the over-representation of Aboriginal people in the Canadian criminal justice system. However, Ms. Gladue was charged with killing her male partner, and there was some evidence the relationship was a violent one (paragraphs 3, 5 and 9). Yet, the Supreme Court barely acknowledges the power relations across genders. The situation of Ms. Gladue as a woman was disappeared throughout almost the entire decision. The fact of Aboriginal over-representation is a reality that directly affects men's lives as they are incarcerated in greater numbers. The gender based violence Ms. Gladue responded to with her own violence is an important reality that should have caused the Supreme Court to stop and more fully acknowledge the context of this sentencing case. This is a caution that perhaps the Court has not fully got its mind around intersectionality—at least not so far as gender is concerned.

Four cases were heard by the federal courts and the Supreme Court of Canada in 1992, during the height of the "Charlottetown Round," of constitutional talks which examined the right of the Native Women's Association of Canada (NWAC) to participate in the constitutional renovation process with the other four designated Aboriginal groups—the Inuit Tapirisat (ITC), the Métis National Council (MNC), the Native Council of Canada (NCC), and the Assembly of First Nations (AFN).[19] At the centre of the dispute between the Association and the Queen, was the issue of equal funding to participate in the constitutional process.

In a discussion tracing the history of Aboriginal rights which also assesses the current state of Canadian law, an analysis of the four Native Women's Association of Canada cases is essential because these are some of the very first cases to address the issue of political rights. In addition, the denial of rights to some Indian women under the *Indian Act* regime, in place since 1876, had a catalytic effect on the way in which section 15 of the *Charter* was drafted. Because in the *Lavell and Bedard* cases, neither of the protections contained in section 1(b) of the *Canadian Bill of Rights*, that is the right to "equality before the law" and "the equal protection of the law," were sufficient to protect the needs of women, section 15 of the *Charter* contains four protections: the two Bill of Rights protections as well as "equal benefit of the law" and "equality under the law." It must not be diminished that Indian women's suffering and experience shaped the positive development of legal guarantees of equality that benefit all women and other so-called disadvantaged groups. These four cases could have been an important opportunity for Aboriginal women to test the gains made under the 1982 constitutional amendments.

The cases are unique as the women are asserting political rights which have been traditionally understood as individual rights belonging to individual women. It is possible that the plaintiffs' position could have included an articulation of collective rights as one of the foundations for their case. However, the degree to which this could have been accomplished was mitigated by the fact that the opposing party was the Crown. In practice, this was also difficult because the case proceeded in the identity of two individual representatives of the NWAC as opposed to the organization as a whole.

Behind the desire of the NWAC to participate equally in the constitutional renovation process and be equally funded was another issue. The NWAC firmly supported the full application of the *Charter* to Aboriginal self-government. The NWAC's desire to ensure that *Charter* protections exist for Aboriginal women is prefaced on the abuse and unequal treatment of women in Aboriginal societies. However, little commentary was generated by the NWAC regarding the manner in which the *Charter* is expected to protect Aboriginal women from the abuses that they face.[20] Most of the documentation generated focuses on the fact abuses do occur (a fact which most Aboriginal people would not dispute). Serious concerns have been raised by at least one noted Aboriginal scholar, Mary Ellen Turpel, who is highly critical, even fearful, of the application of the *Charter* to Aboriginal people (Turpel 1989-90:3–45). Lawyers, activists and academics travelling in the other direction on the pro-*Charter* train, have yet to produce a complete, respectful and systematic response to these concerns.[21]

What is really at issue here is the strategy that ought to be utilized to resolve issues of women's oppression. The NWAC approach is both adversarial and prefaced on a feminist construction of reality. Both of these approaches in my experience do not advance a claim that is based in a cultural understanding of Aboriginal reality.[22]

The issue that is embedded in the NWAC cases is representation and this may not be an issue that should be placed before Canadian courts or legislatures. The mess made by judicial and legislative attempts to deal with the issue of membership is clearly one of the foundational components of representation. And is representation not essentially a question of voice and who legitimately speaks for whom? Is this articulation of "political" voice really not an issue of right(s)? The underlying issue not articulated in this litigation is the colonial interference with unique Aboriginal patterns of governance (and this reality must shape any attempt to bring Aboriginal Peoples more fully into the Canadian state system). Because the NWAC and the AFN are modelled on the colonizers ways of political organization, neither can fully give voice to tradition and therefore they are not necessarily about fully reaching out to the goals of emancipation, freedom and independence. These cases are derailed from the outset because of what they do not and likely cannot incorporate in their positions. Therefore, the cases do not hold transformative potential but rather seek only to access the colonizers' way of distributing power.

For questions of representation (which is really the question of who gets to legitimize political voice and how), the issue is really whether the court is an appropriate forum for the disentanglement of colonial vestiges in Indian systems of governance (including gender based concerns). Because this disentanglement requires skills of crossing cultures, my view is that the courts are not the best place to raise these questions. Courts assume that the organizations are honest about whom they represent. Courts are forced to presume this legitimacy as they have no ability to go underneath the parties' representations; nor do they have the particular experience of cultural insider and the knowledge base that position brings. Therefore, the inquiry that a court can accomplish is merely superficial.[23]

However, the problem really more centrally lies in the fact that there is no other forum[24] to raise these issues in. And this too is not a mere accident but a consequence of colonization.

Representativeness is an important consideration for many Aboriginal Peoples, particularly those seeking to implement "true" forms of self-government.[25] The AFN cannot be said to operate as a true form of Aboriginal government and the Assembly admits this readily. The Assembly represents the majority of *Indian Act* chiefs of Canada. The *Indian Act* is far from an instrument of Aboriginal control. The AFN has also faced internal conflicts. One is the desire of treaty people, particularly of the numbered treaties, to organize in a manner that respects their treaty territories.[26] The degree to which the AFN respects women is also an important question. As of June 1999, 13 percent of all chiefs in Canada were women (81 of 634).[27] As the Canadian parliament is comprised after the 1997 election of 18 percent [28] women (62 of 292) the same criticisms must also be raised about the Canadian political structure's ability to represent women.[29] Both statistics, thirteen percent and seventeen percent, are far away from a goal of reflective representation.

This internal retrospection within Aboriginal organizations should be a fact of life for at least as long as externally defined criteria are forced on Aboriginal Peoples. The federal government has at least once recognized that in the face of its failure to place control in Aboriginal nations to define our own citizenship, the current disputes about representation, including the representation of women, must be worked out in Aboriginal communities. In a letter to Gail Stacey Moore, Joe Clarke notes:

> the concerns you have raised, like those raised by others must be addressed within the community itself. They will not be rectified through the addition of another seat to the constitutional table. (NWAC #1 1992:402)

If in fact Mr. Clarke is correct about process, and I would firmly assert that he is, then the true motivations of the NWAC must be suspect, as the NWAC does not maintain strong ties in First Nations communities (that is, on Indian reserves).[30] This is not to suggest that the NWAC is without purpose as it represents Aboriginal women who through processes of urbanization and disenfranchisement have no voice in either Canadian or Indian political structures. The NWAC's claim of total representation (that is of all Aboriginal women) in fact does a disservice to the voices that are marginalized and the good work of the NWAC over the years.

Although I am uncomfortable challenging an Aboriginal women's association in a public way, the consequences of allowing my voice to drift into silence are significant, as this litigation wrongly represented Aboriginal women as all the same (or similarly situated). The remedy requested (that is, the same amount of funding and the same participation) is one that is based on an "equality is sameness" argument, and I fail to see how such a remedy offers much hope for the redress of gender inequalities that do exist in our communities. Had the relationships between the four designated Aboriginal organizations and the NWAC not been strained, a more interesting case could have been mounted, one that challenged the representation of all five organizations, none of whom were fully satisfied with their allotments. Such a case would have more fully reflected the responsibility owed to Aboriginal Peoples, including women, by the federal government.[31]

The *Charter* is a fairly narrow legal instrument, at least in its application. The *Charter* applies, under the auspices of section 32(1), to all activities of government.[32] It is a fairly simple legal conclusion to assert that the *Charter* will apply to the activities of the Department of Indian Affairs and to First Nations activities under the federal *Indian Act* regime. None of these activities are, however, activities of Aboriginal governments exercising an inherent jurisdiction. It would be an odd conclusion if governments whose independent authority originates outside of any Crown action were forced to submit to the discipline of the *Charter*, itself a Crown act. (It would be odd but not unusual.) Therefore, one must conclude that an unconsented to application of the *Charter* to Indian governments acting in both their traditional capacity and in a traditional way (where gender respect is an absolute requirement) would be an unlawful and unallowable intrusion on the sovereignty of Indian nations. Such an incursion must be seen as a direct threat and a re-entrenchment of colonial patterns of oppression, which many Aboriginal people see as the source of the majority of our present difficulties.

If the inherent activities of Aboriginal governments were deemed to fall under section 32(1) (and this can only happen if and when Aboriginal Peoples place this issue before the courts), the application of *Charter* provisions to Aboriginal governments is not really a difficult problem. Section 25 of the *Charter* provides a shield against the application of *Charter* based rights that abrogate or derogate from Aboriginal and treaty rights (correctly so, as these are rights which pre-exist the 1982 amendments to Canada's constitution). Section 25 is not a specific shield but applies to the entire application of the *Charter*. Therefore, application of the *Charter* question is really one that has been resolved since 1982.[33]

I remain concerned at the ease with which the Canadian courts found that the Charter applies to Aboriginal women. At trial in the NWAC case, no specific factual violations of freedom of expression (section 2(b)), the anti-discrimination provision (section 15) and the gender equality provision (section 28) were found. However, Walsh J. stated:

There is no issue nor can there be, that the *applicants* herein are

> subject to all the rights set out in the *Charter of Rights and Freedoms....* (NWAC #1 1992:405)[34]

Despite the trial court's refusal to issue an order of prohibition, the NWAC was at least partially successful in its *Charter* application quest.[35] The application of the *Charter* to the individual Aboriginal plaintiffs was upheld on appeal where the court found that the right to freedom of expression and gender equality had been violated (NWAC #3 1992:542).[36] Walsh J. sets out the general principle, that the *Charter* applies to the applicants, as an obvious statement of law. If the judge's position is that the *Charter*, particularly section 15, applies to everyone (as individuals), I take no issue with this statement unless it applies to activities on Indian lands[37] or by Indian governments. This is significantly different than asserting the *Charter* applies (automatically) to Aboriginal governments. The NWAC, despite the fact it is an organization, cannot in my opinion be characterized as an Aboriginal government, and because the defendant in these cases was the federal Crown, in my view the sovereignty of Aboriginal governments remains intact. However, I remain concerned because it will not be me but the courts who will ultimately be charged with resolving this issue.

If unequal treatment and abuse of any form are perpetrated by anyone other than a government actor in his official capacity, then the *Charter* provides no protections whatsoever for Aboriginal women caught in a cycle of abuse. Even if the *Charter* were to apply, it would not be a complete remedy. I am here reminded of the small comfort that a peace bond offers to a woman who is in a battering relationship. When that abusive partner shows up at the door, I do not think that holding up her piece of paper offers any woman any real and immediate protection. If she can reach the phone and the police can arrive in time, he surely can be arrested. However, those are probabilities I would not want to risk my own life on.

It is unclear what meaningful gains the NWAC has secured by pursuing this litigation. Its relationship with the other national organizations obviously became more strained than it ever had been before. In this discussion, its uniform characterization of all Aboriginal women as suffering the same discrimination has also been exposed as difficult. For me, this is one of the most disturbing aspects of its case. The NWAC focused on a single issue, one that in practice only affected a minority of Indian women, those who married out. The litigation did not provide a model that educated the judiciary or the Canadian public about the vibrant and diversified roles that Aboriginal women play in our societies.

The series of NWAC cases demonstrated for me the degree to which colonialism is embedded in our communities, organizations, political institutions and citizens. This is the most obvious recognition. I also began to understand how a rights dialogue can operate to cause cultural disconnection and to disguise the true nature of the problem—the impact of colonialism. In fact, relying on rights, particularly constitutionally generated rights (that is, rights in domestic law), obscures the fact that Indigenous claims to sovereignty are not really a proper extension of Canadian constitutionalism. As Patrick Macklem concludes:

> Indian sovereignty is not a domestic constitutional issue. Domestic issues of constitutional interpretation should not obscure the fact that justifications for the recognition of Indian government do not find their source in constitutional documents, but instead transcend national borders. The extent to which Indian sovereignty is respected in North America should not depend on the fortuitousness of a border dividing two nation-states. Indian sovereignty is a matter of distributive justice among nations, and national borders ought to respect, not constrain, distributive justice's demands. (Macklem 1993:1367)

If legal rights and the surrounding rights discourse are to be part of the pathway to the future where Aboriginal nations (and citizens) have the opportunity to co-exist with Canada, then the way rights are understood and defined needs to be culturally inclusive of Aboriginal cultures. I suspect this will not be an easy task.

Notes

1. I do not think of myself as a Canadian as all of those state relations have been forced on Haudenausonee people. I also recognize that not all Aboriginal people share this belief. Consent is the central issue that requires resolution before I could consider myself to be both Kanien'kehaka and Canadian.
2. The latter have no *express* constitutional protection (only French language rights have that). This fact is not lost on Aboriginal people. It is a consequence of the "two founding nations" myth.
3. In other circumstances the Supreme Court has understood that treating unequals alike can result in discrimination. See for example, *Andrews* v. *Law Society of British Columbia*, 1989.
4. I read Professor Lahey's paper, "Legal 'Persons' and the Charter of Rights: Gender, Race, and Sexuality in Canada" (1998), just a few days after I learned that both my editor and publisher thought serious revisions were needed in this chapter. (Thanks Brenda and Errol.) I agreed fully with their assessment but wondered where I was going to find the energy to approach this task. I took the kids to the beach and took the article with me. As I read this article, the structural and theoretical problems in the paper and the need to focus on the idea of representation became clear to me. Much of what is written in this chapter arises because of Professor Lahey's paper and the ideas it generated

in my own process of thought. Thank you Kathleen.

5. *Edwards* v. *A.-G. Canada* (1930). In this decision the definition of the word "persons" in section 24 of the British North America Act, 1867, was found by the Privy Council to include women. The Privy Council's decision overturned the finding of Canada's Supreme Court which reasoned that women were not persons and could not be appointed to the Senate.

6. In a similar way to the process where courts can take judicial notice of historical facts, the court should be forced to deal with their own involvement in colonial oppression. Rules such as precedent allow the courts the opportunity to excuse past cultural blindness (often to the point of overt racism).

7. By way of example, please refer to Janet Silman 1987.
My central concern has never been with issues of membership (perhaps because I have always had my birthright recognized) but with issues of citizenship. Citizenship issues are much broader (and more respectful to the views of Aboriginal nations) than are mere membership issues. Language here is an important issue. Darlene Johnston explains:

> The political status of the First Nations within Canadian Confederation has never been satisfactorily resolved. The prevailing Canadian mythology portrays a transition from ally to subject to ward to citizen. In First Nations circles, this is often referred as "the Big Lie." This theory of transition constitutes a denial of the inherent right of First Nations to be self-governing. Such denial is characteristic of the practice of colonialism. (Johnston 1993:349)

Johnston continues her article by documenting the statutory authority for the various colonial membership provisions that First Nations have survived.

8. In the 1867 *Indian Act*, the following provision is found:

> 12. The term "person" means an individual other than an Indian, unless the context clearly requires another construction.

9. A similar American case provides an interesting comparison, see *Santa Clara Pueblo* v. *Martinez*, (1978).

10. See for example, Kathleen Jamieson 1978, Lilianne E. Krosenbrink-Gelissen 1991, Teressa Nahanee 1993, Douglas Sanders 1975, Mary Ellen Turpel 1993.

11. The case applies only to the situation of Indian women as it questions the application of a section of the *Indian Act* 1970.

12. The sections of the 1876 *Indian Act* provided:

> 3. 3 (a) The term "Indian" means
> *First.* Any male person of Indian blood reputed to belong to a particular band;
> *Secondly.* Any child of such person;
> *Thirdly.* Any woman who is or was lawfully married to such person:
> (c) Provided that any Indian woman marrying any other than an Indian or a non-treaty Indian shall cease to be an Indian in any respect within

the meaning of this Act, except that she shall be entitled to share equally with the members of the band to which she formerly belonged, in the annual or semi-annual distribution of its annuities, interest moneys and rents; but this income may be commuted to her at any time at ten years' purchase with the consent of the band:

(d) Provided that any Indian woman marrying an Indian of any other band, or non-treaty Indian shall cease to be a member of the band to which she formerly belonged, and become a member of the band or irregular band of which her husband is a member:

13. Section 1(b) of the *Canadian Bill of Rights*:

1. It is hereby recognized and declared that in Canada there have existed and shall continue to exist without discrimination by reason of race, national origin, colour, religion or sex, the following human rights and fundamental freedoms, namely ...

(b) the right of the individual to equality before the law and the equal protection of the law;

14. This lesson was repeated in the so-called Oka crisis when then Minister of Justice Kim Campbell used the rule of law to justify the imposition of thousands of members of the Canadian army on a handful of Kanien'kehaka individuals. Kent McNeil also points to his concerns with the application of the rule of law (1993:95).

15. I am a child of such a marriage.

16. It is my understanding that this removal does not reflect traditional Mohawk laws on adoption but ironically reflects old *Indian Act* rules which capitalized on the silence in the Act regarding the status of children adopted. In a Federal Court decision, it was held that adoption of a non-Indian child by Indian parents was not sufficient to confer status on the child. See *Sahanatien* v. *Smith* (1983). Whether or not Canadian law is a proper venue for resolving the question is an appropriate question.

At paragraph 10, the Human Rights Tribunal noted:

This practice [*adoption*] was consistent with the position that existed at that time under the Indian Act (pre-Bill C-31, 1985). There was conflict in the evidence as to whether this practice conformed to the Great Law of Peace.

17. All Indian women were potentially affected by the application of section 12(1)(b), but in reality this section only applied to a portion of that population, those who chose to marry out. Despite the fact that the section disenfranchised only Indian women, it is a mischaracterization to suggest the section was of concern or application to all women.

18. This is not a "slam" off-reserve residents. I understand the pressures that move people toward urban areas. I actually support the acknowledgment of off-reserve residents' voting rights (as the reserve is a colonial distinction in the first place). I see this as an opportunity for Indian nations to reconnect disenfranchised members to our communities.

19. The NWAC did not seek to include any of the four designated organizations in this litigation by including them as defendants. In fact, it opposed the motions of the three organizations that sought intervenor status (NWAC #1 1992:399). This leads to several interesting discussions which have no easy or obvious conclusions. First, the exclusion of the four designated organizations can be applauded. The source of the non-recognition of Aboriginal women's rights has historically been the domain of the federal government, its laws and policies. Former section 12(1)(b) of the federally designed *Indian Act* regime is the most notorious example. By bringing suit only against the federal government, the NWAC establishes a principle of respecting the source of the majority of the discrimination. Therefore, responsibility is put in an appropriate place, at the feet of the offending government.

20. The Native Women's Association of Canada received funding from the Secretary of State to prepare a discussion paper on the application of the *Charter*. The Association produced a booklet of eleven pages, *Native Women and the Charter*, that would be useful as a community education document. I was particularly interested in seeing how this booklet would assert that the *Charter* will protect Aboriginal women from domestic violence and sexual abuse. The booklet provides no assistance in answering this question. The only situation that is described is the section 12(1)(b) discrimination. The *Charter* has thus far only been successful in partially removing the consequences of the section 12(1)(b) discrimination because the grandchildren of a woman who married out are not entitled to regain their status.

21. For example, Teressa Nahanee writes of the concerns of scholars such as Mary Ellen Turpel (a former executive director of the NWAC) in the following paragraph:

> The *Canadian Charter of Rights and Freedoms* is apposite to the collectivist aspirations of some Indian leaders who find themselves supported by legal theoreticians like Boldt and Long, and to a certain extent, Professors Doug Sanders and Mary Ellen Turpel. Their theories, in my view, are largely influenced by American Indian policy and case law and perhaps their own reading of international law and colonized peoples. To a certain extent, Boldt and Long are influenced by the Rousseauian 'Noble Savage' philosophy, and Sanders and Turpel are influenced by the international concept of 'self-determination'. Some of these theoreticians and some male Indian leaders have argued that sovereignty would put Indian governments outside the reach of the *Canadian Charter of Rights and Freedoms*. (Nahanee 1993:370)

22. Some are now referring to an Aboriginal feminist perspective (Nahanee 1993:360). I must confess to not understanding what this is. The author provides no definition of this new concept. Aboriginal feminism is also referred to in the work of Joyce Greene (1993). She also fails to provide a definition. My concern is not merely semantic or definitional. I am concerned with the ability of feminism to represent Aboriginal women's concerns. This is based on my understanding that patriarchy is just one vibrant strategy of colonization.

I have also written extensively on the lives and experiences of Aboriginal women. Regarding feminism, please refer to "The Roles and Responsibilities of Aboriginal Women: Reclaiming Justice," (1992). One section of this paper is entitled "Within a Legal Paradigm: Aboriginal Women and Feminism." I am not an Aboriginal feminist nor do I support such a construction of the world. My problem with feminism is quite simple. The reference point for feminism is the power and privilege held by white men of which I aspire to neither. My work is woman-centred and will continue to be as I can only understand the world through my own experience as a Kanien'kehaka woman.

23. An example of this difficulty is seen in the NWAC case where the judge held that the NWAC was the "bone fide" voice of *all* Aboriginal women (NWAC #2 1992:110).

24. The only forum is within the organizations themselves. Such critical self-reflection is true to traditional values and responsibilities.

25. This form of self-government could also be described as the inherent jurisdiction that Aboriginal people possess.

26. For example, Treaty Six met the summer of 1994 at the Thunderchild First Nation. It had been many years since the Treaty Six First Nations of both Alberta and Saskatchewan formally met.

27. I am grateful to Kelly Whiteduck of AFN's research office for providing these figures. I am also aware that AFN, approximately one year ago, established a Women's Unit and a full-time director of that unit. The AFN has done this by reallocating resources, not by securing new gender specific resources (conversation with Lea MacKenzie on September 2, 1999).

28. Figures provided by Federal Referral Service, telephone conversation, August 30, 1999.

29. It would be interesting to see figures on the representation of various racialized groups within parliament.

30. This reflects the experience of the author who was First Vice-President of the Ontario Native Women's Association in the late 1980s.

31. Such an action could have utilized both treaty rights arguments as well as relied on the fiduciary responsibility of the federal and provincial governments.

32. This section reads as follows:

> 32(1) This *Charter* applies
> (a) to the Parliament and government of Canada in respect of all matters within the authority of Parliament including all matters relating to the Yukon Territory and Northwest Territories; and
> (b) to the legislatures and government of each province in respect of all matters within the authority of the legislature of each province.

33. As section 35 is outside of the *Charter*, none of this discussion applies to that section. It is also important to note that section 35(4) also contains a gender equality provision.

34. Note that the *Charter* is said to apply to the applicants (NWAC) and not the defendants (the Crown). Given the rule set out in section 32 this pronouncement is confused.

35. It is not that I am so fearful about the application of the *Charter*, I would like to see some rigorous analysis done on how to protect collective rights in an individual rights environment before I bow to the *Charter* as a great benefit to Aboriginal Peoples. This criticism may be trivial as section 25 (the non-derogation clause) does fully and finally satisfactorily resolve the individual versus collective rights dilemma in favour of Aboriginal collectives.

36. The difference between the trial court decision and the first appellate decision was that the trial judge completed a purpose of intent analysis of the *Charter* provisions and failed to consider the effect of the governmental decision the NWAC challenged (NWAC #2 1992:120).

37. Whether this is designated reserve lands or Aboriginal title lands is a broad question well beyond the scope of this discussion.

Chapter Seven

Closing This Circle

This book was very difficult for me to write. I have danced for a long time with the notion that I am a lawyer. Writing this book has forced me to realize the degree to which I resist thinking like a lawyer. I went through phases, at times needing to compulsively footnote every idea on the page, and times I was content with my storytelling, responding on a cultural level to the decisions of the Supreme Court. I make no apologies for the somewhat "split-headed"[1] presentation which in the end is neither solely cultural nor solely legal. I have worried endlessly about those who will be unsatisfied with this work and use it to marginalize me further from mainstream institutions. No matter how difficult it becomes, I will always choose to stand with my people.

There were many days when I thought that I just could not write this book. I thought this for a number of reasons. Perhaps the most destructive experience has been trying to write a book on self-determination at the same time as working in an environment where the views of First Nations people are not respected. The ultimate irony is that this is occurring in a Native Studies department. This was very much a personal obstacle that I had to learn to step over.

The other major obstacle, which is not a personal one, is my concern for the people. This book criticizes the governments of Canada, Indian governments and the courts. Even if we as Aboriginal people accept these institutions as imperfect, we have nonetheless built our future hopes within these structures. By choosing to point to their shortcomings, I am very conscious that I am pulling the hope away from many people. I do not feel that this is an acceptable conclusion for this book. It is not my desire to be negative and hurt people. This does not fulfill my obligations as a Kanien'kehaka woman to live in the way of peace.

I have learned one significant lesson. Perhaps it is just a lesson that the process of writing this book has strongly reaffirmed for me. The hope for the future does not lie in institutions because institutions are artificial creations. Institutions do not have as one of the central organizing principles "living in the way of peace." What has been reaffirmed is the fact that the solution lies with the people. Change will come not from institutions but from the people. It is just that simple. Being self-determining is simply about the way you choose to live your life every day. And from the people, comes my hope. I have some stories to tell about just why I have so much faith in the people being able to overcome colonial imposition.

One of my favourite stories is about the vitality and resilience of Indian law. People (of all races) sometimes think that Aboriginal cultures have been destroyed. This can never be true. The songs, the language, the ceremonies all live in the land. They belong to mother. People also often think that Aboriginal law does not exist because it is not formal, professionalized and aggressive, as Canadian law is. This just is not so in my experience.

Take the pow wow for example. When greeting a person you have just met, the first question (and yes, Indians ask questions) is always: "Where are you from?" The follow-up question is: "Who're your mom and dad?" This second question is asked if you recognize that you may have relations at that First Nation. Aboriginal people in fundamental ways are always sharing and affirming these present and ancient kinship relationships. These relationships are the basic fabric of Aboriginal laws. Every time Aboriginal people greet each other, they are affirming the fundamental relationships that exist between them. It is, therefore, safe to say that Aboriginal people are affirming their legal relationships every day. It is part of the subtle ways of who we are.

Aboriginal law is not something that is distant, professionalized and removed from the people. I think it is one reason why Aboriginal ways do not involve relationships where authority is exercised over the people. In fact, the people are the authority.

There are many significant lessons I have learned about Aboriginal cultures and ways by just watching everyday events (often events that are part of my own life and experiences). One time, when doing some child welfare community work for First Nations in what is now known as Manitoba, a friend of mine, a member of the Ojibwe nation and fluent in her language, noted in a very quiet way that she could not say adoption in her own language.[2] This really got me thinking about what the meaning of family is in Aboriginal ways. I started to realize that Aboriginal people are very "reality" based. It is not the biological facts of childbirth and parentage that matter so much in defining family. It is the *actual* relationship that is real and recognized. This is why there is no such word as "adoption" in (at least) the Ojibwe language—it was unnecessary.

There are a number of good examples of this idea that Aboriginal society was based on the actual relationship as opposed to mere biology. Many times the people we refer to as parents, aunts, uncles, brothers and sisters have no biological relationships to us at all. To distinguish these relationships from biological relationships, my friends and I often refer to them as family "by Indian ways." I have two brothers and one sister that

I have taken in this way. However, once "taken" as family the same duties and obligations are "owed" to you as to those you are related to by blood.

In this last story it was language that was the window to a lesson I needed to understand about family. Maintaining good relationships with your family, clan and nation, but the rest of the living world as well (by which I mean the environment and all things around us), means that you are fulfilling one of your basic responsibilities as a human being. It is this web of relationships which provides the support, encouragement and instruction necessary to living a good life. It is this web (or the natural laws) that is the relationship that has been devastated by colonialism. As I have discussed in detail in this book, I no longer believe that Canadian law has a role to play in fixing the damage to this web. This of course forced me to do a lot of thinking about where I (and we) can turn our energies in search of solutions.

I thought a lot in the last few years about how to create change in First Nations communities. I know that in many Aboriginal communities, from reserves to urban enclaves, Aboriginal people have been surviving a number of traumas. Despite this, I do not think that change is that difficult to come by. I am influenced by the teaching of my friend, Leroy Little Bear. Leroy teaches that change will come out of the flux. Flux is a softer word, as I understand it, for chaos. This makes a lot of sense to me. Colonialism is about, among other things, controlling the lives of the individuals who comprise the people. When, for generations, a people have been controlled, their ability to make decisions and advance change is impaired. In order to shake up our communities and get them thinking as communities again, relying on themselves instead of bureaucracies, all that needs to be done is to shift the pieces so the "common" answer, depending on the colonizer, is no longer available. It is out of this chaos that the change will come. I am quite certain that this is a gift brought to the people with the return or continued presence of the trickster.

For example, in a community several years ago, a few days after a young man had committed suicide, members of the justice team, health clinic, and social services and public works departments met to discuss their concerns. Some time into this meeting, people started a list of other young people that they were worried about. One of the women at this meeting sat silently watching. The health director (as it is important to the story, I will share that this director was a non-Aboriginal woman) noted in a frustrated way that she had no money or resources to do anything. She was worried about drafting some emergency proposals for funding quickly. The woman who was watching was not happy about these interventions as they relied on outside sources to secure community wellness. The woman believed that this was not the answer as it actually encouraged the people to embrace and accept that they were helpless. This helplessness the woman understood to be a classic condition of colonialism.

She finally verbally burst her way into the meeting, asking: "Can anyone tell me the name of a single person on that list who is not related to someone in this room?" Her question was followed by an awkward silence. She continued: "What's the matter with us that we are not willing to care for our relatives? My nephew's name is on that list and I have already gone to him and told him how much I care for him and how important it is to me that he is here for us. I made him promise if he ever contemplated suicide he would come and talk to me first." Shortly after this, the meeting broke up with nothing decided. Self-government is really very simple to attain. All it requires is living your responsibilities to your relations.

A similar story makes the same point. A few years ago at an RCMP policing conference, I offended a number of the police officers there, although what I said was not meant as a disrespect to their services. The point was much more fundamental. I suggested to my audience of young people that they should break their dialing fingers. Next time a minor criminal event occurred in their community, such as the theft of property, they ought to consider doing something different (and by no means am I sanctioning any form of vigilante justice). They should sit back and consider what they could do besides calling the police. Why did the theft occur? Were the kids hungry or bored? My son had a bicycle stolen once. It wasn't the only bike he owned. Imagine how frustrated and sad the young man who took the bike felt because he did not even have one. I know if that young man had asked for one of those bikes, my son probably would have given him one (or helped him build one out of the parts Brandon was forever collecting at the time). What I was hoping to encourage was an individual and reserve based analysis of what we can do as self-determining people to make our experiences of our communities different.

It is important to consider why I was suggesting this change (and this is precisely the piece that the offended RCMP officers failed to consider). I was asserting a standard of accepting responsibility. Because it is this responsibility that is the foundation of an Aboriginal justice system as I understand it. If enough people take it upon themselves to do this kind of thinking (that is, how do I fix this?) then Aboriginal justice would be upon us. Aboriginal justice will never come because non-Aboriginal authorities allow us to build and run correctional institutions or police forces. It will come when we start to take responsibility and care for our relations. This is absolutely simple in my mind. Aboriginal aspirations toward self-determination are often frustrated because we do not just "do it!"

More recently, I was forced to amend my opinion about how simple creating Aboriginal justice would be. My son was assaulted (along with another friend) outside the band office by a band employee. Because this band employee also worked at the school and his last words to my son after the assault (my boy was first swung around by his hair and then hit in the head with a closed fist) were "I am going to get you," both my partner and I were worried that unless we did something, our son would be in a very vulnerable position at the school. We laid charges. This, at first blush, will appear contradictory. It was unfortunately the only choice that we believed we had.

We did not believe in the man who was then chief. He has a drinking problem. There was no justice committee active in our community at that time; nor was there an Aboriginal policing agreement. There were no resources available to do things differently. And we believed we needed to do something. Perhaps this does not contradict the first standard that I set out. It might be a specification of the circumstances when you can take matters into your own hands. This situation involved the fact that the man who assaulted our son was in a situation of "power over" that child. As parents we felt we had a duty to act. Further, we also felt that even if the only choice we had was to lay charges, we needed to stand up and speak out against the unacceptable level of violence in our community.

Ironically, the decision to lay charges was based on our desire to see something happen differently in the community. We wanted to ask for a sentencing circle so that our views about the level of violence in our community could become public. Sadly this did not happen. When we arrived in court, the plea was suddenly changed to guilty, and a fine of several hundred dollars levied before we, the victims, had any chance to say a word. No one talked to us; nor did we have an opportunity to speak. If this opportunity passed us by, and I am a lawyer (which means I have significant privilege), then the opportunity to positively impact the way we as individual Indian people experience the criminal justice system is generally not available.

It is also important to remember not to get things backwards. And because of colonial impositions, it's a very easy thing to do. A good number of years ago, I had the opportunity to listen to Oren Lyons speak at a Trent University Elders' conference. Oren has been very concerned about environmental issues. This has never really been one of my callings. However, the fact that I never felt challenged by environmental movements, despite recognizing how important the earth is, had always bewildered me. Oren was able to explain this to me. He explained that the environmental movement was backwards. Environmentalists have as their calling "save the earth." This is inside out because the earth has all the power necessary to save herself. Consider here the frequency with which we have been encountering floods, wind storms of many varieties and other so-called natural disasters. This is the power of the earth (and the winds, and the waters and so on). It is not the earth that needs saving but rather what the people have done to the earth. We are the problem. This is a very good lesson. The answers are dependent on how we define the problem.

I understand that peace requires speaking the truth as you understand it. In this book, I have offered my current understandings of the way forward. But a single voice is not enough to accomplish the re-establishment of the way of the great peace. My goal for this book has been simply to add my voice and present understanding to the "flux."

Notes

1. I would like to thank my friend Sakej Henderson for providing this concept which expresses my experiences of being Kanien'kehaka and legally educated.
2. Thank you Irene Linklater.

Bibliography

Abel, Kerry, and Jean Friesen. 1991. *Aboriginal Resource Use in Canada: Historical and Legal Aspects.* Winnipeg: University of Manitoba Press.

Alfred, Gerald (Taiaiake). 1999. *Peace, Power, Righteousness: An Indigenous Manifesto.* Don Mills: Oxford University Press.

Andrew, Caroline, and Sanda Rodgers. 1997. *Women and the Canadian State.* Montreal and Kingston: McGill-Queen's University Press.

Asch, Michael. 1984. *Home and Native Land: Aboriginal Rights and the Canadian Constitution.* Toronto: Methuen.

_____. 1992. "Aboriginal Self-Government and the Construction of Canadian Constitutional Identity." XXX:2 *Alberta Law Review,* 465–491.

_____ (ed.). 1997. *Aboriginal and Treaty Rights in Canada: Essays on Law, Equality, and Respect for Difference.* Vancouver: UBC Press.

Asch, Michael, and Patrick Macklem. 1991. "Aboriginal Rights and Canadian Sovereignty: An Essay on *R. v. Sparrow.*" XXIX (2) *Alberta Law Review,* 498–517.

Aylward, Carol A. 1999. *Canadian Critical Race Theory: Racism and the Law.* Halifax: Fernwood Publishing.

Backhouse, Constance. 1991. *Petticoats and Prejudice: Women and Law in Nineteenth-Century Canada.* Toronto: Osgoode Society and Women's Press.

Barreiro, Jose. 1992. *Indian Roots of American Democracy.* New York: Akwe:don Press, Cornell University.

Barsh, Russel. 1996. "Anthropology and Indian Hating." 12(1) *Native Studies Review,* 3–22.

Barsh, Russel L., and James Youngblood Henderson. 1997. "The Supreme Court's *Van der Peet* Trilogy: Naive Imperialism and Ropes of Sand." 42 *McGill Law Journal,* 993–1009.

Bartlett, Richard H. 1989. "The Fiduciary Obligation of the Crown to the Indians." 53 *Saskatchewan Law Review,* 301–325.

Becker, Howard. 1973. "Labeling Theory Reconsidered." In *Outsiders: Studies in the Sociology of Deviance.* New York: The Free Press.

Bell, Catherine, and Michael Asch. 1997. "Challenging Assumptions: The Impact of Precedent in Aboriginal Rights Litigation." In Asch.

Binnie, W.I.C. 1990. "The Sparrow Doctrine: Beginning of the End or End of the Beginning." 15 *Queen's Law Journal,* 217–253.

Boldt, Menno. 1993. *Surviving as Indians: The Challenge of Self-Government.* Toronto: University of Toronto Press.

Bibliography

Borrows, John. 1994. "Contemporary Traditional Equality: The Effect of the Charter on First Nations Politics." 43 *University of New Brunswick Law Journal,* 19–48.

_____. 1994. "Constitutional Law From a First Nation Perspective: Self-Government and The Royal Proclamation." 28(1) *University of British Columbia Law Review,* 1–47.

_____. 1997. "Wampum at Niagara: The Royal Proclamation, Canadian Legal History, and Self-Government." In Asch.

Borrows, John, and Leonard Rotman. 1997. "The *Sui Generis* Nature of Aboriginal Rights." 36(1) *Alberta Law Review,* 9–45.

Brodsky, Gwen, and Shelagh Day. 1989. *Canadian Charter Equality Rights for Women: One Step forward or Two Steps Back.* Ottawa: Canadian Advisory Council on the Status of Women.

Bruchac, Joseph. 1989. *New Voices from the Longhouse: An Anthology of Contemporary Iroquois Writing.* New York: The Greenfield Review Press.

Bryant, Michael J. 1993. "Crown-Aboriginal Relationships in Canada: The Phantom of Firduciary Law." 27:1 *U.B.C. Law Review,* 19–49.

Cassidy, Frank. 1992. *Aboriginal Title in British Columbia: Delgamuukw v. The Queen.* Lantzville, BC: Oolichan Books.

Chartier, Clem. 1978–9. "'Indian': An Analysis of the Term as Used in Section 91(24) of the British North America Act, 1867." 43 *Saskatchewan Law Review,* 37–69.

Chrisjohn, Roland, and Sherri Young with Michael Maraun. 1997. *The Circle Game: Shadows and Substance in Indian Residential School Experience in Canada.* Penticton: Theytus Books.

Comack, Elizabeth (ed.). 1999. *Locating Law: Race/Class/Gender Connections.* Halifax: Fernwood Publishing.

Cottam, S. Barry. 1991. "Indian Title as a 'Celestial Institution': David Mills and the *St. Catherine's Milling Case.*" In Abel and Friesen.

Culhane, Dara. 1992. "Adding Insult to Injury: Her Majesty's Loyal Anthropologist." 95 *B.C. Studies,* 66–92.

_____. 1998. *The Pleasure of the Crown: Anthropology, Law and First Nations.* Don Mills: Talonbooks.

Deloria, Vine Jr., and Clifford Lytle. 1984. *The Nations Within: The Past and Future of American Indian Sovereignty.* New York: Pantheon Books.

Devlin, Richard (ed.). 1990. *An Introduction to Jurisprudence.* Toronto: Emond Montgomery.

Engelstad, Diane, and John Bird (eds.). 1992. *Nation to Nation: Aboriginal Sovereignty and the Future of Canada.* Concord: House of Anansi Press.

Friere, Paulo. 1996. *Pedagogy of the Oppressed.* New York: Continuum Publishing.

Funk, Jack. 1989. *Outside, the Women Cried: The Story of the Surrender by Chief Thunderchild's Band of their Reserve Near Delmas, Saskatchewan.* Battleford: TC Publishing.

Goodwill, Jean, and Norma Sluman. 1984. *John Tootoosis.* Winnipeg: Pemmican Publications.

Gosse, Richard, James Youngblood Henderson and Roger Carter (eds.). 1994. *Continuing Poundmaker and Riel's Quest: Presentations Made at a Confer-*

ence on Aboriginal Peoples and Justice. Saskatoon: Purich Publlishing.

Greene, Joyce. 1993. "Constitutionalising the Patriarchy: Aboriginal Women and Aboriginal Government." 4 Constitutional Forum, 110–120.

Hall, Geoff R. 1992. "The Quest for Native Self-government: The Challenge of Territorial Sovereignty." 50:1 University of Toronto Faculty of Law Review, 39–60.

Harring, Sidney L. 1998. White Man's Law: Native People in Nineteenth-Century Canadian Jurisprudence. Toronto: University of Toronto Press.

Hauptman, Laurence M. 1986. The Iroquois Struggle for Survival: World War II to Red Power. Syracruse: Syracruse University Press.

Henderson, James Youngblood. 1994. "Conclusion: All Is Never Said." In Gosse, Henderson and Carter.

Highway, Thomson. 1998. Kiss of the Fur Queen. Toronto: Doubleday Canada.

Hildebrandt, Walter, and Brian Hubner. 1994. The Cypress Hills: The Land and Its People. Saskatoon: Purich Publishing.

Hill, Richard. 1992. "Continuity of Haudenosaunee Government." In Barreiro.

Hodgson, Maggie. 1992. "Rebuilding Community After the Residential School Experience." In Englestad and Bird.

Hogg, Peter. 1985. Constitution Law of Canada. Second Edition. Toronto: Carswell.

hooks, bell. 1995. Killing Rage: Ending Racism. New York: Henry Holt and Company.

Hulan, Renee (ed.). 1999. Native North America: Critical and Cultural Perspectives. Toronto: ECW Press.

Hutchins, Peter W., and David Schulze with Carol Hilling. 1995. "When Do Fiduciary Obligations to Aboriginal People Arise." 59 Saskatachewan Law Review, 97–137.

Indian Affairs and Northern Development: Unknown. "Registration Manual of the Department of Indian Affairs." Ottawa: INAC.

Jaine, Linda, and Drew Taylor (eds.). 1992. Voices: Being Native in Canada. Saskatoon: University of Saskatchewan, Extension Division.

Jamieson, Kathleen. 1978. Indian Women and the Law in Canada: A Citizens Minus. Ottawa: Supply and Services.

Jennings, Francis, William N. Fenton, Mary A. Druke and David R. Miller (eds.). 1985. The History and Culture of Iroquois Diplomacy: An Interdisciplinary Guide to the Treaties of the Six Nations and Their League. Syracuse: Syracuse University Press.

Johansen, Bruce E. 1982. Forgotten Founders: How the American Indian Shaped Democracy. Boston: The Harvard Common Press.

Johnston, Darlene. 1993. "First Nations and Canadian Citizenship." In Kaplan.

Kane, Marlyn (Ossennonton), and Sylvia Maracle (Skonaganleh:ra). 1989. "Our World." 10:2 & 3 Canadian Woman Studies, (summer/fall) 7–19.

Kaplan, William (ed.). 1993. Belonging: The Meaning and Future of Canadian Citizenship. Montreal and Kingston: McGill-Queen's University Press.

Krosenbrink-Gelissen, Lilianne E. 1991. Sexual Equality as an Aboriginal Right: The Native Women's Association of Canada and the Constitutional Process on Aboriginal Matters, 1982–1987. Sarrbrucken: Verlag Breithenback.

Lahey, Kathleen A. 1998. "Legal 'Persons' and the Charter of Rights: Gender, Race, and Sexuality in Canada." 77 Canadian Bar Review, 402–427.

Bibliography

Little Bear, Leroy. 1976. "A Concept of Native Title." 17:3 *C.A.S.N.P. Bulletin,* 30–34.

Locke, John, edited by C.B. Macpherson. 1980. *Second Treatise of Government.* Indianapolis: Hackette Publishing.

Lyon, Noel. 1988. "An Essay on Constitutional Interpretation." 26 *Osgoode Hall Law Journal,* 95–126.

Lyons, Oren, John Mohawk, Vine Deloria, Jr., Laurence Hauptman, Howard Berman, Donald Grinde, Jr., Curtis Berkey and Robert Venables. 1992. *Exiled in the Land of the Free: Democracy, Indian Nations and the U.S. Constitution.* Sante Fe: Clear Light Publishers.

Macklem, Patrick. 1991. "First Nations Self-Government and the Borders of the Canadian Legal Imagination." 36 *McGill Law Journal,* 382–456.

_____. 1993. "Distributing Sovereignty: Indian Nations and Equality Peoples." 45(5) *Stanford Law Review,* 1311–1367.

_____. 1995. "Normative Dimensions of an Aboriginal Right of Self-Government." 21 *Queen's Law Journal,* 173.

Mandell, Louise. 1987. "Native Culture on Trial." In Martin and Mahoney.

Mann, Barbara A. 1997. "The Lynx in Time: Haudenosaunee Women's Traditions and History." 21(3) *American Indian Quarterly,* 423–449.

Martin, Calvin (ed.). 1987. *The American Indian and the Problem of History.* New York: Oxford University Press.

Martin, Sheilagh, and Kathleen Mahoney (eds.). 1987. *Equality and Judicial Neutrality.* Toronto: Carswell.

McConney, Denise. 1996. "Dear Wynonah (First Daughter)." 12(1) *Native Studies Review,* 116–124.

McMurtry, William R., and Alan Pratt. 1986. "Indians and the Fiduciary Concept, Self-Government and the Constitution: Guerin in Perspective." 3 *C.N.L.R.* 19–46.

McNeil, Kent. 1982. "The Constitutional Rights of the Aboriginal People of Canada." 4 *Supreme Court Review,* 25.

_____. 1993. "Envisaging Constitutional Space for Aboriginal Governments." 19:1 *Queen's Law Journal,* 95–136.

_____. 1997. "The Meaning of Aboriginal Title." In Asch.

_____. 1998. *Defining Aboriginal Title in the 90's: Has the Supreme Court Finally Got it Right?* Toronto: York University, Robarts Centre for Canadian Studies.

Mead, Sidney Moko. 1997. *Landmarks, Bridges and Visions.* Wellington: Victoria University Press.

Minister of Indian Affairs and Northern Development. 1997. *Gathering Strength—Canada's Aboriginal Action Plan.* Ottawa: Indian and Northern Development Canada (Catalogue No. R32-189-1997E).

Mohawk, John. 1989. "Origins of Iroquois Political Thought." In Bruchac.

Monture, Patricia. 1990. "Reflecting on Flint Woman." In Devlin.

Monture-Angus, Patricia. 1995. *Thunder in My Soul: A Mohawk Woman Speaks.* Halifax: Fernwood.

_____. 1995. "The Familiar Face of Colonial Oppression: An Examination of Canadian Law and Judicial Decision Making." Paper prepared for the Royal Commission on Aboriginal Peoples.

_____. 1999a. "Standing Against Canadian Law: Naming Omissions of Race, Culture and Gender." In Comack.

_____. 1999b. "Native America and the Literary Tradition." In Hulan.

_____. 1999c. "On Being Homeless: One Aboriginal Woman's 'Conquest' of Canadian Universities." In Valdez et al.

Monture-Okanee, Patricia. 1992a. "Self-Portrait: Flint Woman." In Jaine and Taylor.

_____. 1992b. "The Roles and Responsibilities of Aboriginal Women: Reclaiming Justice." 56(2) *Saskatchewan Law Review*, 237–266.

_____. 1994. "Thinking About Aboriginal Justice: Myths and Revolution." In Gosse.

Morse, Bradford W. 1997. "Permafrost Rights: Aboriginal Self-Government and the Supreme Court in *R. v. Pamajewon*." 42 *McGill Law Journal*, 1011–1042.

Nahanee, Teressa. 1993. "Dancing with a Gorilla: Aboriginal Women, Justice and the Charter." In Royal Commission on Aboriginal Peoples.

O'Brien, Brendan. 1992. *Speedy Justice: The Tragic Last Voyage of Her Majesty's Vessel Speedy*. Toronto: University of Toronto Press.

Parker, A.C. 1991. *The Constitution of the Five Nations or the Iroquois Book of the Great Law*. Ohsweken, Ontario: Iroqrafts Ltd.

Penner, Keith. 1993. *Indian Self-Government in Canada: Report of the Special Committee*. Ottawa: Queen's Printer.

Pentney, William. 1987. "The Rights of the Aboriginal People of Canada in the Constitution Act, 1982, Part II, Section 35: The Substantive Guarantee." 22 *University of British Columbia Law Review*, 207.

Porter, Robert B. 1998. "Building a New Longhouse: The Case for Government Reform within the Six Nations of the Haudenosaunee." 46(3) *Buffalo Law Review*, 805–945.

Pratt, Alan. 1992. "Aboriginal Self-Government and the Crown's Fiduciary Duty: Squaring the Circle or Completing the Circle." 2 *National Journal of Constitutional Law*, 163–195.

Raczack, Sherene. 1998. *Looking White People in the Eye: Gender, Race, and Culture in Courtrooms and Classrooms*. Toronto: University of Toronto Press.

Ross, Rupert. 1996. *Returning to the Teachings: Exploring Aboriginal Justice*. Toronto: Penguin Books.

Rotman, Leonard. 1996. *Parallel Paths: Fiduciary Doctrine and the Crown–Native Relationship in Canada*. Toronto: University of Toronto Press.

Royal Commission on Aboriginal Peoples. 1993a. *Partners in Confederation: Aboriginal People, Self-Government and the Constitution*. Ottawa: Government of Canada.

_____. 1993b. *Aboriginal Peoples and the Justice System: Report of the National Round Table on Aboriginal Justice Issues*. Ottawa: Government of Canada.

_____. 1996a. *Bridging the Cultural Divide: A Report on Aboriginal People and Criminal Justice in Canada*. Ottawa: Supply and Services Canada.

_____. 1996b. *People to People, Nation to Nation: Highlights from the Report of the Royal Commission on Aboriginal Peoples*. Ottawa: Supply and Services Canada.

_____. 1996c. *Final Report of the Royal Commission on Aboriginal Peoples*. Volumes 1–6. Ottawa: Supply and Services Canada.

Bibliography

Salisbury, Neal. 1987. "American Indians and American History." In Calvin Martin.

Sanders, Douglas. 1975. "Indian Women: A Brief History of their Roles and Rights." 21(4) *McGill Law Journal,* 656–672.

_____. 1991. "Collective Rights." 13 *Human Rights Quarterly,* 368–386.

Sharma, Parnesh. 1998. *Aboriginal Fishing Rights: Law, Courts, Politics.* Halifax: Fernwood Publishing.

Silman, Janet (ed.). 1987. *Enough is Enough: Aboriginal Women Speak Out.* Toronto: The Women's Press.

Slattery, Brian. 1987. "Understanding Aboriginal Rights." 66 *Canadian Bar Review* 726.

_____. 1991. "Aboriginal Sovereignty and Imperial Claims: Reconstructing North American History." 29 *Osgoode Hall Law Journal,* 681.

_____. 1992. "The Legal Basis of Aboriginal Title." In Cassidy.

Stonechild, Blair Bill Waiser. 1997. *Loyal till Death: Indians and the North-West Rebellion.* Calgary: Fifth House.

Surtees, Robert. 1985. "The Iroquois in Canada." In Jennings et al.

Swartz, Bryan. 1986. *First Principles, Second Thoughts: Aboriginal Peoples and Constitutional Reform and Canadian Statecraft.* Montreal: The Institute for Research on Public Policy.

Thomas, Chief Jacob (with Terry Boyle). 1978. "The Friendship Treaty Belt and the Two Row Wampum Treaty." Mimeographed copy on file with author.

_____. 1994. *Teachings from the Longhouse.* Toronto: Stoddart Publishing Company.

Treaty Commissioner, Office of the. 1998. *Statement of Treaty Issues: Treaties as a Bridge to the Future.* Saskatoon: Office of the Treaty Commissioner.

Tully, James. 1995. *Strange Multiplicity: Constitutionalism in an Age of Diversity.* New York: Cambridge University Press.

Turpel, Mary Ellen. 1989–90. "Aboriginal Peoples and the Canadian Charter: Interpretive Monopolies, Cultural Differences." 6 *Canadian Human Rights Yearbook,* 3–45.

_____. 1991. "Home/Land." 10 *Canadian Journal of Family Law,* 17.

Turpel-Lafond, Mary Ellen. 1993. "Patriarchy and Paternalism: The Legacy of the Canadian State for First Nations Women." 6(1) *Canadian Journal of Women and the Law,* 174–192, and in Andrew and Rogers.

Valdez, Frank, Jerome Culp and Angela Harris. 1999. *Critical Race Theory Conference Proceedings.* New Haven: Yale University Press.

Vizkelety, Beatrice. 1987. *Proving Discrimination in Canada.* Toronto: Carswell.

Wallace, Paul (with John Kahionhes Fadden, Chief Leon Shenandoah and John Mohawk). 1994. *The Iroquois Book of Life: White Roots of Peace.* Sante Fe: Clear Light Publishers. (Paul Wallace first published this book in 1946.)

Warrior, Robert. 1995. *Tribal Secrets: Recovering American Indian Intellectual Traditions.* Minneapolis: University of Minnesota.

Weinrib, Ernest. 1975. "The Fiduciary Obligation." 25 *University of Toronto Law Journal,* 1.

Wilkinson, Charles F. 1987. *American Indians, Time and the Law.* New Haven: Yale University Press.

Zlotkin, Norman. 1984. "Judicial Recognition of Aboriginal Customary Law in Canada." 4 *Canadian Native Law Reporter,* 1–17.

Cases Cited

Andrews v. *Law Society of British Columbia*, [1989] 1 S.C.R. 141 (S.C.C.).
Baker Lake v. *Minister of Indian Affairs and Northern Development*, [1980] 5 W.W. R. 193, 107 D.L.R. (3d) 513), [1979] 3 C.N.L.R. 17.
Bear Island Foundation (see Ontario (Attorney General)).
Bhinder v. *C.N.E.* (1985), 23 D.L.R. (4th) 481 (S.C.C.).
Bliss v. *Attorney General of Canada*, [1979] 1 S.C.R. 183, 92 D.L.R. (3d) 417 (S.C.).
Bluebery River Indian Band v. *Canada*, [1995] 2 C.N.L.R. (S.C.C.). sub nom. *Apsassin* v. *Canada* (Dept. of Indian Affairs and Northern Development).
Calder (1973), 34 D.L.R. (3d) 145; 74 W.W.R. 1 (S.C.C.).
Canada (Attorney General) v. *Giroux* (1916), 53 S.C.R. 172.
Canada (Attorney General) v. *Inuit Tapirisat of Canada* (1980), 115 D.L.R. (3d) 1, [1980] 2 S.C.R. 735.
Canada (Attorney General) v. *Lavell and Bedard*, [1974] 1 S.C.R. 1349 (S.C.C.).
Cherokee Nation v. *Georgia*, 30 U.S. (5 Pet.) 1 1831.
Connolly v. *Woolrich* (1867), 17 Rapports Judiciaries Revises de la Province De Quebec, 75.
Corbiere v. *Canada (Minister of Indian and Norther Affairs)*, Court file No: 25708, May 20, 1999.
Delgamuukw (Muldane et al.) v. *The Queen*, [1991] 5 C.N.L.R., 1 (B.C.S.C.).
Delgamuukw v. *British Columbia*, [1993] 5 C.N.L.R. 1 (B.C.C.A.).
Delgamuukw v. *British Columbia*, [1998], 1 C.N.L.R 14 (S.C.C.).
Dreaver v. *The King* (1935), 5 C.N.L.C. 92 (Ex. Ct)
Dumont et al. v. *Attorney General of Canada and Attorney General of Manitoba*, [1990] 2 R. v. Agawa, [1988] 3 C.N.L.R. 73.
Edwards v. *Attorney General Canada*, [1930] A.C. 124 (J.C.P.C.)
Guerin v. *The Queen*, [1984] 2 S.C.R. 335, [1985] 1 C.N.L.R. 120 (S.C.C.)
Jack and Charlie v. *The Queen* (1985), 21 D.L.R. (4th) 641 (S.C.C.) (also cited as *Jack and Charlie*).
Jacobs v. *Mohawk Council of Kahnawake*, T.D. 3/98, March 11, 1998.
Johnson v. *McIntosh*, (1823), 8 Wheaton 543 (U.S.S.C.).
Kruger v. *R.* (1985), 17 D.L.R. (4th) 591 (F.C.A.).
Lavell and Bedard (see *Canada (Attorney General)*).
Logan v. *Styres* (1959), 20 D.L.R. (2d) 416 (Ont. H.C.).
Manitoba Language Reference (1985), 1 S.C.R. 721.
Manitoba Métis Federation Inc. v. *Attorney General of Canada*, [1988] C.N.L.R. 39.
Martin v. *Chapman* [1983] 1.S.C.R. 365 (S.C.C.).
Martineau v. *Matsqui Institution Inmate Disciplinary Board* (1976), 31 C.C.C. (2d), 39–56.
Native Women's Association of Canada et al. v. *The Queen* (Case #1) (1992), 90 D.L.R. (4th) 394 (F.C.T.D.).
Native Women's Association of Canada et al. v. *The Queen* (Case #2) (1992), 95 D.L.R. (4th) 106 (F.C.A.).
Native Women's Association of Canada v. *Canada* (Case #3) (October 16, 1992), 97 D.L.R. (4th) 537.

Bibliography

Native Women's Association of Canada v. *Canada* (Case #4) (November 13, 1992) 97 D.L.R. (4th) 548.

Nowegijick v. *The Queen*, [1983] 2 *C.N.I.R.* 89.

O'Malley v. *Simpson-Sears Ltd.*, [1985] 2 S.C.R. 536 (S.C.C.).

Ontario Education Reference, [1987] 1 S.C.R. 1148, 40 D.L.R. (4th) 18 (S.C.C.).

Ontario (Attorney General) v. *Bear Island Foundation et al.* (1984), 15 D.L.R. (4th) 321.

Pasco v. *Canadian National Railway Co.*, [1986] 1 C.N.L.R. 35.

R. v. *Adams*, [1996] 4 C.N.L.R. 1 (S.CC.).

R. v. *Agawa*, [1988] 3 C.N.L.R. 73.

R. v. *Cote*, [1996] 4 C.N.L.R. 26 (S.CC.).

R. v. *Eninew*, [1984] 2 C.N.L.R. 122.

R. v. *Gladstone*, [1996] 4 C.N.L.R. 64 (S.CC.).

R. v. *Gladue*, Court File No: 26300, April 23, 1999.

R. v. *Hare and Debassige*, [1985] 3 C.N.L.R. 139.

R. v. *Jones and Nadjiwon*, [1993] 3 C.N.L.R. (O.C.J.).

R. v. *N.T.C. Smokehouse Ltd*, [1996] 4 C.N.L.R. 130 (S.CC.).

R. v. *Pamajewon*, [1996] 4 C.N.L.R. 164 (S.CC.).

R. v. *Simon*, [1986] 1. C.N.L.R. 153 (S.C.C.).

R. v. *Sioui*, [1990] 3 C.N.L.R. 127 (S.C.C.).

R. v. *Sparrow*, [1990] 3 C.N.L.R. 160, 70 D.L.R. (4th) 385.

R. v. *Sundown*, [1999] 2 C.N.L.R. 289 (S.C.C.).

R. v. *Van der Peet*, [1996] 4 C.N.L.R. 177 (S.CC.).

R. v. *White* (1964), 13 S.C.R. 613 (B.C.C.A.) (also cited as White and Rob).

Re Beaulieu (1969), 67 W.W.R. 669 (N.W.T. Terr.Ct.).

Re Eskimos, [1939] S.C.R. 104, [1993] 2 D.L.R. 417 (S.CC.).

Re Katie's Adoption Petition (1961), 38 W.W.R. 100 (N.W.T. Terr.Ct.).

Re Steinhauer v. *The Queen*, [1985] 3 C.N.L.R. 187.

Re Tagornak, [1984] 1 C.N.L.R. 185 (N.W.T. S.C.).

Re Wah-Shee (1975), 21 R.F.L. 156 (N.W.T. S.C.).

Retail Wholesale and Department Store Union Local 580 v. *Dolphin Delivery Ltd.* (1986), 33 D.L.R. (4th) 174 (S.C.C.).

Sahanatien v. *Smith* (1983), 134 D.L.R. (3d) 172 9 F.C.T.D.).

Santa Clara Pueblo v. *Martinez*, (1978) 436 U.S. 49.

St. Ann's Island Shooting and Fishing Club v. *R.*, [1992] 2 D.L.R. 225.

St. Catharines Milling and Lumber Company v. *The Queen* (1888), 14 App. Cas. 46, 4 Cart. 107 (P.C.).

The Queen v. *Drybones*, [1970] S.C.R. 282.

Twinn v. *Canada* (1986), 6 F.T.R. 138.

Statutes Cited

British Columbia Fishery (General) Regulations, SOR/84-248, s. 27(1).
British North America Act, 1867.
Canadian Bill of Rights, R.S.C. 1960, c.44.
Canadian Human Rights Code, R.S.C. 1985, c. H-6.
Constitution Act, 1867, R.S.C. 1985, AppII, No. 5.
Constitution Act, 1982, R.S.C. 1985, AppII, No. 44.
Criminal Code of Canada, R.S.C. 19485, c. C-46, Part XXIII, [repl. 1995, c.22,
    s. 6], ss 718.2 [am. 1997, c. 23, s.17).
Crown Procedure Act, R.S.B.C. 1960, c.89.
Fisheries Act, R.S.C. 1970, c. F-14, R.S.C. 1985, C.F-14.
Indian Act, R.S.C. 1970, c. I-6.
Indian Act, R.S.C. 1985, c. I-5.
Indian Act, R.S.C.1927, c.98.
Indian Act, S.C. 1876, c.18.
Indian Act, S.C.1951, c.29.
Manitoba Act,
Royal Proclamation of 1763
Salmon Fishery Regulations for British Columbia, 1878

Index

Index